Supervising Paraeducators
in School Settings

Supervising Paraeducators in School Settings

A Team Approach

· ·

Edited by
Anna Lou Pickett
and
Kent Gerlach

8700 Shoal Creek Boulevard
Austin, Texas 78757-6897

This book is designed in Avant Garde and Goudy.

Production Manager: Alan Grimes
Production Coordinator: Karen Swain
Managing Editor: Tracy Sergo
Art Director: Thomas Barkley
Reprints Buyer: Alicia Woods
Editor: Lorretta Palagi
Editorial Assistant: Claudette Landry
Editorial Assistant: Suzi Hunn

Printed in the United States of America

3   4   5   6   7   8   9   10   01   00   99

To
Hugh Pickett
and
Laurence Gerlach,
who encouraged us
to accept challenges

Contents

Foreword

During the past 20 years, educational practices and systems in the United States have changed, most particularly in the area of the delivery of special education and related services. The number of support and ancillary personnel delivering services to children and adolescents with diverse special needs has increased significantly. This increased reliance on paraeducators and other support staff is attributable to several factors. The changing roles of teachers together with continuing shortages in the ranks of school professionals are two major reasons for greater employment of paraprofessionals. Additionally, the expansion of educational and related services for children from birth to kindergarten and for youth in secondary/transition programs has required policymakers to turn to paraeducators to assist teachers, speech–language pathologists, and occupational and physical therapists. The shift of educational programming nationwide to delivery models serving *all* children in inclusive classrooms has also had a significant impact on paraeducator utilization.

Data from the U.S. Department of Labor, the National Center for Education Statistics, and other sources indicate that employment of paraeducators will be one of the fastest growing occupational areas in the job market for the foreseeable future. In addition, a recent study conducted by the Federal Resource Center for Special Education, Issues and Trends in Special Education, predicted that paraeducator roles and responsibilities will continue to expand well into the 21st century.

As teacher roles evolve into that of managers of education programs, with less time devoted to providing direct services, it is important for teachers to be able to supervise and work effectively with paraeducators and other support personnel. Traditionally, teachers have been solely responsible for providing the educational experiences within the classroom. The employment of paraeducators to assist school professionals adds a new set of dynamics to the educational process.

Personnel policies and administrative procedures in school districts need to be restructured to recognize new role definitions for all members of education and related services teams. Formal opportunities for staff development and professional growth are critical for both the supervising professionals and paraeducators and paratherapists. Effective integration of paraprofessionals into the classroom and other education settings requires extensive cooperation among administrators and practitioners at the district and building levels and in institutions of higher education. It is very important that roles be defined and standards for paraeducator supervision established.

This text provides a much needed resource for policymakers, administrators, educators, and personnel in colleges and universities. It will support their efforts to develop policies and infrastructures to strengthen the performance of educational and related services teams.

Phyllis Kelly, Team Leader
The Educate America Act Program
Kansas State Board of Education

Preface

The roles and responsibilities of teachers and related services personnel are being redefined. The result is that they are becoming increasingly responsible for supervising paraeducators and other support personnel. *Supervising Paraeducators in the School Setting: A Team Approach* is intended to provide teachers, related services personnel including physical and occupational therapists and speech–language pathologists, and administrators with the skills and knowledge necessary to work more effectively with paraeducators in the schools.

Although several texts have been written about collaboration and communication in the schools, this is the first one written about issues associated with the management and supervision of paraeducators. It is intended to provide guidelines and methods to prepare school professionals to understand the contributions paraeducators make to the delivery of education services, and the need for role clarification, effective supervision and management, good communication, and teamwork.

This text was written for a broad audience. Our goal is to provide teacher educators and other personnel developers, policymakers, administrators, general and special educators, and related services practitioners with information they can build on to address the issues and practices surrounding the employment, supervision, and preparation of paraprofessionals. The text stresses a team approach.

OVERVIEW

Over the years, we have worked with many dedicated teachers, paraeducators, parents, administrators, and providers of related services who have encouraged us to write and edit this book. We have tried to make the contents clear and practical. The information you will read is the outgrowth of many years of experience working with paraeducators and the teachers or therapists who supervise them.

Chapter 1 begins with a historical perspective and overview of paraeducators working in today's schools. It provides the framework for the issues school administrators and practitioners are facing today. Chapter 2 focuses on team roles in instructional settings and examines the roles of school professionals and paraeducators. The term *paratherapist* is introduced in Chapter 3, Team Roles in Therapy Services. This chapter is devoted to speech–language pathology, physical and occupational therapy, and the paratherapist's role in the delivery of these services. The management of paraeducators and paratherapists is discussed in Chapter 4. The role of teachers and therapists with regard to supervision and evaluation is emphasized. The importance of team building, communication, and problem solving is the focus of Chapter 5, while Chapter 6 deals with the professional and ethical responsibilities of team members. Administrative issues are examined in Chapter 7, and strategies for developing standards and infrastructures to address policy questions and systemic issues are discussed in Chapter 8.

Our primary objective was to produce a reader-friendly, thoughtful guide that would enable personnel to work effectively with paraeducators. Each chapter consists of instructional objectives, a summary, discussion questions, suggested exercises, and/or case studies. It is our hope that you will find useful the information provided in this book.

ACKNOWLEDGMENTS

We are indebted to many colleagues who assisted with the writing and preparation of this text. First and foremost we want to thank the chapter authors for their commitment to this project. Their individual and collective contributions provide information and insight into current best practices associated with paraeducator and paratherapist roles, their supervision, and their preparation.

We greatly appreciate the willingness of several friends to review the chapters. They include Barbara Jo Stahl, Minnesota Department for Children, Families and Learning; Marilyn Likins, Utah State University at Logan; Joan Clair, Puget Sound Education Service District, Seattle; Paula Leitz, Pacific Lutheran University, Tacoma; and Mary Radaskzewski-Byrne, Southwest Missouri State University, Springfield.

Ross Graham and Paula Magluyan did yeoman service editing the first draft and the final copy and Dana Shoecraft provided word processing services.

Lucille Mascetti, the administrative assistant at the National Resource Center for Paraprofessionals in Education and Related Services, deserves our special thanks. Her patience and sense of humor remained constant throughout the entire process.

The staff of PRO-ED has given us guidance, encouragement, and advice. We especially appreciate the support received from Jim Patton, Tracy Sergo, and Annie Koppel.

We also want to recognize the thousands of paraeducators and their teacher partners who inspired us.

CHAPTER 1

$\cdots\cdots\cdots\cdots\cdots\cdots\cdots\cdots\cdots\cdots\cdots\cdots\cdots\cdots\cdots$

Paraeducators in School Settings: Framing the Issues

$\cdots\cdots\cdots\cdots\cdots\cdots\cdots\cdots\cdots\cdots\cdots\cdots\cdots\cdots\cdots$

Anna Lou Pickett
*National Resource Center for Paraprofessionals
in Education and Related Services,
City University of New York*

SETTING THE STAGE

Rose G., an instructional assistant with 20 years of experience in elementary and special education, has been assigned to work with Ruby C., a first-year teacher. Ruby decided to go on for her master's degree in special education immediately after she received her baccalaureate in elementary education. She feels confident that she has the skills she needs to plan for and teach the students. Because she was not prepared at either the undergraduate or the graduate level to plan for, assign, or delegate tasks to another adult, she is uncertain about her ability to integrate Rose into the curriculum and other classroom activities. Over the years, Rose has assisted teachers in all aspects of the instructional process. Rose is becoming increasingly unhappy, because she feels that Ruby does not appreciate the skills she has learned during the last 20 years. Further complicating the situation is the fact that there is no designated time in the weekly schedule for them to discuss their concerns or plan together.

For the first time in her 10-year career as a speech–language pathologist (SLP), Perri S. is working with a therapy aide. She is pleased that Maria H. has been added to the team because many of the students in her caseload have limited English. Perri feels strongly that it is her responsibility as the SLP to involve parents in all aspects of their children's treatment. Recently,

1

Perri has become aware that many parents seem to feel more comfortable speaking with Maria about their children than to her. While she and Maria work well together, Perri is afraid she will offend Maria if she asks her not to communicate with the parents.

Joan W. is a teacher's aide who was employed to facilitate the inclusion of five students with disabilities into general education programs. She works with several teachers who all have different expectations about what she should do in "their" classrooms. The duties assigned to Joan range from being fully responsible for teaching "the special education kids" in one class, to assisting *all* students in another classroom who the teacher feels will benefit from personalized attention, to escorting "her students" to another class, and then sitting in the back of the room and doing routine recordkeeping, preparing instructional materials, and occasionally scoring papers. Joan is confused about what her role and responsibilities are supposed to be. Of greater importance, however, is that she is concerned that she needs training because she does not have the skills she needs to work effectively with students who have so many ability levels. She has asked other teacher's aides about job descriptions and training opportunities and has been told that neither exist. She is uncertain about who she should speak to about her concerns.

Gloria R. is an administrator with responsibility for staff development in a school district. Several district-wide focus groups were held to establish staff development priorities. Analysis of the results indicates the need to build the capacity of teachers and paraeducators to work together as effective teams. She has contacted the leader of the state department of education's comprehensive system of personnel development to obtain resources and information that she can use to design and implement professional development opportunities for both teachers and paraeducators. She has discovered that there are no statewide guidelines for employment, placement, and supervision of paraeducators, nor are there standards for competency-based training for paraeducators or for preparing teachers to work with them.

OVERVIEW

These and similar scenarios are played out daily in schools and other education settings across our country. They reflect the emerging management roles of teachers and other school professionals who are responsible for planning, assigning, and/or delegating tasks and providing on-the-job coaching to paraprofessionals. They are also indicative of the growing need for policymakers and administrators in state and local education agencies to join forces with their colleagues in colleges and universities and professional organizations representing different disciplines to (a) improve policies, systemic procedures, and personnel practices that influence the employment, placement, supervision, and performance of paraprofessionals; (b) prepare school professionals to supervise paraprofessionals; and (c) develop standardized, ongoing opportunities for training and career development for paraprofessionals.

The purpose of this book is to provide stakeholders in different jurisdictions with different responsibilities with information they can build on to strengthen the performance of school-based education and related services delivery teams. This chapter identifies the broad range of issues connected with paraprofessional employment, supervision, and preparation, and lays the foundation for the seven chapters that follow.

Instructional Objectives

After studying this chapter and participating in discussions and the exercise, the reader will be able to:

1. Describe the historical basis for the employment of paraprofessionals in education and related services.

2. Discuss contemporary factors that contribute to continued reliance on paraprofessionals.

3. Explain why development of standards, policies, and mechanisms for paraprofessional employment, placement, supervision, and preparation is important.

4. Describe the unique role of state departments of education (SDEs) in promulgating and implementing standards for paraprofessional employment, placement, supervision, and preparation.

5. Explain why it is important for SDEs, local education agencies (LEAs), institutions of higher education (IHEs), and other stakeholders to work together to ensure that professional development opportunities are available to prepare teachers and other school professionals to supervise paraprofessionals.

6. Discuss why SDEs, LEAs, and IHEs need to collaborate in the design and implementation of comprehensive, articulated systems of training and career development for paraprofessionals.

DEFINING THE TERMS

Local education agencies nationwide use many titles to describe school employees who (a) provide instructional and other direct services to children, youth, and/or their parents or other caregivers, and (b) are supervised by certificated, licensed professionals who are responsible for diagnosing student needs, planning and evaluating programs designed to meet these needs, and assessing student performance and progress (Pickett, 1989). Paraeducator, paraprofessional, paratherapist, instructional teacher assistant/aide, occupational and physical therapy aide/assistant, speech–language pathology aide/assistant, education technician, transition trainer, job coach, and home visitor are just a few of the titles assigned to personnel who support the administrative and program functions of school professionals. Throughout the different chapters, for the most part we will use the terms *paraeducator* and *paraprofessional*. There are times, however, when it is more appropriate to use other titles or to use various titles interchangeably.

HISTORICAL PERSPECTIVE:
THE 1950s TO THE PRESENT

The current employment of paraprofessionals throughout education, health, mental health, and other human services has its roots in the social and political history of the 20th century. Paraprofessional auxiliary workers were first employed in the settlement house movement of the early 1900s: Henry Street in New York City and Hull House in Chicago. Later various New Deal programs, initiated during the Great Depression, utilized "nonprofessional" workers to provide services. Chief among these programs were the Social Security Act of 1935, the Works Progress Administration, and the National Youth Administration. Little attention was paid to retaining and enhancing the status of these workers through the war years of the 1940s (Gartner, 1971).

The 1950s

Recognition of the contributions paraprofessionals could make in education began in the 1950s when local school boards, confronted by post–World War II shortages of teachers, were forced to find alternative resources for providing education services. One of the most significant programs during that era was supported by the Ford Foundation and took place in Bay City, Michigan. The school district recruited and trained uncredentialed, college-educated teacher aides to perform clerical, monitoring, and other routine administrative tasks in order to enable teachers to spend more time on instructional activities (Bowman & Klopf, 1968; Gartner, 1971).

At about the same time as the Bay City experiment, Cruickshank and Herring (1957) documented a project undertaken at Syracuse University that tested the efficacy of utilizing teacher aides to work alongside special education teachers. Although results were positive, just as they were in Bay City, it was not until almost 10 years later that the benefits of paraprofessional employment would be more fully tested and realized.

The 1960s and 1970s

The mid-1960s and early 1970s were a time of social, political, and institutional change. During that period, many significant events occurred that touched the lives of most Americans in one way or another. These events included the growth of the civil rights movement, efforts of women and senior citizens to achieve financial and political equity, the campaign to ensure human and legal rights for children and adults with disabilities, emergence of strong antiwar feelings sparked by our country's participation in the Vietnam War, and more.

Separately and together, advocates pressured public officials to reorder fiscal priorities and reassess the role of government in expanding and improving education and other human services. As a result, under the leadership of President Lyndon Johnson, several "Great Society" initiatives came into being. A war on poverty was launched. Medicare and Medicaid were created. Title I and Head Start programs were established to increase education and support services for economically and educationally disadvantaged children and youth. Several community action programs were put in place to help major urban and rural areas restore neglected neighborhoods. In the mid-1970s, advocates for the rights of people with disabilities achieved their goal of passing P.L. 94-142 (Education for All Handicapped Children Act of 1975). This landmark legislation required schools to provide a free appropriate education for all children and youth with disabilities. Reauthorized in 1990, it is now called the Individuals with Disabilities Education Act (IDEA).

With the advent of several new entitlement programs, including Title I, Head Start, Model Cities, and other community action programs, funds were

allocated specifically for the employment of paraprofessionals and the movement gained momentum.

Bowman and Klopf (1967, 1968), reporting on two studies conducted
by the Bank Street School of Education, identified the following benefits
derived from the presence of teacher aides in classrooms. Teacher time was
increasingly redirected toward the central goal of instructional improvement in that more time was available

- for giving students individual and small group attention,
- for cooperative planning and learning opportunities for students,
- for attention to students' personal–social needs, and
- for innovation in teaching.

Gartner and Riessman (1974) reported other factors that were also instru-
mental in increasing the use of paraprofessionals. Foremost among them was a
growing lack of confidence on the part of both parents and policymakers in the
ability of traditional educational delivery systems, in which teachers and
administrators were predominantly white and middle class, to meet the needs
of ethnic, language minority, and economically and educationally disadvantaged students. To bridge the widening gap between the schools and communities, policymakers in both urban and rural areas began to recruit workers from
local neighborhoods who understood the community's cultural and ethnic heritages and could facilitate communication with pupils and other parents.

As a result, the job of the teacher's aide began to evolve from being primarily clerical or custodial to one in which the aide served as a liaison
between the school and the community, tutored individual and small
groups of students, or provided other direct and indirect services to students
and their parents. Unlike those in Bay City and other early programs who
were usually white and had some college education, these new paraprofessionals were black, Latino, or Native American. And many viewed their
job as an opportunity to gain experience and eventually earn teaching credentials (Gartner & Riessman, 1974; Kaplan, 1977).

As the employment of paraprofessionals began to expand, there was
also a growing awareness of the need to reduce the barriers that prevented
workers from ethnic and language minority heritages, young people from
disadvantaged backgrounds, and women from achieving professional status.
In *New Careers for the Poor* (1965), Arthur Pearl and Frank Riessman
charted a course for developing programs in higher education that would

reach out to paraprofessionals and encourage them to enter the professional ranks. They also provided the expanding movement with a name—New Careers. The career development efforts undertaken during the 1960s and 1970s were based on several assumptions. Among the most important were the following:

- Employment of paraprofessionals could ease the impact of shortfalls in personnel at all levels on the availability and quality of education and health and social services.

- It is possible to differentiate tasks performed by personnel in different disciplines and separate them into different functions, some of which must be performed by certificated/licensed professionals and others which can be shared with or carried out by paraprofessionals.

- Providing increased access to higher education for individuals who need to work at the same time they are earning academic credentials would open up opportunities for career advancement for people underrepresented in the professional workforce (Cohen, 1976; Gartner & Riessmann, 1974; Kaplan, 1977).

Beginning in the early 1970s, the federal government was a major facilitator of the New Careers Movement. Support came through legislative actions, funding, and administrative guidelines. In *From Aide to Teacher: The Story of the Career Opportunities Program* (1977), George Kaplan reported on one of the most creative comprehensive programs undertaken during the era: the Career Opportunities Program (COP). Established in 1970 by the U.S. Office of Education, COP involved more than 20,000 people in career advancement programs. The mission of COP was to provide opportunities for indigenous community residents, working as teacher aides in the nation's low-income urban and rural areas, to advance within various education disciplines and ultimately to improve the learning of the children in those schools. One of the most creative aspects of the COP was that all programs were developed cooperatively by school districts and teacher education programs to support committed, talented paraprofessionals who wanted to become teachers.

The COP design for teacher training represented a sharp break from established teacher education programs. Participating school districts helped the IHEs plan and conduct the program. The school selected the people who were to be trained and described the skills they needed to be effective teachers. The colleges and universities adapted their programs to the needs of prospective teachers by removing potential barriers. They scheduled required coursework at night, provided financial assistance, tutored candidates for high school equivalency tests, and conducted classes off campus near participants' homes.

In analyzing the 7-year program, Kaplan reported the COP was an effective way to provide an alternative route to teacher certification for paraprofessionals and other school employees who wanted to achieve professional status. His conclusions were based on the following:

- The COP training model was generally shaped to the practical needs and demands of its participants.

- Early introduction to and immersion in classrooms was a quick and natural method of career selection. (There were some aides for whom the management of an entire class was a nightmare. They learned this early, and were able to leave the field before their investment of time and money had become irretrievable. Those who took to teaching were spared the usual confusion about career choice.)

- For teacher aspirants and permanent paraprofessionals alike, the career ladder/lattice (i.e., mobility across or in program positions) that was part of many COP programs was a source of personal security and an assurance of an orderly career in public education. (The combination of lattice and ladder was ideal for individuals with professional aspirations who continued to be concerned on a day-to-day basis with their existing careers. The lattice was a powerful device in itself for strengthening the legitimacy of paraprofessionalism in education.)

- COP's decided preference for indigenous participants, as opposed to outsiders who had traditionally staffed inner-city or other low-income schools, contributed to internal accountability. (The aides' own children or their neighbors' children were often in those schools and, as neighborhood people, they knew and were part of the scene in which they lived and worked.)

- When hiring time came, school principals could draw on experienced practitioners whom they knew both personally and professionally and in whose training they had taken an active interest.

- The participants liked the COP formula. (It demanded sacrifice and it stretched physical and intellectual capacities, but it rewarded honest effort and was almost equally demanding of project staff, university instructors, and others involved in the process.)

At the same time that higher education was actively engaged in developing flexible degree programs designed to recruit and support paraprofessionals, a few states began to create credentialing procedures that set guidelines for the employment and preparation of paraprofessionals. Some of these systems included criteria for career advancement; most did not. States that developed paraprofessional credentialing systems in the late 1960s and early 1970s included Alabama, Delaware, Georgia, Illinois, Kansas, New Hampshire, New York, Ohio, and Vermont. Rather than develop regulatory procedures, some states chose to establish administrative guidelines that defined appropriate duties for paraprofessionals and in some rare cases delineated supervisory responsibility. To a more limited extent, local school districts began to develop job descriptions and personnel practices that included career ladders and training opportunities for staff whose personal career choices were to remain in paraprofessional positions (Pickett, 1989).

The 1980s

As federal support for all education programs declined during the 1980s, interest in developing standards and infrastructures for improving paraprofessional performance and fostering opportunities for career development receded. As the years passed, policies and administrative guidelines concerned with paraprofessional employment, roles, placement, supervision, and preparation became more and more unstructured. As a result, in some states and locales, standards for paraprofessional utilization and staff development mechanisms are almost nonexistent (Pickett, 1989, 1996).

The 1990s

Several events and trends have converged to create a resurgence of interest in the paraeducator workforce. New laws enacted in the late 1980s and early 1990s increased demands for highly skilled personnel at all levels. These legislative actions include the mandates contained in P.L. 99-457, the Education of the Handicapped Act Amendments of 1986 (known informally as the Handicapped Infant and Toddlers Act), that require public schools to provide services to children ages 3 through 5 who have disabilities or chronic health needs that place them at risk. The provisions in IDEA requiring schools to serve all students in the least restrictive environment and to provide transition and vocational educational services to teenagers have also contributed to increased paraeducator employment. Title I of the Elementary and Secondary Education Act (ESEA) of 1994 contains new guidelines for the employment and preparation of teacher aides/assistants. Title II of the same act enables school districts to use funds to train paraprofessionals as well as teachers to build capacity in order to help students reach rigorous content and performance standards. Title II also allows LEAs to use funds to develop career ladder programs that assist paraeducators to earn teacher certification in all core subject areas. Title VII of ESEA contains several provisions that support both the employment and professional development of paraeducators who work in programs serving linguistic-minority students. And Goals 2000: Educate America Act of 1994 calls on states to set professional development standards for all educational personnel.

In addition to these legislative actions, other factors have also caused policymakers to once again turn to paraeducators:

- continuing efforts to integrate effectively children and youth with disabilities into general education and the life of their community (Blalock, 1991; Hales & Carlson, 1992; Hofmeister, 1993; Morehouse & Albright, 1991; Pickett, 1996)

- growing need for occupational and physical therapy and speech–language pathology services for children and youth of all ages (American Speech-Language-Hearing Association [ASHA], 1995; Council for Exceptional Children [CEC], 1996; Fenichel & Eggbeer, 1990)

- increasing numbers of students who come from ethnic and language minority heritages in school systems nationwide (Buenaventura & Donlin, 1992; Ebenstein & Gooler, 1993; Haselkorn & Fideler, 1996; Office of Special Education Programs and Rehabilitation Services [OSEPRS], 1993)

- ongoing shortages of teachers and related services personnel, particularly with regard to recruiting and retaining school professionals from racial, cultural, and language-minority heritages (Haselkorn & Fideler, 1996; National Center for Educational Statistics [NCES], 1993; OSEPRS, 1993)

- changing and expanding roles of school professionals as classroom and program managers (French & Pickett, in press; Pickett, Vasa, & Steckelberg, 1993; Putnam, 1993; Snodgrass, 1991)

Changing Roles of Teachers

While all of these issues and concerns have contributed to a renewed interest in employing paraprofessionals to work alongside school professionals, the evolution of school professionals' roles from providers of direct services to program managers is one of the most significant but underrecognized reasons for increased reliance on paraprofessionals.

The introduction of various reform initiatives to restructure education systems and practices has had an impact on the roles and professional development needs of all members of instructional and related services teams. Many of these efforts are connected with two interrelated sets of issues. The first is school governance and administration. The second is concerned with empowering teachers and other school professionals by involving them more directly in setting education priorities (Carnegie Forum on Education and the Economy, 1986; Darling-Hammond, 1994; Darling-Hammond & McLaughlin, 1995; Lieberman, 1995).

In many local school districts, approaches to these changes have centered on building (site) based management and shared decision making as ways to renew and improve our country's schools. As a result of these efforts, the roles of teachers are being redefined and restructured. In addition to their traditionally recognized responsibilities as diagnosticians of students' education needs, program and lesson planners, instructors, and assessors of student progress, teachers increasingly are becoming frontline managers. These new management responsibilities for school professionals require them to work in partnership with principals and other members of shared decision-making teams to identify and allocate human, fiscal, and technological resources. Moreover, the roles of school professionals are becoming more collaborative in nature. Thus, more time is required for multidisciplinary planning of individualized instructional and therapeutic treatment plans (French & Pickett, in press; Friend & Cook, 1996; Villa, Thousand, Nevin, & Malgeri, 1996). Another new dimension added to school professionals' portfolios is their increased leadership in developing curriculum content and curriculum activities that enable all students to solve real-world problems, think conceptually and creatively, and work cooperatively (Alper, Fendel, Fraser, & Resek, 1996; Carnegie Forum on Education and the Economy, 1986; Darling-Hammond, 1994; David, 1996; Shor, 1992; Simpson, Whelan, & Zabel, 1993).

Changing Roles of Paraeducators

The evolution of teacher and other professional practitioner roles in education and related services has had a profound impact on paraeducator roles and duties. Although they still perform clerical tasks, duplicate materials, and monitor students in nonacademic settings, paraeducators are increasingly expected to work at higher levels of independence and to participate in all phases of the instructional process. In early childhood, elementary, and secondary education, paraeducators are assigned to Title I, multilingual, and inclusive general and special education and transition services programs. Under the direction of teachers and other licensed school professionals, paraeducators instruct individual and small groups of students; assist with functional assessment activities; administer some standardized tests; and document student behavior and performance (Blalock, 1991; Lyons, 1995; Passaro, Pickett, Latham, & HongBo, 1994; Snodgrass, 1991; Stahl & Lorenz, 1995). Nationwide, employment is increasing of paratherapists (therapy aides and assistants) who assist speech–language pathologists and occupational and physical therapists to carry out therapy treatment plans for children and youth who have sensory, physical, and speech–language disabilities (ASHA, 1995; CEC, 1996; Coufal, Steckelberg, & Vasa, 1991; Fenichel & Eggbeer, 1990; Longhurst & Witmer, 1994). Duties assigned to paratherapists range from performing clerical tasks, to observing and documenting student needs, to maintaining adaptive equipment and safe environments, to providing therapeutic treatment under the direction of a licensed professional.

Indeed as Pickett noted in 1989, the roles and responsibilities of teacher aides have changed dramatically since they were introduced in classrooms a little more than 40 years ago. In today's schools, they are technicians who are more accurately described as paraeducators, just as their counterparts in law and medicine are designated as paralegals and paramedics.

POLICY QUESTIONS AND SYSTEMIC ISSUES

Despite increased reliance on paraeducators and increased emphasis on the instructional nature of their jobs, most SDEs, LEAs, and other provider agencies have not established administrative policies or systems that set standards for their employment, roles and responsibilities, preparation, and supervision. Where policies and systems do exist, they have not been revised since the late 1960s or early 1970s when interest in paraprofessionals was at its peak (Pickett, 1996). Thus, they do not acknowledge the changes in paraeducator roles that are occurring in response to the evolving roles of teachers. The most critical issues confronting policymakers and implementers in state and local education agencies and institutions of higher education can be summarized as follows:

- The vast majority of paraeducators in our country's schools spend all or part of their time providing instructional and other direct services to children, youth, their parents, or other caregivers (Blalock, 1991; Fenichel & Eggbeer, 1990; Longhurst & Witmer, 1994; Lyons, 1995; Passaro et al., 1994; Rubin & Long, 1994; Snodgrass, 1991; Stahl & Lorenz, 1995).

- During the last 15 years, SDEs, LEAs, and IHEs have paid scant attention to (a) determining the hierarchy of skills and knowledge paraeducators require to carry out their new, more demanding duties; (b) defining experiential and education qualifications for paraeducator employment; (c) establishing criteria for advancement to different levels of paraeducator positions; and (d) setting standards for evaluating paraeducator performance (Pickett, 1996).

- Training for paraeducators when it is available is usually highly parochial, is not competency based, and is rarely part of a comprehensive system of career development that includes (a) systematic on-the-job coaching; (b) structured, standardized opportunities for staff development; and (c) access to flexible degree programs that enable paraeducators to earn professional certification/licensure while they continue to work (Pickett, 1996).

- At the present time, fewer than half (24) of the state departments of education (which includes the District of Columbia and the territories) have standards or guidelines for employment, roles and duties, placement, supervision, and preparation of paraeducators. Twelve of these 24 states have credentialing mechanisms. These systems range from multilevel certification/permit systems that define roles, training, and career advancement criteria to one-dimensional systems that do not specify duties or training requirements (Pickett, 1996).

- Contemporary education reform efforts increasingly emphasize the team and management responsibilities of teachers. These efforts have, however, overlooked the roles of teachers as leaders of instructional teams and supervisors of paraeducators. As a result, most teacher education programs have not revised curriculum content to prepare teachers to plan for, delegate, or assign tasks, assess paraeducator skills and performance, and provide on-the-job training (French & Pickett, in press; French, 1996; Lindemann & Beegle, 1988; Pickett et al., 1993).

- The need to recruit and train committed teachers is well documented. The need to attract more ethnic, cultural, and language-minority men and women into the field is particularly acute (Haselkorn & Fideler, 1996; McDonnell & Hill, 1993; NCES, 1993; OSEPRS, 1993).

Although paraeducator personnel represent high percentages of the diverse ethnic, cultural, and language-minority populations in their communities, they are frequently overlooked as resources for recruitment into teacher education and other professional preparation programs (Genzuk, Lavadenz, & Krashen, 1994; Haselkorn & Fideler, 1996).

ADDRESSING THE ISSUES
AND ESTABLISHING THE SYSTEMS

Establishing standards for paraeducator employment—roles and duties, supervision, preparation, and maintaining articulated comprehensive career development systems to ensure that paraeducators have the skills they require—is not an easy task. The broad range of issues linked to paraeducator utilization, professional development, and supervision cannot be addressed in isolation. One of the keys to focusing attention on these issues successfully is to establish partnerships among state and local education agencies, 2- and 4-year institutions of higher education, professional organizations representing different disciplines, and unions—all of which have different responsibilities for improving the performance and preparation of paraeducators and their supervising professionals.

In this section, the roles of SDEs in developing paraeducator standards and systems are discussed. The emerging interest in paraeducator/paratherapist issues in various professional organizations and unions is outlined. In addition, the roles and responsibilities of teacher education and other personnel preparation programs in providing school professionals with supervisory skills and removing obstacles to professional development for paraeducators are reviewed.

The Role of State Departments of Education

Policymakers and implementers in SDEs have important leadership roles in establishing policies, developing standards, and creating mechanisms to improve paraeducator utilization and preparation. Policy, systemic, and personnel development issues, described in the previous section, need to be explored by SDE personnel in concert with their colleagues in LEAs, IHEs, professional organizations, and unions. Because of their ongoing relationships with the various entities regarding other administrative and regulatory issues,

SDEs are in a unique position to establish and nurture partnerships. A primary role of SDE personnel is to spearhead collaborative efforts among the different players with responsibility for and interest in improving the performance, supervision, and preparation of school professionals and paraprofessionals.

Creation of statewide standards for employment, roles and duties, supervision, and preparation and mechanisms for implementing them expands the capacity of LEAs to integrate paraeducators/paratherapists effectively into education and related services teams. This is achieved by providing local district personnel with information they can build on to develop (a) functional job descriptions that recognize the changing roles and duties of paraeducators in different program areas; (b) competency-based staff development opportunities for paraeducators; and (c) structured supervisory and evaluation procedures. (The roles and responsibilities of local district and school administrators are addressed in Chapter 7.) Statewide standards also provide policymakers and faculty in IHEs with guidelines they can use to revise curriculum content to prepare supervising professionals to more fully tap the resources of the paraeducator workforce.

For partnerships to work collaboratively and to find effective solutions to policy questions and systemic issues, states must have databases that identify who paraeducators are, where they work, and what they do in different program areas or educational settings. Once this has been accomplished, the stakeholders will have access to information they can use to

- delineate appropriate duties and tasks for paraeducators and the non-delegable responsibilities of school professionals;

- determine similarities and distinctions in the roles and duties of paraeducators assigned to different programs;

- identify a common core of skills for all paraeducators, and a hierarchy of performance skills and the knowledge base needed by paraeducators working in more advanced levels of paraeducator positions;

- set standards for paraeducator training, professional development, and education and/or experiential qualifications for employment;

- establish standards for paraeducator supervision and performance evaluation;

- make recommendations for developing and implementing comprehensive systems of staff development and career advancement for paraeducators; and

- identify the supervisory roles and responsibilities of teachers and other school professionals and establish standards for preparing them to assume their duties.

In addition to addressing these needs, there is a growing awareness among the various constituencies of the need for paraeducator credentialing systems or other regulatory procedures to ensure that paraeducators have the skills necessary to meet the requirements of their roles. The need for paraeducator credentialing is not a new idea; it is, however, highly controversial. As noted earlier, only 12 states have criteria for hiring, training, and career advancement for paraeducators they regard as credentialing systems. Other states have chosen to develop administrative guidelines rather than more formal, mandatory credentialing procedures—and the majority have not moved to adopt either system.

Pickett (1986) identified four reasons for developing new or strengthening current credentialing systems for paraeducators:

1. By setting standards and mandating specified levels of training and performance, credentialing would guarantee that paraeducators have the skills and knowledge required to perform their assigned duties.

2. Effective credentialing procedures would be based on realistic viable opportunities for upward mobility on various levels of a paraeducator career ladder and, therefore, would serve as an incentive for retaining skilled paraeducators.

3. Credentialing would establish clear distinctions in the tasks associated with different certificate/licensure levels, matching responsibilities with training/education and competency.

4. Credentialing would serve as a method for providing formal recognition of the contributions paraeducators make to the delivery of instructional and related services.

Roles of Professional Organizations and Unions

Until recently, professional organizations representing teachers in different education disciplines have not actively engaged in assessing the need to differentiate distinctions in teacher and paraeducator roles, or to establish supervisory responsibility. This is beginning to change, albeit slowly. In 1995, CEC approved a resolution prepared by the Teacher Education Division (TED) calling on IHEs, SDEs, and LEAs to work together to develop standards and guidelines that address:

1. role distinctions among teachers, therapists, or other credentialed licensed specialists and paraeducators;

2. supervision of paraeducators and other support staff;

3. preservice training, inservice training, and professional development combined with career advancement opportunities for paraeducators;

4. job descriptions that articulate the knowledge and skills required by paraeducators to perform their assigned tasks;

5. strategies for structured, systematic management and supervision of paraeducators; and

6. ethical and legal responsibilities for paraeducators working in a variety of positions.

CEC has also recognized the importance of preparing teachers to plan for and supervise paraeducators by developing knowledge and skill standards for entry into the profession.

Professional organizations representing occupational and physical therapists and speech–language pathologists have been in the forefront of efforts to develop certification systems for therapy aides and assistants. These mechanisms clearly delineate distinctions in the roles and responsibilities of professional and paratherapist roles. They also identify differences in therapy aide and therapy assistant roles, and establish standards for community college associate of arts degree programs for certified occupational and certified physical therapy assistants (American Occupational Therapy Association [AOTA], 1990; American Physical Therapy Association [APTA], 1995). Although the American Speech, Language and Hearing Association (ASHA) has delineated distinctions in SLP roles and those of SLP assistants and has established guidelines for the supervision and training of assistants (ASHA, 1995), no AA degree programs for SLP assistants are currently in place. (These systems and strategies are discussed in greater depth in Chapter 3.)

In addition to the roles and concerns of professional organizations, it is important not to overlook the roles of unions. In most cases, unions (employee organizations) are the primary representatives of paraeducators. In addition to their collective bargaining responsibilities concerned with salaries, health coverage, and other benefits, unions increasingly are addressing other issues that affect the performance and status of paraeducators.

Nationwide, they are providing leadership in the development of standards to improve employment practices and training systems for paraeducators.

The Roles of Institutions of Higher Education

Some of the most underappreciated support systems available to SDEs and LEAs are the expertise and resources available from colleges and universities. Three issues are connected with paraeducator employment, supervision, and preparation that directly concern administrators and faculty in 2- and 4-year colleges and universities. The first (and the primary focus of this text) is related to strengthening and improving the quality of education practices by preparing school professionals to supervise and work effectively with paraeducators. The second is the role of IHEs in the preparation of paraeducators and paratherapists. The third reason is linked to the continuing shortages of teachers and related services personnel to provide services to children and youth who have disabilities and other special needs that place them at risk of failure and ultimately dropping out.

Although there is mounting evidence that the supervisory role of teachers and other school professionals is expanding, few professional preparation programs have assessed current curriculum content and instructional methods. Analysis of several recent reports indicates that teachers in general, special, and early childhood education and school professionals in transition and other related services programs have little or no preparation to supervise paraprofessionals (French, 1996; Lindemann & Beegle, 1988; Pickett et al., 1993; Rubin & Long, 1994; Salzberg & Morgan, 1995). Moreover, reluctance on the part of teachers to supervise paraeducators has been documented in a small study of 26 teacher–paraeducator teams (French, 1996).

French and Pickett (in press) identified eight policy questions that require the attention of teacher educators and administrators in SDEs and LEAs related to preparing teachers and other school professionals to supervise paraprofessionals:

1. Are both entry-level and experienced professionals receiving preparation for their supervisory roles?

2. If so, is the information that prospective professionals get from their preservice programs accurate and current?

3. What knowledge, attitudes, and skills should professionals demonstrate regarding paraprofessional supervision?

4. Is the reluctance to supervise paraprofessionals that was found in one study a generalizable phenomenon? If so, to what can it be attributed? How should it be managed?

5. Are there differences in the ways that professionals who have and have not had preservice or inservice training regarding paraprofessional supervision actually carry out their supervisory responsibilities?

6. How does the type of supervision provided to a paraprofessional affect the performance of assigned duties?

7. What role should teacher educators play in staff development provided by LEAs to improve professionals' skills regarding paraprofessional supervision?

8. Should standards be established regarding the amount or type of experience and preparation required for professionals to supervise paraprofessionals?

In addition to these questions, faculty and curriculum developers in IHEs and policymakers and staff developers in SDEs and LEAs must be concerned about ethical issues. What are the ethical issues that emerge when distinctions in the roles of school professionals and paraprofessionals are not clear; when paraprofessional duties are assigned or delegated inappropriately; when opportunities for systematic staff development for paraprofessionals do not exist; and when school professionals are not prepared to supervise paraprofessionals?

The second issue that requires the attention of all stakeholders is the role of community colleges and other IHEs in providing systematic standardized pre- and inservice training and opportunities for career advancement for paraprofessionals. The dilemma confronting policymakers in SDEs, LEAs, and IHEs is how to develop systems that interface and are flexible enough to meet the needs of school employees whose career choices are either to remain in the field as paraprofessionals or to move into the professional ranks and still continue to work while earning a credential.

Since the beginning of the new careers movement, community colleges have provided leadership in developing AA degrees and 1-year certificate programs for paraprofessionals in education and other human services. As noted earlier, both AOTA and APTA recognize AA degrees for certified therapy assistants. Community colleges have also been deeply involved in preparing paraeducators to work in early childhood, elementary, and special education and adult services provider agencies.

In all too many cases, however, the resources of community colleges are not acknowledged in efforts to establish and maintain comprehensive systems of personnel development for paraprofessionals. This and other issues related to paraprofessional preparation must be addressed cooperatively by the various constituencies in order to enhance the on-the-job performance of paraprofessionals and facilitate professional advancement based on career preferences.

Finally, the third significant issue associated with paraprofessionals that confronts policymakers in our nation's schools, colleges, and universities is the growing need to attract more women and men from ethnic, cultural, and language-minority heritages into education and related services. Paraprofessionals are an important but underrecognized resource for the recruitment of minority candidates into the professional ranks: The vast majority of paraprofessionals are women entering or reentering the workforce, who work in schools located near their homes. They are generally representative of the ethnic, cultural, and language-minority populations in their local community. They are familiar with community concerns and school concerns and, therefore, they help to bridge gaps in trust and communication between schools, homes, and the wider community. Moreover, because their roots are in the community, they are likely to remain or return there after they have completed their education (Emig, 1986; Genzuk et al., 1994; Haselkorn & Fideler, 1996; Miramontes, 1990; Pickett, 1989; Rubin & Long, 1994).

SUMMARY

Haselkorn and Fideler (1996) point out that the strategies developed and tested by different Career Opportunities Programs in the 1970s are highly relevant to the field today. In their report *Breaking the Class Ceiling: Paraeducator Pathways to Teaching,* they describe reemerging efforts between schools and IHEs to recruit and support paraeducator career advancement. Across the country teacher educators are once again trying to reduce barriers to career advancement for paraeducators. They are scheduling required, undergraduate work at night, tutoring candidates for high school equivalency tests, granting credit for life and work experience, and conducting classes either off campus or through distance learning technologies. Thus, we have come full circle and are ready to take a closer look at several issues that influence the employment, roles and duties, supervision, and preparation of paraeducators and paratherapists.

Discussion Questions

1. What were the most significant factors that caused school districts to test the efficacy of paraprofessional utilization in the 1950s?

2. Why did the "paraprofessional movement" expand in the 1960s and 1970s?

3. What are the major factors that have contributed to continuing and growing reliance on paraeducators and paratherapists in more complex and demanding roles?

4. What are today's most critical issues connected with paraprofessional employment and preparation confronting policymakers and implementers in SDEs, LEAs, and IHEs? Why is it important for different agencies and organizations to collaborate to address these issues?

5. What is the current state of the art with regard to the employment, placement, supervision, and preparation of paraeducators in your state?

Exercise

Obtain copies of your state's administrative guidelines and regulatory procedures that address the employment, supervision, roles and duties, and preparation of paraprofessionals. Divide into groups of five or six. Working together, analyze the documents to determine if your state has (a) established criteria/guidelines for education and experiential qualifications for paraprofessional employment; (b) identified appropriate roles and duties for paraprofessionals; (c) established paraprofessional training; (d) developed a comprehensive plan that includes inservice staff development and opportunities for career advancement for paraprofessionals; (e) established standards for paraprofessional supervision; and (f) established standards for preparing school professionals to supervise paraprofessionals. (To obtain this information, it may be necessary to contact state departments of education, human services, health, and/or other state agencies with responsibility for the licensure and credentialing of education and related services personnel.)

REFERENCES

Alper, L., Fendel, D., Fraser, S., & Resek, D. (1996). Problem-based mathematics: Not just for the college-bound. *Educational Leadership, 53*(6), 18–25.

American Occupational Therapy Association. (1990). Entry-level role delineation for registered occupational therapists (OTRs) and certified occupational therapy assistants (COTAs). *American Journal of Occupational Therapy, 44*, 1091–1102.

American Physical Therapy Association. (1995). *Guide for professional conduct.* Alexandria, VA: Author.

American Speech-Language-Hearing Association. (1995). *Guidelines for the training, credentialing, use and supervision of speech-language pathology assistants.* Rockville, MD: Author.

Blalock, G. (1991). Paraprofessionals: Critical team members in our special education programs, *Intervention in School and Clinic, 26*(4), 200–214.

Bowman, G. W., & Klopf, G. J. (1967). *Auxiliary school personnel: Their roles, training and institutionalization.* New York: Bank Street College of Education.

Bowman, G. W., & Klopf, G. J. (1968). *New careers and roles in the American school: A study of auxiliary personnel in education.* New York: Bank Street College of Education.

Buenaventura, L., & Donlin, M. (1992). *The Seattle public schools department of transitional, bilingual education and the G-Step program.* Paper presented at the annual meeting of Colleges for Teacher Education, San Antonio, TX.

Carnegie Forum on Education and the Economy. (1986). *A nation prepared: Teachers for the 21st Century.* The report on the Task Force on Teaching as a Profession. New York: The Carnegie Corporation of New York.

Cohen, R. (1976). *New careers grow older: A perspective on the paraprofessional experience, 1965–75.* Baltimore: John Hopkins University Press.

Coufal, K. L., Steckelberg, A. L., & Vasa, S. F. (1991). Current trends in the training and utilization of paraprofessionals in speech and language programs: A report of an eleven state survey. *Language, Speech, and Hearing Services in Schools, 22*(1), 51–59.

Council for Exceptional Children. (1996). *Report of the consortium of organizations on the preparation and use of speech-language paraprofessionals in early intervention and education settings.* Reston, VA: Author.

Cruickshank, W., & Herring, N. (1957). *Assistants for teachers of exceptional children.* Syracuse, NY: Syracuse University Press.

Darling-Hammond, L. (1994). *The current status of teaching and teacher development in the United States.* Background paper prepared for the National Commission on Teaching and America's Future. New York: Teachers College–Columbia.

Darling-Hammond, L., & McLaughlin, M. W. (1995). Policies that support professional development in an era of reform. *Phi Delta Kappan, 76*(8), 597–604.

David, J. L. (1996). The who, what and why of site-based management. *Education Leadership, 53*(4), 4–9.

Ebenstein, W., & Gooler, L. (1993). *Cultural diversity and developmental disabilities workforce issues.* New York: Consortium for the Study of Disabilities, City University of New York.

Education for All Handicapped Children Act of 1975, 20 U.S.C. §1400 *et seq.*

Emig, C. (1986). *A report on certification of paraprofessionals in education.* Washington, D.C.: National School Paraprofessional, School Related Personnel Committee, American Federation of Teachers.

Fenichel, E., & Eggbeer, L. (1990). *Preparing practitioners to work with infants, toddlers and their families: Issues and recommendations for educators and trainers.* Arlington, VA: National Center for Clinical Infant Toddler Programs, Zero to Three.

French, N. K. (1996). *Teachers as supervisors: What they know and what they do.* Manuscript in preparation. University of Colorado at Denver.

French, N. K., & Pickett, A. L. (in press). The utilization of paraprofessionals in special education: Issues for teacher educators. *Teacher Education and Special Education.*

Friend, M., & Cook, L. (1996) *Interactions: Collaboration skills for school professionals* (2nd ed.). White Plains, NY: Longman.

Gartner, A. (1971). *Paraprofessionals and their performance: A survey of education, health and social services programs.* New York: Praeger.

Gartner, A., & Riessman, F. (1974). The paraprofessional movement in perspective. *Personnel and Guidance Journal, 53,*253–256.

Genzuk, M., Lavadenz, M., & Krashen, S. (1994). Paraeducators: A source for remedying the shortage of teachers for limited-English-proficient students. *The Journal of Educational Issues of Language Minority Students, 14.* Boise, ID: Boise State University.

Hales, R. M., & Carlson, L. B. (1992). *Issues and trends in special education.* Stillwater, OK: National Clearinghouse of Rehabilitation Training Materials.

Haselkorn, D., & Fideler, E. (1996). *Breaking the class ceiling: Paraeducator pathways to teaching.* Belmont, MA: Recruiting New Teachers, Inc.

Hofmeister, A. (1993). Paraprofessionals in special education: Alternatives to casteism. *Utah Special Educators, 14*(3), 1.

Individuals with Disabilities Education Act of 1990, 20 U.S.C. §1400 *et seq.*

Kaplan, G. (1977). *From aide to teacher: The story of the career opportunities program.* Washington, DC: U.S. Government Printing Office.

Lieberman, A. (1995). *The work of restructuring schools.* New York: Teachers College Press.

Lindemann, D. P., & Beegle, G. P. (1988). Preservice teacher training and the use of the classroom paraprofessional. *Teacher Education and Special Education, 11*(4), 183–186.

Longhurst, T. M., & Witmer, D. M. (1994). *Initiating therapy aide/assistant training in a rural state.* Paper presented at the 13th annual conference on the Training of Paraprofessionals in Education and Rehabilitative Services, Albuquerque, NM.

Lyons, D. (1995). *Training for special education funded paraprofessionals: A report on the education and responsibility study.* Federal Way, WA: Washington Education Association.

McDonnell, L., & Hill, P. (1993). *Newcomers in American schools: Meeting the needs of immigrant youth.* Santa Monica, CA: RAND.

Miramontes, O. B. (1990). Organizing for effective paraprofessional services in special education: A multilingual/multiethnic instructional service team model. *Remedial and Special Education, 12*(1), 29–36.

Morehouse, J. A., & Albright, L. (1991). Training trends and needs of paraprofessionals in transition services delivery agencies. *Teacher Education and Special Education, 14*(4), 248–256.

National Center for Educational Statistics. (1993). *Language characteristics and schooling in the United States: A changing picture.* Washington, DC: U.S. Department of Education, Office of Educational Research and Improvement.

Office of Special Education Programs and Rehabilitation Services. (1993). *Fifteenth annual report to Congress on the implementation of the Individuals with Disabilities Act.* Washington, DC: United States Department of Education.

Passaro, P., Pickett, A. L., Latham, G., & HongBo, W. (1994). The training and support needs of paraprofessionals in rural and special education settings. *Rural Education Quarterly, 13*(4), 3–9.

Pearl, A., & Riessman, F. (1965). *New careers for the poor: The non-professional in human services.* New York: Free Press.

Pickett, A. L. (1986). Certified partners: Four good reasons for certification of paraprofessionals. *American Educator, 10*(3), 31–34.

Pickett, A. L. (1989). *Restructuring the schools: The role of paraprofessionals.* Washington, DC: Center for Policy Research, National Governor's Association.

Pickett, A. L. (1994). *Paraprofessionals in the education workforce.* Washington, DC: National Education Association.

Pickett, A. L. (1996). *A state of the art report on paraeducators in education & related services.* New York: National Resource Center for Paraprofessionals, City University of New York.

Pickett, A.L., Vasa, S. F., & Steckelberg, A. L. (1993). *Using paraeducators effectively in the classroom.* Fastback #358. Bloomington, IN: Phi Delta Kappa Foundation.

Putnam, J. W. (1993). *Cooperative learning and strategies for inclusion: Celebrating diversity in the classroom.* Baltimore: Paul H. Brookes.

Rubin, P., & Long, R. M. (1994). Who is teaching our children? Implications of the use of aides in Chapter 1. *ERS Spectrum* (Spring), 28–34.

Salzberg, C. L., & Morgan, J. (1995). Preparing teachers to work with paraeducators. *Teacher Education and Special Education, 18*(1), 49–55.

Shor, I. (1992). *Empowering education: Critical teaching for social change.* Chicago, IL: University of Chicago Press.

Simpson, R. L., Whelan, R. J., & Zabel, R. H. (1993). Special education personnel preparation in the 21st century: Issues and strategies. *Remedial and Special Education, 14*(2), 7–22.

Snodgrass, A. S. (1991). *Actual and preferred practices of employment, placement, supervision, and evaluation of teacher aides in Idaho school districts.* Unpublished doctoral dissertation, University of Idaho, Moscow.

Stahl, B. J., & Lorenz, G. (1995). *Views on paraprofessionals.* St. Paul, MN: Minnesota Department of Education.

Villa, R. A., Thousand, J. S., Nevin, A. I., & Malgeri, C. (1996). Instilling collaboration for inclusive schooling as a way of doing business in public schools. *Remedial and Special Education, 17*(3), 169–181.

CHAPTER 2

. . . .

Team Roles in Instructional Settings

. . . .

Lynn Safarik
California State University, Long Beach

OVERVIEW

Educators are increasingly challenged to provide instruction and services—often with scarce resources—to children and youth who are diverse in terms of cultural background, primary language, and special learning needs. Most teachers, administrators, and parents recognize the critical role of the paraeducator in contributing to student success and well-being under these conditions. What is not clear, however, is the definitive role of the paraeducator; in many local education agencies discrepancies are seen between school district job descriptions, teacher expectations, and student needs. Paraeducator skill levels and the extent of formal education can also be disparate. Formal training options for paraeducators are frequently piecemeal and are not necessarily based on accurate assessments of training needs.

Generally, paraeducators have less formal education than professionals and, therefore, it is presumed that they provide services that are relatively concrete, routine, and under the supervision of professionals. In reality, they sometimes function independently and, in underserved areas (rural and inner-city schools), they are often the primary service providers. This is likely to be particularly true for paraeducators working with students with special needs, including those with limited English proficiency (Harper, 1994). It is not uncommon for paraeducators to be assigned one title, that is, instructional assistant, and actually perform beyond the parameters of that role, often with little or no formal training. Fully cognizant of the implications of this state of affairs, teachers and administrators, grateful for the much needed help, tend to look the other way.

In schools and other education settings, the primary duties of paraeducators are to provide instruction and other direct services (Passaro, Pickett, Latham,

& HongBo, 1994; Pickett, Vasa, & Steckelberg, 1993; Snodgrass, 1991; Stahl & Lorenz, 1995), which may include providing information and referrals; support and advocacy; and mediation for individuals, families, and communities. Their role is characterized by terms such as *assist, support,* and *facilitate.* In areas such as inclusive education programs for children and youth with disabilities, transition services, multilingual/multiethnic instructions, and early childhood education, paraeducators, like their professional colleagues, are experiencing role transformations as the lines between school, home, and community become blurred. The trend toward education and human service integration has broadened the scope of the paraeducator's role to include job titles such as job coach, technology assistant, case aide, outreach worker, youth worker, residential case worker, and community liaison, in addition to the traditional titles of instructional aide or assistant.

Instructional Objectives

After studying this chapter and participating in discussions and exercises, the reader will be able to:

1. Describe educational settings and programs where paraeducators are employed.

2. Describe similarities and distinctions in the roles and duties of paraeducators working in special education, multilingual and multiethnic programs, Title I and other compensatory (remedial) education programs, early childhood education, transitional services, and orientation and mobility programs.

3. Compare and contrast competencies shared by paraeducators and school professionals.

4. Describe competencies primarily for paraeducators.

5. Describe competencies required by school professionals only.

6. Compare and contrast knowledge and functional competencies for school professionals and paraeducators.

7. Compare and contrast core competencies and specialized competencies required by paraeducators working in early childhood, multilingual/multiethnic, special and compensatory education, transition services, and orientation and mobility programs.

INTRODUCTION

Despite the lack of uniformity in the deployment and training of paraeducators, efforts to ascertain how the roles and responsibilities of paraeducators who work in elementary and secondary level programs have evolved suggest that progress is under way. The National Resource Center for Paraprofessionals in Education and Related Services has identified competencies for paraeducators who work in three programmatic areas: inclusive classrooms, early childhood home- and center-based programs, and vocational and transition services (Pickett, Faison, & Formanek, 1993; Pickett, Faison, Formanek, & Semrau, 1993; Pickett, Faison, Formanek, & Woods, 1993). These competencies were developed through expert consultation and analysis and field tested by practitioners across the nation. Two nationally based competency studies have focused on transition services professionals and paraprofessionals (DeFur & Taymans, 1995; Safarik, Prather, Hanson, Guzman, & Schwan, 1991). Position papers have been developed by the National Association for the Education of Young Children (NAEYC, 1994) and the Association for Education and Rehabilitation of the Blind and Visually Impaired (Wiener et al., 1990) to establish guidelines for paraeducator training.

Clearly, more research is needed to ensure the integrity of current paraeducator training models and to provide a foundation from which school districts can establish personnel policy. School reform efforts that do not recognize and include paraeducator issues ignore a critical resource for effecting change. Yet without an empirical basis for understanding the roles and responsibilities of paraeducators, policy is ill conceived. A few studies have been conducted to validate paraeducator competencies (Morehouse & Albright, 1991; Pickett, Faison, & Formanek, 1993; Pickett, Faison, Formanek, & Semrau, 1993; Safarik et al., 1991); however, the proposed frameworks are based mainly on position papers and the recommendations of various experts. The great regional disparity in the need for paraeducators and requisite skills of paraeducators portends further research, which will provide an accurate picture of what paraeducators do.

The purpose of this chapter is to synthesize the current literature on paraeducator competencies and to propose a conceptual framework on which supervisors, trainers, administrators, and researchers can build. This review encompasses competencies and models for training paraeducators to work in diverse educational settings such as inclusive general and special education programs, transition services, multilingual and multiethnic instruction, Title I and other compensatory programs for disadvantaged children and youth, and early childhood education.

PARAEDUCATORS IN INCLUSIVE SPECIAL EDUCATION PROGRAMS

The number of children and youth with disabilities being served in public schools has increased significantly since the enactment of the Education for All Handicapped Children Act in 1975. Passage of the Individuals with Disabilities Education Act in 1990 emphasizes the need for collaboration among general, special, and vocational education and the agencies providing services to young children and adults. These federal guidelines reflect the evolution of instructional approaches designed to serve students with special needs in inclusive classrooms and other instructional settings. Addressing personnel training needs for the 21st century created by these changes in service delivery, Simpson, Whelan, and Zabel (1993) cited three critical priorities that require the attention of teacher educators and other personnel developers. The first is to train special educators from underrepresented groups. The second is the need to develop nontraditional approaches to teacher education. The third is the need to prepare teachers who are qualified to serve children and youth with new and emerging disabilities. A framework for determining knowledge and skill outcomes/standards for special education personnel training is provided in Figure 2.1.

These three sets of issues have implications for the preparation of paraeducators as well as certified/licensed personnel. The first two, which focus on teacher education, support the expansion of paraeducator training programs that provide career-ladder opportunities. Innovative approaches (e.g., credit for work experience, mentor training programs) that are designed to meet the needs of nontraditional students in higher education are sorely needed. The third priority underscores the increased demand for individual instruction; it follows that a team approach, which includes paraeducators, is highly desirable. These broader training issues, however, are beyond the scope of this chapter.

Several authors have emphasized the need for special educators to be prepared to consult and collaborate with general education teachers and related services personnel (Friend & Cook, 1996; Simpson et al., 1993). Increasingly school professionals and paraeducators are being called on to establish part-

1. Special education foundations

2. Population characteristics

3. Preinstructional assessment

4. Instructional content and media

5. Instructional presentations/methods

6. Planning learning environments

7. Developing student–teacher relationships

8. Behavior management procedures

9. Program evaluation procedures

10. Consultation/collaboration skills

11. Involving families in programming

12. General program management and legal requirements

Figure 2.1. **Skill outcome areas for education preparation programs.** Adapted from "Special Education Personnel Preparation in the 21st Century: Issue and Strategies," by R. L. Simpson, R. J. Whelan, and R. H. Zabel, 1993, *Remedial and Special Education*, *14*(2), 7–22.

nerships between education, business and industry, and rehabilitative and social services agencies in order to maximize successful outcomes for students with disabilities as they leave high school (DeFur & Taymans, 1995; Gajar, Goodman, & McAfee, 1993; Safarik et al., 1991).

Similarly, training should include strategies for facilitating linkages with postsecondary institutions. In the future, special education personnel will need to assume greater responsibility for those students who are not classified as special education recipients, but who are at risk of educational failure. Knowledge of cultural and linguistic diversity and family dynamics as they relate to educational success, and knowledge of the factors that create risk and their influence on children and youth, are essential competency areas. Special education personnel need to be familiar with the roles of others who are involved with at-risk students and learn to collaborate with them. Skills in policy and systemic change processes relative to at-risk students are necessary for professionals who can then facilitate these changes when working with the educational team members, including paraeducators.

Collaboration skills are essential for educators charged with effectively including children and youth with learning, physical, sensory, and other disabilities into general education programs. Both intra-agency collaboration (between special educators and general educators) and interagency collaboration (among parents, families, related service personnel, mental health and medical provider agencies, and political leaders) are necessary for successfully including students with disabilities in general education programs.

In "A Core Curriculum and Training Program to Prepare Paraeducators to Work in Inclusive Classrooms Serving School Age Students with Disabilities," Pickett, Faison, & Formanek (1993) categorized paraeducator competencies in six instructional components: strengthening the instructional team; human and legal rights of children and youth with disabilities and their families; human development; the instructional process; appreciating diversity; and emergency, health, and safety procedures. Figure 2.2 contains the core competencies that serve as the basis for the curriculum content. These competencies are required by all paraeducators who work with young children and school-age students with special needs.

In addition to the core competencies, the curriculum specifies additional competencies for paraeducators working in inclusive general/special education classrooms, early intervention/childhood programs, and transition services. Additional competencies for paraeducators assigned to inclusive classrooms serving school-age students are listed in Figure 2.3.

In the core curriculum and the training program that accompanies it, the role of the paraeducator is distinguished from that of the teacher. Seven major teacher responsibilities identified in the curriculum are highlighted in italics: *assessing* the performance level of students; *consulting* with colleagues and participating in the preparation of education plans; *determining* instructional objectives for individual students and the entire class; *implementing* the instructional programs along with paraeducators; *evaluating* the effectiveness of individual programs; *involving* parents in all aspects of their child's education; and *supervising* the work of paraeducators and other support staff.

Describing the teacher's role, in turn, clarifies the role of the paraeducator. Paraeducators are defined in this curriculum as those

1. whose positions are either instructional in nature or who deliver other direct services to students and/or their parents; and

2. who work under the supervision of teachers or other professional staff who have the ultimate responsibility of the design, implementation, and evaluation of instructional programs and student progress (Pickett, Faison, & Formanek, 1993, p. 9).

Competencies in the curriculum content areas are intended to be interpreted within the parameters set by this definition. Therefore, although paraeduca-

To work in education and related services programs for children and youth with special needs, paraeducators will demonstrate

- an understanding of the value of serving children and youth with disabilities in integrated settings;

- an understanding of differentiated staffing patterns and the distinctions among the roles and responsibilities of professional and paraprofessional personnel;

- an ability to communicate with colleagues, follow instructions, and use problem solving and other skills that will enable them to work as effective members of the instructional teams;

- a knowledge of legal and human rights of children and youth with special needs and their families;

- an ability to practice ethical and professional standards of conduct established by the agency where they are employed;

- a sensitivity to diversity in cultural heritages, lifestyles, and value systems among the children, youth, and families they serve;

- a knowledge of patterns of human development and milestones typically achieved at different ages; and of risk factors that may prohibit or impede typical development;

- an ability to motivate and assist children and youth with disabilities to build self-esteem; develop interpersonal skills that will help them avoid isolation in different learning and living environments; and strengthen skills to become more independent by monitoring and controlling their behavior;

- an ability to follow health, safety, and emergency procedures developed by the agency where they are employed; and

- an ability to use assistive technology and adaptive equipment and to provide the special care that infants, children/youth with disabilities may require (e.g., positioning, transferring, and feeding).

Figure 2.2. **Core competencies for paraeducators.** From *A Core Curriculum and Training Program to Prepare Paraeducators to Work in Inclusive Classrooms Serving School Age Students with Disabilities,* by A. L. Pickett, K. Faison, and J. Formanek, 1993, New York: The National Resource Center for Paraprofessionals in Education and Related Services, Center for Advanced Study in Education, City University of New York.

tors must be skilled in data collection, assessment, and instructional strategies, for example, they are not responsible for design or evaluation of methods or programs. Paraeducators are responsible, however, in several legal and ethical competency areas. Among the primary skill/knowledge requirements for paraeducators are the following: maintaining confidentiality; respecting the legal and human rights of children, youth, and their families; following district policy; understanding role distinctions; and appreciating diversity.

To work in inclusive programs for school-age students, paraeducators will demonstrate

- an ability to instruct students in academic subjects using lesson plans and instructional strategies developed by teachers or other professional support staff;

- an ability to gather and record data about the performance and behavior of individual students; and to confer with special and general education practitioners about student schedules, instructional goals, progress, and performance;

- an ability to use developmentally and age-appropriate instructional procedures and reinforcement techniques; and

- an ability to operate computers, assistive technology, and adaptive equipment that will enable students with disabilities and other special needs to participate more fully in general education.

Figure 2.3.   **Additional competencies for paraeducators working in programs for school-age students.** From *A Core Curriculum and Training Program to Prepare Paraeducators to Work in Inclusive Classrooms Serving School Age Students with Disabilities,* by A. L. Pickett, K. Faison, and J. Formanek, 1993, New York: The National Resource Center for Paraprofessionals in Education and Related Services, Center for Advanced Study in Education, City University of New York.

PARAEDUCATORS WHO PROVIDE MULTILINGUAL/MULTIETHNIC INSTRUCTION

In addition to inclusive classrooms and other special education programs, paraeducators are assigned to other programs administered by schools. During the last decade they have become a major contributor to the delivery of instruction and other services for children and youth from multilingual and multiethnic heritages.

Paraeducators who provide multilingual/multiethnic instruction for children and youth are often the only members of instructional teams who speak the students' primary languages and are familiar with their cultural heritages. Consequently, role clarification is essential for effective instruction. Miramontes (1990) developed a triadic model for serving multilingual/multiethnic children with disabilities, in which responsibility for instruction is shared by a team comprising the resource specialist, paraeducator, and student. To avert the problem of a two-tiered system of education that results when the paraeducator becomes the primary instructor for language-minority students, the model emphasizes that instruction be the ultimate responsibility of school professionals. Team resource specialists with expertise in multilingual instruction function as consultants, sharing information with special educators and other school personnel, as well as collaborating with paraeducators for whom they provide assistance to develop lessons and try different instructional strategies. The resource specialist also conducts ongoing evaluations of the paraeducator's performance, providing feedback on a weekly or biweekly basis.

Paraeducators in multilingual/multiethnic programs perform tasks in three general categories: instruction, home contacts, and assessment. The primary responsibility of paraeducators is instructional. In addition to serving as a positive and linguistic role model, the paraeducator who speaks the student's home language can provide critical information about the knowledge base on which the student builds to learn the second language. With support from resource specialists, the paraeducators also identify specific objectives from the Individualized Education Program (IEP) and collaborate to provide in-depth instruction. Miramontes (1990) cautions against diminishing instructional time by using the bilingual paraeducator as an on-the-spot multipurpose translator, which results in decreased time for instructors.

The triadic model utilizes weekly or biweekly planning sessions as an opportunity to communicate about education guidelines and the overall needs of the school, and to promote cross-cultural understanding. Working under the direction of the team resource specialist, as a school-to-community liaison, paraeducators are often responsible for making home visits and calling parents. This capacity is frequently extended to create linkages with other social service agencies in the community. As community advocates, ethnic minority paraeducators may feel the strain of the dual responsibility of representing institutional and cultural perspectives. When the scope of the ethnic paraeducator's responsibilities is not formally stated in a job description, and adequate time and compensation are not provided for these multiple demands, frustration and burnout can occur.

Miramontes (1990) incorporates additional skill requirements for paraeducators on the multilingual/multiethnic team that address issues of selection and retention. These include interpersonal skills (the ability to relate to students and parents from a range of economic and educational backgrounds; ability to work well on a team), awareness (knowledge of school policies and systems; knowledge of community needs and interests), and literacy (verbal, reading, and writing fluency in their own language; adequate oral fluency in English).

Critical skills areas for school professionals working on multilingual/multiethnic teams include knowledge about how to assess and interpret difficulties with the translation process. An understanding of first and second language acquisition and of the sociocultural effects on learning are also important; the model emphasizes frequent discussions related to these matters during team meetings. School professionals also need to be knowledgeable about the community they serve and are required to strengthen school–community interactions. Collaboration skills are essential for all personnel, as are professional development skills; both can be enhanced during reflective discussions about student progress between team members.

Based on a review of best practices and research in the area, Pickett and Safarik (in press) have proposed a set of competencies for paraeducators who work with children and youth with special needs, including limited English proficiency. The competencies are listed in Figure 2.4.

To work in programs serving children and youth who have limited English, paraeducators will demonstrate

1. an understanding of differentiated staffing patterns and the distinctions among the responsibilities of professional and paraeducator personnel who work in bilingual and English as a Second Language programs;

2. an understanding and respect for the rights of all people, including those who have disabilities, are culturally different, or who have limited English proficiency;

3. an ability to meet legal, ethical, and professional standards of conduct established by the agency;

4. an ability to describe the distinctions among the various levels of English proficiency, including levels of conversational and academic proficiency;

5. an ability to use family and community outreach strategies to promote the full integration of children and youth who have limited English proficiency, are culturally different, and who have disabilities in school and society;

6. an ability to participate in the instructional team to implement appropriate instructional techniques that are natural, content-based, interactive, and promote inclusion of children and youth who have limited English proficiency and have disabilities;

7. an ability to participate in the instructional team to implement multidimensional formal and informal assessment procedures that are direct, accurate, and not culturally biased and to use assessment data to meet students learning needs;

8. an understanding of language acquisition theory; and

9. an understanding of the unique transition services needs of secondary students who have limited English proficiency and who have disabilities.

Figure 2.4.   **Competencies for paraeducators who provide instruction and support for children and youth who have limited English proficiency.** From *A Core Curriculum and Instructional Program to Prepare Paraeducators to Work with Children and Youth Who Have Limited English*, by A. L. Pickett and L. Safarik, in press, New York: The National Resource Center for Paraprofessionals in Education and Related Services, Center for Advanced Study in Education, City University of New York.

PARAEDUCATORS WHO WORK IN TITLE I AND OTHER COMPENSATORY EDUCATION PROGRAMS

The Office of Educational Research and Improvement, U.S. Department of Education (1990), developed the *Paraprofessional Training Manual* for paraeducators and teachers to use in forming an instructional team to help students from disadvantaged backgrounds succeed in a regular school program. The manual provides general guidelines for the clarification of the teachers' and paraeducators' roles and legal responsibility for instruction of these students. The preparation and oversight of lesson plans, as well as the supervision of the paraeducator staff, are teacher-designated functions. The role of paraeducators includes carrying out lesson plans, adding creative ideas and suggestions, maintaining discipline, and serving as a positive liaison to the community. Other paraeducator duties are the development of enrichment activities for students, assisting with creating an attractive learning environment, and sharing in clerical and other routine classroom management tasks. Understanding the legal and ethical rights of students and their families and the professional standards of conduct for working in schools and in the community are emphasized as key elements of both paraeducator and professional roles. Student welfare and safety are primary responsibilities.

This model also promotes a collaborative relationship between school professional and paraeducator staff, and identifies the importance of regularly scheduled meetings for planning and professional development purposes. Student assessment and progress, lesson planning, teaching strategies, parent–teacher conferences, behavior management, recordkeeping, school–community events, material and resource identification, community outreach, and special student needs were among the appropriate topics for planning meetings.

The potential for strengthening student skills when paraeducators are part of the team is stressed in this model. By delivering small group instruction, preteaching in support of the regular classroom activities, and assisting with the coordination of instruction with the regular program, the paraeducator can provide much needed individualized instruction. Doing reinforcement activities, providing additional assistance with instruction, administering teacher-developed tests, and overseeing long-term projects or homework are ways in which the paraeducator can support the instruction of students who are educationally or economically disadvantaged.

Serving as a link to the community is identified as a crucial function for paraeducators. By participating on community–school advisory groups, making home visits to encourage attendance (and to accompany other school staff on home visits), interpreting policies to non–English-speaking parents, making culturally appropriate visual aids, and providing instruction in home languages, paraeducators help foster a positive partnership between the school and the community.

EARLY CHILDHOOD PARAEDUCATORS

The NAEYC (1994) has developed a conceptual framework to promote "a coordinated, articulated system of high-quality early childhood professional preparation and development" (p. 77). This position statement identified key assumptions, guiding principles, and a common body of knowledge and skill competencies to be used in personnel preparation at levels ranging from entry-level paraeducator to doctoral-level professional. The paper identified the common "core" elements required for all early childhood personnel. Guidelines for expanding and adding depth to these core competencies for specialization such as administration and parent education, as well as higher levels of professional development, are established. The core competencies comprised eight domains and are listed in Figure 2.5.

These core competency areas are used as a foundation on which personnel training programs at various levels can build. At the *entry level*, the indi-

---

1. Demonstrate an understanding of child development and apply this knowledge in practice.

2. Observe and assess child behavior.

3. Establish and maintain a safe, healthy environment.

4. Plan and implement a developmentally appropriate curriculum.

5. Establish supportive relationships with children and implement developmentally appropriate guidance and group management techniques.

6. Establish and maintain positive and productive relationships with families.

7. Support the development and learning of individual children in the context of family, culture, and society.

8. Demonstrate an understanding of the early childhood profession and make a commitment to professionalism.

Figure 2.5. **Core competency domains for early child personnel.** Adapted from "NAEYC Position Statement: A Conceptual Framework for Early Childhood Professional Development," by National Association for the Education of Young Children, 1994, *Young Children*, pp. 68–77.

vidual with a Child Development Associate credential has demonstrated "competency to meet the specific needs of children and to work with parents and other adults to nurture children's physical, social, emotional, and intellectual growth in child development" (NAEYC, 1994, p. 72). Personnel at the *associate level* are able to perform independently with a group of children. Those at the *baccalaureate level* can apply and analyze the core knowledge to plan and develop curriculum, whereas the *doctoral-level* graduate conducts research contributing to the best practices body of knowledge.

This model also includes a continuum of professional development that identified six levels of early childhood professional preparation programs for which standards have been established nationally. Levels I through III are comparable to paraeducator levels in models developed by other disciplines, since they represent formal education levels below the baccalaureate degree. Level I requires supervision or support including linkages with the provider agency or enrollment in a supervised practicum. Level II requires the successful completion of a 1-year early childhood certificate program; and level III requires the successful completion of an associate degree program that conforms to the NAEYC guidelines. An interesting feature of this position paper is the recommendation that early childhood professionals with comparable qualifications, experience, and job responsibilities receive comparable compensation regardless of the setting of their job (i.e., public school, part-day or full-day centers, Head Start, before-school and after-school programs) or the age of the children they serve (pp. 75–76).

The National Resource Center for Paraprofessionals in Education and Related Services has developed training competencies for paraeducators who work with children with disabilities from birth to age 5 in classrooms and home-based programs (Pickett, Faison, Formanek, & Semrau, 1993). The competencies build on the core competencies for all paraeducators described earlier (see Figure 2.2). The team roles of early intervention/childhood paraeducators were differentiated from those of paraeducators in other settings. Specific training objectives were developed for paraeducators who work in home-based programs for infants and toddlers (Figure 2.6) and those who work in early childhood classrooms (Figure 2.7).

PARAEDUCATORS IN TRANSITION SERVICES

Key reform initiatives of the 1990s—for example, the School-to-Work Opportunities Act of 1994, the Individuals with Disabilities Education Act of 1990,

In addition to the core competencies required by all paraeducators, to work in early intervention and home visitor programs, paraeducators will demonstrate

- an ability to participate as a member of the Individualized Family Service Plan (IFSP) team responsible for developing service plans and education objectives for parents and their children;

- an ability to listen to and communicate with parents in order to gather information which the service delivery team can build on to meet the needs of the child and family;

- a knowledge of health care providers, social services, education agencies, and other support systems available in the community to assist parents and their child; and an ability to support parents and provide them with the skills and information they require to gain access to these services; and

- an ability to enhance parent interactions with their child by using/demonstrating effective techniques and materials to stimulate cognitive, physical, social, and language development.

Figure 2.6. **Competencies for paraeducators working in home visitor programs.** From *A Core Curriculum and Training Program to Prepare Paraeducators to Work in Center and Home Based Programs for Young Children with Disabilities from Birth to Age Five*, by A. L. Pickett, K. Faison, J. Formanek, and B. Semrau, 1993, New York: The National Resource Center for Paraprofessionals in Education and Related Services, Center for Advanced Study in Education, City University of New York.

Goals 2000: Educate America Act of 1994, and other related legislation in vocational education, rehabilitation human services, and employment and training (e.g., Carl D. Perkins Vocational and Applied Technology Education Act of 1990, Job Training Partnership Act of 1982, and its Amendments in 1992, Americans with Disabilities Act of 1990)—have an impact on the types of services schools are required to provide and on the need to establish systematic mechanisms for linking school and adult services.

Transition services, aimed at preparing and supporting students for transition from school to work and independent adult life, is an area within education that reflects significant changes in the traditional educator/human service provider role (DeFur & Taymans, 1995). With an emphasis on coordination, facilitation, and an interdisciplinary approach, this area of specialization requires competence in domains that have not been widely recognized for teacher effectiveness.

Since transition services are by definition cross-disciplinary, the need for role clarification is particularly important. The use of consultative collaboration is a useful model for integrating the work of paraeducators and professionals in providing transition services for persons with disabilities (Gajar

In addition to the core competencies required by all paraeducators, to work in center-based programs for young children, paraeducators will demonstrate

- an ability to use developmentally appropriate instructional interventions for curriculum activities in the areas of cognitive, motor, self-help, social/play, and language development for infants and young children ages 0–5;

- an ability to gather information about the performance of individual children and their behaviors and to share it with professional colleagues;

- an ability to prepare and use developmentally appropriate materials; and

- an ability to communicate and work effectively with parents and other primary caregivers.

Figure 2.7. **Competencies for paraeducators working in center-based programs.** From *A Core Curriculum and Training Program to Prepare Paraeducators to Work in Center and Home Based Programs for Young Children with Disabilities from Birth to Age Five,* by A. L. Pickett, K. Faison, J. Formanek, and B. Semrau, 1993, New York: The National Resource Center for Paraprofessionals in Education and Related Services, Center for Advanced Study in Education, City University of New York.

et al., 1993). The authors described the process as "an interactive process which enables people with diverse expertise to generate creative solutions to mutually defined problems. The outcome is enhanced, altered, and produces solutions that are different from those that the individual team members would produce independently" (p. 61). This model relies on the systematic coordination of services, stressing an individualized, holistic approach to service and instruction; personnel are not limited to prescribed functions.

DeFur and Taymans (1995) identified 12 competency domains for transition services professionals. They are listed in Figure 2.8. When individual competencies were ranked, those relating to coordination, communication, and collaboration were among the highest. The direct service competencies such as those involving instruction, curriculum, and learning theory were ranked lowest. The authors suggest that "Perhaps these areas constitute specialty areas where a working knowledge of these skills is needed by the transition specialist practitioner, but the direct application of these important skills is performed by someone else" (p. 46). This statement indicates a team approach to staff differentiation, involving the transition service specialist as a facilitator with school professionals and paraeducators from within and outside the local education agency contributing in various capacities. The authors also identified 7 essential or "core" competencies for the transition services specialist, from a total of 116. These core competencies are included in Figure 2.9.

1. Philosophy and historical considerations

2. Knowledge of agencies and systems changes

3. Professionalism, advocacy, and legal issues in transition

4. Working with others in the transition process

5. Development of management and individualized plans

6. Curriculum, instruction, and learning theory (general)

7. Assessment (general)

8. Career counseling and vocational theory

9. Vocational assessment and job development

10. Job training and support

11. Transition administrative functions

12. Program evaluation and research

Figure 2.8. **Transition services specialist competency domains.** Adapted from "Competencies Needed for Transition Specialists in Vocational Rehabilitation, Vocational Education and Special Education," by S. H. DeFur and J. M. Taymans, 1995, *Exceptional Children, 62*(1), pp. 38–51.

In a similar study, Safarik et al. (1991) identified competencies for paraeducator transition service providers who were at various stages of training and career development. Their work was based on prior research (Morehouse & Albright, 1991) which identified competencies for transition services paraprofessionals as reported by 95 paraprofessionals and 45 administrators in schools and agencies serving Southern California youth and adults with disabilities. Safarik et al. used a three-phased competency validation process. A

1. Knowledge of systems change

2. Development and management of Individualized Transition Plans

3. Working with others in the transition process

4. Vocational assessment and job development

5. Professionalism, advocacy, and legal issues

6. Job training and support

7. Assessment (general)

Figure 2.9. **Transition services specialist competency domains.** Adapted from "Competencies Needed for Transition Specialists in Vocational Rehabilitation, Vocational Education and Special Education," by S. H. DeFur and J. M. Taymans, 1995, *Exceptional Children, 62*(1), pp. 38–51.

national panel of 18 experts who represented secondary and 2- and 4-year postsecondary programs that provided training for transition services personnel reviewed the original set of competencies as developed by the research team. A sample of 21 practitioners (paraprofessionals enrolled in a university training program) was surveyed to identify (a) criticality, (b) relative time spent using, and (c) perceived need for training in each of the competencies. The study yielded 54 competencies, which were organized into eight categories. The competency categories are displayed in Figure 2.10.

The purpose of the study was to develop a comprehensive curriculum for paraeducators at three training levels: secondary, community college, and university. (Training at the secondary level included vocational training and inservice education typically conducted at regional occupational programs and centers which serve both high school students and adults in the state of California.) Reviewers were asked to identify competencies as "essential," "important," "somewhat important," and "not important" for training at each level. The three training levels corresponded roughly to three levels of personnel: *entry-level* paraeducators were trained at the secondary level for positions such as job coach; *midlevel* paraeducators were trained at the community college level for positions such as job developer and independent living instructor; and *professional-level* training was conducted at the university for roles such as transition coordinator. The analysis resulted in a set of training competencies for each of the three levels.

Paraeducators training to become transition services practitioners at the professional level complete a bachelor's degree program encompassing the entire range of competencies. Articulated programs at entry level and midlevel

---

1. Foundations of transition services

2. Assessing transition program needs

3. Assessing learner needs

4. Planning transition programs for special needs learners

5. Implementing training/instructional components

6. Job development and placement

7. Job site training and instruction

8. Developing professional skills

Figure 2.10. **Competency categories for all transition services personnel.** Adapted from *A Career Ladder Program for Transition Services Personnel: A Collaborative Curriculum Development Approach*, by L. Safarik et al., 1991, Long Beach: California State University, Long Beach.

emphasize applied competencies. The curriculum for training transition services paraeducators uses the competency differentiation framework shown in Table 2.1.

Certain competencies are essential at all training levels (demonstrating professional, ethical, and legal standards of conduct). Others are only essential at the professional level (developing management skills and program evaluation skills; participating in local, state, and national professional organization activities). In certain competency areas, such as implementing training instructional components, the collaborative role is emphasized at all levels (i.e., entry, mid, and professional). Assessment and program planning functions are "essential" training areas for professionals, but are "important" or "somewhat important" for entry-level and midlevel training. In other categories, such as job development and placement and job site and community training, training in the development and implementation of behavior management, data collection, training, task analysis, and communication with employers and employees is "essential" at the midlevel (community college) for paraeducators. By design, this model is flexible and recognizes that discrete training boundaries are not realistic. Conceptually, this approach assumes that the professional must be competent in all areas, but as a facilitator is likely to be less involved in direct instruction and services. However, paraeducators who provide transition services must be competent in providing direct instruction and services in the community where they are likely to be the sole service providers.

PARAEDUCATORS IN ORIENTATION AND MOBILITY PROGRAMS

Paraeducators may work with individuals with disabilities in settings outside of the classroom. For example, paraeducators who work with blind or visually impaired individuals frequently conduct training in the community or other natural settings. A position paper on the training and certification of orientation and mobility (O&M) assistants (Wiener et al., 1990) put forth recommendations for defining the roles, responsibilities, and training and supervision needs of these paraeducators. Consensus for implementing these recommendations was reached by the Association for Education and Rehabilitation (AER) of the Blind and Visually Impaired, Division IX, in 1988.

Among the key considerations reported as affecting the functioning of O&M professionals and, therefore, O&M assistants are (a) the need for a

Table 2.1

Transition Services Competencies for Entry-Level and Midlevel Paraprofessionals and Professionals (Sample from Category A Only)

Transition Services Foundations	Entry Level	Midlevel	Professional
1. Demonstrate knowledge of the unique transition service needs of individuals with disabilities.	E	E	E
2. Demonstrate knowledge of the professional, ethical, and legal standards of conduct in relationships with students, parents, school personnel, adult service providers, clients, employers, and coworkers.	E	E	E
3. Compare and contrast the theoretical models and current practices for providing transition services to youth and adults with disabilities.	I	I	E
4. Identify, describe, and differentiate between various systems, agencies, businesses, communities, their use of terms, and the roles of personnel that participate in the transition process.	I	I	E
5. Demonstrate communication, conflict resolution, and negotiation skills that facilitate interagency and intra-agency collaboration.	I	I	I
6. Demonstrate knowledge of the legislative history and current mandates that address the provision of transitional services and the rights and entitlement of students/clients with disabilities and their families.	S	S	E

Note. E = essential; I = important; S = somewhat important.

Adapted from *A Career Ladder Program for Transition Services Personnel: A Collaborative Curriculum Development Approach* by L. Safarik et al., 1991, Long Beach, California State University, Long Beach.

trusting relationship between student and service provider, (b) thorough assessment and evaluation of each student's abilities and needs, (c) analysis and selection of instructional environments, (d) individualized programming for each student, (e) appropriate sequencing of instruction, and (f) instruction in appropriate and effective decision making (Wiener et al., 1990, p. 70).

O&M professionals are certified through university training in child development, adult learning, psychosocial aspects, learning and teaching principles, and the special needs of individuals who are blind and visually impaired. This training qualifies O&M professionals to perform the essential functions of assessment and evaluation, program planning, direct teaching, public education, and supervision of the assistant. Employing O&M assistants as part of the service delivery team serves several important purposes. These include freeing professionals to do more direct instruction, providing increased opportunities for application of skills for the client, and providing reinforcement of key concepts and skills through frequent practice.

O&M paraeducator roles include following prescriptive programs written by supervising professionals and providing input for, but not making, programmatic decisions. The primary responsibilities of O&M assistants are to provide ongoing, frequent repetition and reinforcement of skills and concepts in the areas of body-image training, sensory training, sensory-motor development, spatial environment, and basic skills such as diagonal cane techniques. The specialist is responsible for the introduction and initial instruction in all of these areas with the exception of the sighted-guide technique due to the tremendous need for this basic training.

ANALYSIS AND SYNTHESIS: COMPETENCY MODEL REVIEW PROCESS

The compilation of paraeducator competencies summarized in the previous sections was analyzed at two levels. In level 1, competencies were analyzed within specific disciplines to identify role distinctions between paraeducators and professionals. In level 2, a cross-disciplinary analysis was used to derive a common set of "core" competencies, as well as competencies which are unique for paraeducators employed in specific areas. The resulting conceptual framework for staff differentiation may be useful for educators (professionals and paraeducators), curriculum developers, trainers, and agency administrators.

Level 1 Analysis: Parameters for Paraeducator Competencies

At the first level of analysis, competencies within each discipline were examined to identify the parameters for professional and paraeducator roles and responsibilities. Competencies for paraeducators and professionals were listed for each specialty area, then labeled according to five categories:

1. competencies shared by both paraeducators and professionals

2. competencies primarily designated for the paraeducator

3. competencies designated for the professional only

4. competencies that require different functional capacities for paraeducators and professionals

5. knowledge competencies that are broad-based and theoretical for professionals and applied for paraeducators

Competencies in similar categories for each specialty area were collapsed. The descriptions that follow summarize the results.

1. *Competencies shared by both paraeducators and school professionals:* Some competencies are essentially the same for both paraeducators and professionals. Both personnel groups are responsible for knowing and adhering to legal, ethical, and professional standards; both must demonstrate effective communication skills and human relation skills in their work with students and coworkers within and outside of their agency, and with families and parents of their students. Both groups must know the boundaries and expectations for paraeducators and professionals and carry out their responsibilities accordingly. Advocacy skills, which may be considered within the realm of legal, ethical, and professional standards, are essential for both groups.

There are slight differences in how these competencies are to be demonstrated by the team members. Communication with family members specifically regarding programmatic decisions, treatment, and diagnoses is the sole responsibility of the professional. Also, while both need to consult with other staff within and outside their agencies, the professional's mode of communication is one of a *facilitator,* who must ensure that communication between all participating individuals is coordinated efficiently. Finally, the ultimate legal responsibility for providing services and instruction for students lies with the professional. Further, professionals must apply legal, ethical, and professional standards in developing and managing programs.

2. *Competencies primarily for paraeducators:* Some competencies are designated primarily as paraeducator duties, although the professional member of the team is likely to be involved in these tasks as well. Maintaining a safe, healthy, and attractive environment; performing clerical duties; and maintaining equipment and supplies (including assisting students with adaptive devices) are among the routine, noninstructional responsibilities of the paraeducator. Ongoing professional development is important for all school personnel; paraeducators who usually lack formal training prior to employment should be able to enhance their skills through structured on-the-job coaching, inservice training, conferences, or formal education.

3. *Competencies for school professionals only:* Aside from responsibilities related to instructional and therapeutic assessment, planning, and programming duties (which are described in the "Different Functional Capacity" category), professionals are responsible for the supervision, on-the-job coaching, and mentoring of paraeducators with whom they work. Ongoing and formal evaluations and consultative planning meetings are to be conducted by the professional in an effort to guide the paraeducator in the development and proper application of skills.

Professionals, who are increasingly expected to perform as program managers, often have duties that go beyond the direct instruction of students. Knowledge of systems' change processes, marketing strategies and public education, program evaluation, and grant writing is within the scope of the professional's competency. Finally, the professional must have content knowledge; that is, the teacher or other professional must have a sufficient level of general education that enables him or her to create curriculum and design programs, make critical decisions, and ensure quality standards of education and services. This content knowledge is acquired through formal education, or in the case of employment training and transition services, through experience in an occupational field.

4. *Competencies with different functional capacities for professionals and paraeducators:* Paraeducators and professionals work together as a team to provide instruction and services to their students and clients. Although it may appear that paraeducators and professionals are involved in virtually the same role as they interact with children, youth, and adults, there are subtle, yet critical differences in the nature of their work. In all instructional matters, such as assessment, planning, instruction, service intervention, and behavior management, the professional functions as the developer, decision-maker, interpreter, prescriber, and manager. The paraeducator provides input at each instructional phase, implements the instructional or behavior man-

agement strategies, and provides feedback to the other members of the team about the strategy or intervention.

The quality of services or instruction depends on the creativity and observation skills of all team members, but the paraeducator does not make major modifications to the instructional or related services program plan without consultation with the professional. A major function of paraeducators is to provide reinforcement of instruction and provide practice opportunities to facilitate mastery. Remedial assistance, orientation of new students, and assisting absent or tardy students with instructions are examples of how paraeducators implement instruction as developed by the professional.

Paraeducators may administer teacher-made assessment instruments and formal standardized tests as directed by the professional, but the interpretation and scoring of nonstandardized assessments must be conducted by the professional. Paraeducators must be skilled in making nonjudgmental behavioral observations and in monitoring student/client progress. Professionals must be skilled in using these data to make sound programmatic decisions and in communicating the results to the student, parents, administrators, and other members of the instructional and service delivery team.

Both paraeducators and professionals provide instruction and other direct services to individuals and groups on a daily basis. In most cases, paraeducators perform these tasks in the presence of a supervising professional. However, there are exceptions which are related to the instructional or service delivery setting. Paraeducators who make home visits or who do community outreach (such as early childhood workers, multiethnic/multilingual workers, and transition services paraprofessionals) are expected to work more independently and make decisions in their interactions with employers, parents, and other community representatives. Competency in client or student supervision and behavior management are necessary for paraeducators who work in these settings.

5. *Knowledge competencies: broad-based and theoretical for school professionals; applied for paraeducators:* Knowledge competency includes theory in human development, child development, instructional technology, and language acquisition, and the models or best practices accepted by the respective disciplines. In all areas, paraeducators and professionals are required to have knowledge of the theoretical basis and best practices relative to their discipline. The depth, breadth, and way in which the knowledge is used varies significantly for the two groups.

Professionals are expected to have thorough knowledge of the theory on which they base diagnostic and programmatic decisions. Professional knowledge is informed by other disciplines (breadth) and is intensive (depth). Paraeducators are required to have a general, practical knowledge of human growth and development, for example, as it relates to their students' needs and to apply best practices knowledge as modeled by the professional. For paraeducators who have limited formal education in theoretical or best practices knowledge, systematic staff development and on-the-job coaching are essential.

Level 2 Analysis: Core Competencies Versus Specialized Competencies

Finally, competencies from all disciplines were analyzed to identify a set of common or core competencies that transcend specialty areas. A previously developed set of core competencies (Pickett, Faison, & Formanek, 1993) was used as a frame of reference. The core competencies developed by the NRC for Paraprofessionals in Education and Related Services encompass seven general categories as seen in Figure 2.11. The competency models

1. Strengthening the instructional team
   a. Understanding distinctions in the roles and duties of teachers and paraeducators
   b. Understanding professional and ethical responsibilities of paraeducators
   c. Using effective communication and problem-solving techniques
2. Legal and human rights of children, youth, and their parents
3. Human growth and development
4. Components of the instructional process
   a. IEP/IFSP/ITP lesson plans
   b. Assessment
   c. Goals and objectives
   d. Behavior management
   e. Instructional strategies
5. Appreciating diversity
6. Working with families
7. Emergency/health/safety procedures

Figure 2.11. **Core curriculum for paraeducators.** From *A Core Curriculum and Training Program to Prepare Paraeducators to Work in Inclusive Classrooms Serving School Age Students with Disabilities*, by A. L. Pickett, K. Faison, and J. Formanek, 1993, New York: The National Resource Center for Paraprofessionals in Education and Related Services, Center for Advanced Study in Education, City University of New York.

reviewed in this chapter were examined to determine their consistency with the NRC model.

Figure 2.12 lists the 11 competency areas that were derived from the analysis of paraeducator competencies. These competency areas were common to all disciplinary models. Within specific disciplines, paraeducators are required to obtain specialized competencies in addition to theoretical foundation knowledge discussed in the previous section. Transition services paraeducators need specialized training in *vocational assessment, job development, and job training and support.* Those who work with multiethnic and multilingual students need to *understand sociocultural effects on learning, community outreach techniques, and have higher levels of community awareness* than other paraeducators. Those paraeducators who specialize in working with individuals who have special needs, such as sensory impairments, physical disabilities, or other learning problems, need to be *knowledgeable about specialized teaching strategies or treatments and assistive devices.*

This analysis validates prior work in identifying core competencies for paraeducators in education and related services. An additional outcome is the observation that several disciplines recognize both an entry-level and *certified* or experienced paraeducator level (NAEYC, 1994; Safarik et al., 1991). Sarkees-Wircenski and Scott (1995) developed a schematic that delineated personnel preparation levels in three categories: vocational,

---

Paraeducators will be able to

1. work effectively with students, clients, coworkers, employers;

2. use effective professional skills;

3. demonstrate instructional skills;

4. develop instructional skills;

5. provide instructional support (e.g., prepare instructional materials);

6. maintain a safe and healthy environment;

7. demonstrate behavior management skills;

8. demonstrate effective communication;

9. demonstrate assessment and planning skills;

10. demonstrate knowledge of legal, ethical, and professional standards; and

11. demonstrate the ability to develop and maintain relationships with families.

Figure 2.12.   **Core paraeducator competencies.**

technical education, and professional levels (p. 43). The skilled worker or craftworker is trained at the vocational education level and receives training in technical skills and knowledge. This "practice-oriented" worker is comparable to the entry-level paraeducator. The specialist or paraeducator at the certified level receives technical education. At this technician level, the worker possesses knowledge of technology and technical skills. The professionally educated worker (i.e., the teacher) is "theory oriented" and has specialized knowledge and technical skills.

SUMMARY

Paraeducators and professionals working together can be a powerful team. When roles and responsibilities are not clarified, however, the best efforts of both are compromised, resulting in a poor quality of services that does not meet the needs of children and youth. The benefits of defining the competencies and role parameters for paraeducators are quality programs and enhanced opportunities for professional development. A cross-disciplinary approach to the training and professional development of paraeducators is a natural outgrowth of the movement toward integrated services, which characterizes recent educational reform efforts. Also, finding the common ground of paraeducator competency models forms the basis for designing articulated secondary and postsecondary education programs in the education, human services, and allied health "career major" areas as defined in the 1994 School-to-Work Opportunities Act. As new models of paraeducator competencies are created and existing models are refined, program developers, trainers, and program administrators will be better equipped to efficiently train and deploy both paraeducators and professionals.

Discussion Questions

1. What are the responsibilities typically performed by teachers and other school professionals who provide education, transitional, and early childhood services?

2. Are there any duties that are solely the responsibilities of paraeducators?

(*Continues*)

Discussion Questions (Continued)

3. What responsibilities are shared by school professionals and para-educators?

4. Compare and contrast the distinctions in the functions and roles of school professionals and paraeducators.

5. Is there an identifiable hierarchy of skills for paraeducators working in different areas? If so, what are the implications for developing comprehensive articulated systems of staff development and career advancement for paraeducators?

Exercises

1. Divide into groups of five or six. Using the Teacher/Paraeducator Role Perception Activity form on the next page, discuss the various tasks with your group to determine whether a specific task is exclusively performed by the teacher or the paraeducator or if it is a shared responsibility. Be prepared to share the results of this activity with the entire class.

2. Working as a group, obtain examples of job descriptions for para-educators from early childhood provider agencies, local school districts, and vocational and other provider agencies in your community. Then use the Competency Model Review Process, discussed in this chapter, to (a) compare and contrast the similarities and differences in the tasks assigned to paraeducators in different programs/agencies; (b) identify competencies required by paraeducators working in the different program areas; (c) compare the similarities and differences between these competencies and those contained in this chapter; (d) determine if duties to be performed exclusively by teachers are clearly specified; and (e) evaluate the similarity and distinctions in the levels (depth and breadth) of skills required by paraeducators in the different program levels. Learners will use the results of this analysis after they study the next chapter.

Teacher/Paraeducator Role Perception Activity

Directions: Discuss the following tasks with the members of your group. When the group reaches consensus about whether a task should be performed exclusively by the teacher or the paraeducator or if it could be a shared responsibility place an "X" in the appropriate column.

Task	Teacher	Paraeducator	Shared
Recording and charting data			
Administering standardized tests			
Scoring standardized tests			
Grading tests and papers			
Analyzing and interpreting the results of various assessment activities			
Setting goals and objectives for the class and individual students			
Planning lessons			
Introducing new skills/concepts			
Modifying/adapting instructional plans			
Carrying out lesson plans			
Instructing individual or small groups of students			
Developing behavior management plans			
Implementing behavior management programs			
Disciplining students			
Developing instructional materials			
Preparing instructional materials			
Evaluating student performance and progress			
Conducting training in community learning sites			
Recording attendance and maintaining other records			
Setting up and maintaining learning centers/ adaptive equipment			

(Continues)

Task	Teacher	Paraeducator	Shared
Inventorying and ordering supplies			
Participating in individualized program planning meetings, parent conferences, and other school-based meetings			
Meeting and conferring with parents			
Consulting with professional staff about a student's program and behaviors			
Maintaining a clean, safe learning environment			

Note. Based on activities contained in *Handbook for Special Education Paraprofessionals*, by A. L. Pickett and J. Formanek, 1982, New York: New York City Public Schools, and in *Issues and Responsibilities in Utilizing, Training, and Managing Paraprofessionals*, by S. F. Vasa and A. L. Steckelberg, 1991, Lincoln: University of Nebraska.

REFERENCES

DeFur, S. H., & Taymans, J. M. (1995). Competencies needed for transition specialists in vocational rehabilitation, vocational education and special education, *Exceptional Children*, 62(1), 38–51.

Education for All Handicapped Children Act of 1975, 20 U.S.C. §1400 *et seq.*

Friend, M., & Cook, L. (1996). *Interactions: Collaboration skills for school professionals* (2nd ed.). White Plains, NY: Longman.

Gajar, A., Goodman, L., & McAfee, J. (1993). *Secondary schools and beyond: Transition of individuals with mild disabilities.* New York: Macmillan.

Harper, V. (1994). Multicultural perspectives in the classroom: Professional preparation for educational paraprofessionals. *Action in Teacher Education*, XVI(3), 66–78.

Individuals with Disabilities Education Act of 1990, 20 U.S.C. §1400 *et seq.*

Miramontes, O. B. (1990). Organizing for effective paraprofessional services in special education: A multilingual/multiethnic instructional service team model. *Remedial and Special Education*, 12(1), 29–36.

Morehouse, J., & Albright, L. (1991). Training trends and needs of paraprofessionals in transition service delivery agencies. *Teacher Education and Special Education*, 14(4), 248–256.

National Association for the Education of Young Children. (1994). NAEYC position statement: A conceptual framework for early childhood professional development. *Young Children*, pp. 68–77.

Office of Educational Research and Improvement, U.S. Department of Education. (1990). *Paraprofessional training manual* (Report No. TAC-B-140). Portland, OR: Chapter 1 Rural Technical Assistance Center, Regions 6 and 7; Northwest Regional Educational Laboratory. (ERIC Document Reproduction Service No. ED 334 151).

Passaro, P., Pickett, A. L., Latham, G., & HongBo, W. (1994). The training and support needs of paraprofessionals in rural special education settings. *Rural Special Education Quarterly, 13*(4) 3–9.

Pickett, A. L., Faison, K., & Formanek, J. (1993). *A core curriculum and training program to prepare paraeducators to work in inclusive classrooms serving school age students with disabilities.* New York: The National Resource Center for Paraprofessionals in Education and Related Services, Center for Advanced Study in Education, City University of New York.

Pickett, A. L., Faison, K., Formanek, J., & Semrau, B. (1993). *A core curriculum and training program to prepare paraeducators to work in center and home based programs for young children with disabilities from birth to age five.* New York: The National Resource Center for Paraprofessionals in Education and Related Services, Center for Advanced Study in Education, City University of New York.

Pickett, A. L., Faison, K., Formanek, J., & Woods, J. (1993). *A core curriculum and training program to prepare paraeducators to work in transitional services and supported employment programs.* New York: The National Resource Center for Paraprofessionals in Education and Related Services, Center for Advanced Study in Education, City University of New York.

Pickett, A. L., & Formanek, J. (1982). *Handbook for special education paraprofessionals.* New York: New York City Public Schools.

Pickett, A. L., & Safarik, L. (in press). *A core curriculum and instructional program to prepare paraeducators to work with children and youth who have limited English.* New York: The National Resource Center for Paraprofessionals in Education and Related Services, Center for Advanced Study in Education, City University of New York.

Pickett, A. L., Vasa, S. F., & Steckelberg, A. L. (1993). *Using paraeducators effectively in the classroom.* Bloomington, IN: Phi Delta Kappa Foundation.

Safarik, L., Prather, M., Hanson, G., Guzman, G., Ryan, C., & Schwan D. (1991). *A career ladder program for transition services personnel: A collaborative curriculum development approach.* Long Beach: California State University, Long Beach.

Sarkees-Wircenski, M., & Scott, J. L. (1995). *Vocational special needs.* Homewood, IL: American Technical Publishers.

Simpson, R. L., Whelan, R. J., & Zabel, R. H. (1993). Special education personnel preparation in the 21st century: Issues and strategies. *Remedial and Special Education, 14*(2), 7–22.

Snodgrass, A. S. (1991). *Actual and preferred practices of employment, placement, supervision and evaluation of teacher aides in Idaho school districts.* Unpublished doctoral dissertation, University of Idaho, Moscow.

Stahl, B. J., & Lorenz, G. (1995). *Views on paraprofessionals.* St. Paul, MN: Minnesota Department of Education.

Steckelberg, A. L., & Vasa, S. F. (1996). *A world wide web delivery model for paraeducator training.* Lincoln: University of Nebraska.

Vasa, S. F., & Steckelberg, A. L. (1991). *Issues and responsibilities in utilizing, training, and managing paraprofessionals.* Lincoln: University of Nebraska.

Wiener, W. R., Deaver, K., DiCorpo, D., Hayes, J., Hill, E., Manzer, D., Newcomer, J., Pogrund, R., Rosen, S., & Usland, M. (1990). The orientation and mobility assistant. *RE: View, XXII,* 69–77.

CHAPTER 3

· ·

Team Roles in Therapy Services

· ·

Thomas M Longhurst
Idaho State University, Pocatello

OVERVIEW

The focus of this chapter is on employees who serve in partnership with or alongside professional-level therapists as *aides* or *assistants* in schools and other education settings. In this chapter these aides and assistants are designated *paratherapists* (Longhurst & Witmer, 1994). The chapter includes discussions of occupational, physical, and speech therapy services; distinctions in the roles and duties of therapists, aides, and assistants; preservice and inservice training for paratherapists including paratherapist career pathways; and a discussion of appropriate utilization standards. The chapter concludes with a discussion of therapist supervision of aides and assistants. Because there is considerable specialized terminology in this chapter that may be new to teachers, administrators, and paraeducators, a glossary of key terms is provided at the end of the chapter.

Instructional Objectives

After studying this chapter and participating in discussions and exercises, the reader will be able to:

1. Describe changes in education and early intervention programs that have increased the need for therapy aides and assistants in these settings.

2. Describe the practice of speech–language pathology and physical and occupational therapy in the schools.

3. Describe the differences between aide and assistant roles in therapy services.

55

4. Describe responsibilities of the therapy team that are reserved for the therapists.

5. Describe standards for paratherapist employment and training across the three disciplines.

6. Compare and contrast different forms of credentials in use for paratherapists.

7. Describe career pathways for paratherapists.

8. Describe therapist responsibilities in the supervision and management of paratherapists.

. . . .

THE NEED FOR PARATHERAPISTS IN EDUCATION AND EARLY INTERVENTION

Two major factors in the last two decades have significantly increased the need for paratherapists. First, the number of children and youth in the schools with disabilities has increased over this time period. The schools are serving more children with more severe, multiple disabilities than ever before. Our school systems are also serving much younger children. The advent of increased services to infants, toddlers, preschoolers, and their families has increased the need for therapists and the paratherapists who work alongside them. This need for increased quantity and quality of services has occurred at the same time as state governments and schools are being faced with cuts in education funding and generally decreased resources.

As the therapy professions have developed and their practice consists both of technical, routine tasks and executive, diagnostic or decision-making tasks, the technical or routine tasks are increasingly assigned or delegated to paratherapists. Also, when there are therapist personnel shortages, the use of paratherapists to extend the services of therapists becomes more attractive. A therapist can serve more students and serve them better because of increased diversity of therapy sites, frequency of services, and daily follow-through, with the appropriate use of paratherapists.

The administrative aspects of therapy services must concern all therapists as well as school administrators. The quality of therapy services and their relevance to the educational goals of students, families, and administrators must be paramount. With increasing costs for therapists working either as school employees or contractees, the cost-effectiveness and clinical efficacy of therapy services take on increasing importance. Using paratherapists appropriately can decrease costs and thereby increase clinical efficiency. The frequency of an individual's therapy can be increased, which often increases effectiveness.

A philosophy of appropriate paratherapist utilization in the schools should be that well-trained, appropriately assigned or delegated, and well-supervised paratherapists can be an effective and efficient adjunct to therapist services. Appropriate paratherapist utilization can stabilize increasing costs or even decrease costs while maintaining high-quality services (Spahr, 1995).

SCHOOL THERAPISTS

The professionals that provide therapy services in schools are known as (a) *speech–language pathologists* or SLPs, (b) *physical therapists* or PTs, and (c) *occupational therapists* or OTs. Sometimes SLPs may be called speech therapists, speech–language clinicians, or even communication disorders specialists, as well as other titles, but the generally accepted title is speech–language pathologist. Often therapists list their degree(s) after their name and designate their credential(s) as in Carrie L. Mori, MS, OTR/L, which means that she has a master of science degree, is registered by the American Occupational Therapy Association, and is licensed by the state. Speech–language pathologists often list their degree and then designate CCC-SLP after their degree to indicate they hold a certificate of clinical competence in speech–language pathology from the American Speech-Language-Hearing Association.

Speech–language pathologists have a long history of service in the schools. In that setting they are the therapists with whom teachers, administrators, students, and their families are most likely to be familiar. Although SLPs work in a variety of settings with all age groups, the greatest proportion work in the schools. Changes in education service delivery systems, increasing numbers of children and youth who need services for communication disorders, and technological advances have resulted in an expanding scope of practice for the profession of speech–language pathology. SLPs are integral to the rehabilitation of students with traumatic brain injury (TBI) and for students developing communication skills through augmentive/alternative communication (AAC) systems.

They work with many students with hearing disabilities, students with learning disabilities and language impairment, and students with speech articulation and phonologic problems. Although they traditionally worked mostly with younger children, more recently they have moved into secondary education where they have experienced great success in developing better communication skills in adolescents and facilitating transitions to work or postsecondary training or education.

Physical therapists often contract their services to the schools and occasionally may be employees of a district. They are specialists in the use of assistive and supportive devices that improve mobility, in positioning students and performing therapeutic modalities, and in using exercises with and without equipment that improve strength of muscles and range of motion of joints. They teach use of safety harnesses, walkers, and other adaptive equipment. They teach the skills of safely lifting and transferring students. Their work is designed to develop strength and range of motion that can then be used in walking, sitting, feeding, writing, using a keyboard, and other activities of daily living.

Occupational therapists are often employed by the schools or may have contracts for service with the schools. They are skilled at using the muscle strength and range of joint movement developed by physical therapists to adapt and teach activities of daily living. They determine effective adaptive equipment needs and classroom modifications. Some school employees or families question the need for occupational therapists in the schools because they assume that OTs are trained to focus on adults who are undergoing vocational rehabilitation to reenter the workforce after an accident or other physical trauma. Occupational therapists are skilled at these types of tasks sometimes employed with adolescent TBI students, but their greatest value is working with infants, toddlers, preschool children, and early elementary children in teaching daily living skills that most educators take for granted in their typical students. It tends to improve understanding of the role of OTs to say that the occupation of young children is play and the occupation of students is learning and acquiring skills. Occupational therapists teach play and learning skills as well as activities of daily living such as oral feeding and swallowing, crawling, sitting, standing, and walking. They are skilled in the use of adaptive devices that augment skills or provide alternative means for accomplishing school tasks.

Often therapists from these three disciplines work together collaboratively on a related services team to support teachers and improve classroom learning for students. They provide educationally relevant services. Their intervention skills are complementary and closely interrelated, and the therapists are trained to work together in an interdisciplinary fashion. Each therapy discipline uses a multiskilled, multilevel workforce that incorporates the use of aides and assistants.

AIDE VERSUS ASSISTANT DISTINCTIONS
IN THERAPY SERVICES

Within the disciplines of occupational, physical, and speech therapy there are clear distinctions between aides and assistants (Figure 3.1). These two paratherapist categories differ in the amount of preservice education or training of the paratherapists, their *credentials*, the extent of their *scope of practice*, amount and type of *supervision* they require, and the pay and fringe benefits they receive.

Aide is a paratherapist title given to individuals with a minimum level of training and a limited scope of practice in student treatment. The aide is typically an unlicensed, uncertified school employee who works under the direction of the therapist. On-site, *close supervision* by the therapist of sessions where an aide is in contact with a child or youth is recommended for best practice. The aide carries out designated or specifically *assigned* routine tasks. These tasks include transporting, transferring, and positioning students; maintaining, cleaning, and assembling materials, devices, and equipment;

Therapy Aides

1. Minimum level of formal training

2. Limited scope of practice

3. Uncertified/unlicensed

4. Prescribed, specifically *assigned* routine tasks

5. On-site supervision with therapist present

6. Usually hourly/often near minimum wage and minimal fringe benefits

Therapy Assistants

1. Associate degree from accredited program

2. Expanded scope of practice

3. Certified/licensed

4. *Delegated* expanded treatment functions

5. Supervised but may provide treatment without therapist present

6. On-site and distant work settings

7. Usually a salaried employee with fringe benefits comparable to therapist's

---

Figure 3.1. **Distinctions between aide and assistant roles.**

performing clerical duties; and working with students as assigned in a closely monitored and supervised therapy environment. In most circumstances the aide is required to have a high school diploma or GED, to be at least 18 years of age, and to have completed some occupational training in high school, in a postsecondary training facility, or during on-the-job training in the school. Aides are often hourly employees with near minimum wage pay and few fringe benefits. Some states recognize additional training or experience through pay grades or levels (I, II, III) within the aide category.

Assistant is a paratherapist title given to individuals with an associate degree (or equivalent) from a physical therapist assistant (PTA), certified occupational therapy assistant (COTA), or speech–language pathology assistant (SLPA) program. The American Physical Therapy Association (APTA, 1994a) and the American Occupational Therapy Association (AOTA, 1991) have formal accreditation standards for such programs. There are only a few associate degree programs in speech–language pathology, although the number is increasing. The American Speech-Language-Hearing Association (ASHA) approves training programs and registers SLPAs. PTAs and COTAs are typically certified and in most states are a licensed or registered employee of either the school, therapist, or agency who contracts with the school. Thirty states certify or license SLPAs, and ASHA is planning to start offering national registration for SLPAs in June 1998 (Paul-Brown, 1995); they will be referred to as *registered SLPAs* (R-SLPAs).

Assistants also work under supervision of the therapist. In many cases the therapist is not present while the experienced assistant is working with students. Their scope of practice is significantly expanded from that of the aide. Their education, expertise, and clinical training allow them to focus their efforts on executing treatment protocols with students and their families. Although they do not diagnose, develop, or change treatment protocols without permission, an experienced assistant may work somewhat independently in carrying out treatment protocols planned by the therapist.

DISTINCTIONS IN TEAM ROLES

Therapists, aides, and assistants work as a team (see Chapter 5). Each has his or her own scope of practice, but they share many duties and work together to accomplish common goals and objectives.

Responsibilities of therapists fall into two basic categories: (a) assessing and developing, implementing, and modifying treatment plans, and (b) supervision and providing on-the-job training to paratherapists. Responsibilities defined in the scope of practice of therapists are outlined in Figure 3.2. The professional organizations (AOTA, APTA, ASHA) representing the three disciplines have specific guidelines for credentialing therapists prior to supervising aides or assistants.

The therapist who will be responsible for supervising an aide or assistant should participate in interviews with potential employees. Participation in this process encourages involvement of the therapist because they are helping select the paratherapist(s) with whom they will work. It is also the therapist's responsibility to inform students, families, teachers, and administrators of the training and scope of practice of the paratherapist.

1. Complete supervisor training and participate in continuing education.
2. Participate in interviewing paratherapist.
3. Document preservice training and credentials of paratherapist.
4. Inform students, families, and coworkers about paratherapist roles.
5. Determine frequency and duration of therapy.
6. Represent the team in meetings, correspondence, and reports.
7. Make significant clinical decisions.
8. Determine caseload assignments.
9. Communicate with students and family members regarding diagnosis, prognosis, eligibility, and dismissal.
10. Conduct diagnostic evaluations and interpret results.
11. Initiate treatment.
12. Prepare the intervention plan and approve modifications with other team members.
13. Delegate specific intervention tasks.
14. Review intervention plan implementation.
15. Refer to and communicate with other professionals.
16. Provide on-the-job training and mentoring to paratherapists.
17. Approve and document paratherapist inservice training and continuing education.
18. Provide and document paratherapist supervision.
19. Ensure that paratherapist provides services within the scope of practice.

Figure 3.2. **Therapist's responsibilities.**

The therapist has primary responsibility for making all decisions related to referrals, diagnosis, eligibility for therapy, prognosis, assessment, proposed frequency and duration of therapy, plan development, implementation, modification, and eventual dismissal from therapy. The therapist represents the team in meetings and prepares, edits, and signs all correspondence and reports. Specific intervention tasks are assigned to the aide or delegated to the assistant—first through written prescription and then through weekly and daily *protocols*. The therapist is responsible for discipline-specific on-the-job training, mentoring, and supervision of paratherapists. Ensuring that paratherapists provide only services consistent with their level of training and experience and within the established scope of practice is an important responsibility of the therapist. The therapist should participate in ongoing and annual performance evaluations of paratherapists.

Duties of paratherapists at either the aide or assistant level are subsets of therapists' responsibilities (see Figure 3.3). The aide is *assigned* only a very small portion of the therapist's treatment duties. Typically, aides assist the therapist with tasks such as maintaining and generalizing behaviors and the therapist is present to provide close supervision. Assistants are *delegated* a significant portion of the therapist's treatment duties and can work more independently (if experienced) in expanded functions consistent with their more extensive training and experience when compared to the aide. With regard to *nontreatment duties* such as clerical and housekeeping tasks, the aide and then the assistant perform most of these tasks leaving time for the therapist to complete those duties that are exclusively his or hers.

Therapists and paratherapists share many responsibilities (see Figure 3.4). All team members must know and adhere to legal, ethical, and confidentiality standards when interacting with students, family members, and their coworkers. They must demonstrate effective communication skills, appropriate human relations, leadership and advocacy skills, and respect for their coworkers. All are responsible for providing a healthy and safe therapy environment and for dealing appropriately with emergencies.

With respect to treatment all members of the team must understand their respective scope of practice and carry out their responsibilities within prescribed boundaries. All members of the team must work together to provide efficient and effective intervention services in support of educational goals for students and families. All participate in on-the-job training, inservice training, and continuing education in the schools and through colleges or universities and participate in their respective state and national professional organizations.

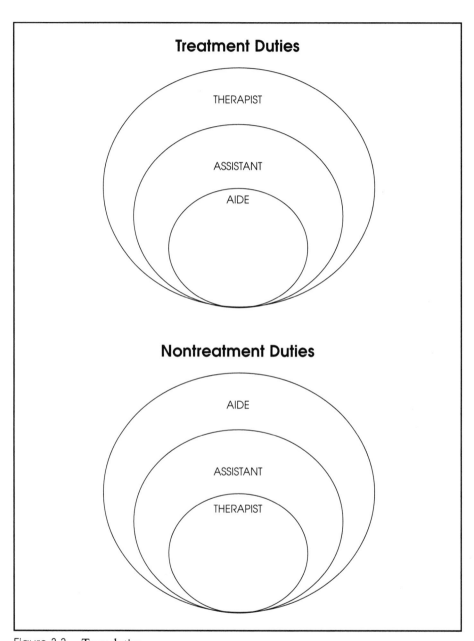

Figure 3.3. Team duties.

1. Knowledge of typical growth and development

2. Knowledge of developmental and acquired disabilities

3. Knowledge of educational service system

4. Ethical conduct

5. Effective communication

6. Human relations skills

7. Leadership and advocacy skills

8. Infection control, safety precautions, and procedures for dealing with emergencies

9. Appropriate behavior management

10. Efficient/effective intervention

11. Observation and reporting skills

12. Intervention documentation skills

13. Ability to use assistive devices

14. Psychosocial support to students and families

15. Administrative/clerical skills

16. Participation in continuing education and professional growth

Figure 3.4.   **Shared responsibilities of therapy teams.**

There are differences in the hierarchy of the shared responsibilities of members of the therapy team. For example, communication with students, family members, and other service providers regarding referrals, diagnoses, intervention, and other programmatic decisions such as eligibility and dismissal are the responsibility of the therapist. An aide or assistant should refer questions or comments about these matters to the therapist by saying, "Ms. Jones will be here tomorrow at 2:00 and I'm sure she would be happy to answer that question for you," *or* "Ms. Jones, my supervisor, is available at this telephone number and she can answer that question for you." Representing the therapy team in a Child Study Team, Individualized Education Program or Individualized Family Service Plan meetings, or staffings is the responsibility of the therapist although aides or assistants may participate at the request of the family, the student, or therapist. Another example of how shared duties may be applied at different levels is that while all team members must practice ethical conduct and work within school regulations and legal standards, it is the therapist who is ultimately responsible for all activities performed by paratherapists in the work setting. Many duties are primarily paratherapist responsibilities, although they are shared by the therapist who has responsibility for overall management. Clearly, many therapist duties with respect to intervention can be carried out by trained and experienced paratherapists when they are assigned or delegated and supervised by the therapist. Maintaining a safe and healthy work environment is an important task for all team members. Paratherapists may assist with cleaning and disinfecting work surfaces, materials, and equipment. They may also collect and construct materials and maintain bulletin boards. They may help with organizing therapy materials and keeping equipment and therapy apparatus in good working order. They also collect or construct equipment designed by the therapist and team.

In addition, paratherapists contribute significantly to the efficiency and effectiveness of the team by performing clerical duties such as scheduling appointments and meetings, answering the telephone and documenting messages, requesting preevaluation documents, filing and retrieving reports and charts, photocopying documents, and word processing reports.

They also assist in training students, teachers, and family members to use assistive devices and AAC systems. As members of the team, paratherapists must have a general knowledge of typical patterns of growth and development as well as disabilities of both a developmental and acquired nature. Behavior management, treatment protocol implementation, and intervention procedure skills are critical paratherapist competencies, along with skillful nonjudgmental observation, documentation, and reporting to the therapist. Both aides and assistants need to be knowledgeable about assertive and adaptive devices within their discipline and across the therapies. The ability to provide psychosocial support for children and youth and their families is also a very important skill, when applied within the paratherapists' scope of practice. Paratherapists are also expected to develop personally and professionally and to facilitate team success by assisting with a variety of administrative functions and to maintain their employability. Enabled through their training and experience, and consistent with their aide or assistant scope of practice, paratherapists supplement the therapist's ability to work with the sizable caseloads typical in the schools, and therapists thereby have more time to fulfill responsibilities that are exclusively theirs.

STANDARDS FOR PARATHERAPIST TRAINING AND UTILIZATION

All three therapy professions recognize paratherapists at the aide and assistant levels. All three professions (AOTA, APTA, and ASHA) have established a formal scope of practice statement and personnel preparation standards for aides and assistants. These standards have been used successfully for more than two decades. The AOTA and APTA, and individual states, recognize paratherapists through formal credentials. The AOTA and APTA also accredit training programs. ASHA registers SLPAs and approves training programs. Appropriate assignment of paratherapist roles in all three therapy disciplines is addressed in state practice acts, licensure statutes or certification regulations, and scope of practice statements of the AOTA, APTA, and ASHA or of individual states.

Granting credentials such as *certification, registration,* or *licensing* are formal methods of recognizing the education and experience of individuals, whereas *accreditation* or *approval* are processes of recognizing educational programs that meet minimum standards of space, faculty, learning resources, and practica for training individuals. Certification may be in the form of a "completion certificate" that documents that a student has completed a course of study. Certification can also mean the individual has completed formal training and passed a board examination as in certified occupational therapy assistant (COTA). Certification may either be administered nationally or by a specific state agency or even a training program. Licensure or registration are typically awarded through state statute or through a regulatory board. Licensure legally protects the public from untrained practitioners and prohibits persons from using the title or designation without first having met all of the requirements (education, clinical experience, and board examinations). Registration is a less stringent form of credentialing than certification or licensure but serves many of the same purposes.

Until recently, the profession of speech–language pathology has had fewer formal guidelines than occupational or physical therapy with no nationally recognized credentialing or program accreditation procedures. That has changed. In 1996, ASHA approved formal guidelines for SLPAs at either the associate degree (or equivalent) or bachelor's degree level.

The Idaho Board of Vocational Education (IBVE, 1994a, 1994b, 1994c, 1994d, 1994e, 1994f) has developed technical committee reports and curriculum guides in occupational, physical, and speech therapy that will be used as examples in this chapter. These documents include performance standards, work setting task lists (competencies), duty areas, enabling objectives, practica suggestions, scope of practice statements, and supervision standards for occupational, physical, and speech therapy aides and assistants. The information contained in the Idaho curriculum guides and in this chapter should be useful to persons who prepare personnel in occupational, physical, and speech therapy as well as those charged with maintaining current therapy programs and planning and implementing new models of therapy service delivery in the schools.

PHYSICAL THERAPIST ASSISTANT (PTA)

Training Outcomes

Idaho PTA training outcomes from IBVE (1994d) are shown in Figure 3.5. More detailed information regarding the PTA's competencies and roles may be found in IBVE (1994d), *Evaluative Criteria for Accreditation Programs for the Preparation of Physical Therapist Assistants* (APTA, 1994a) or *Guidelines for Role Delineation in Physical Therapy* (Minnesota Chapter, APTA, 1993). Note that the title is physical *therapist* assistant rather than physical *therapy* assistant. There is an extensive and very successful history of educating and utilizing PTAs. Probably because of this experience, it was a relatively easy matter for the members of the PT Technical Committee in Idaho to produce their report and curriculum guide. There are many basic similarities between occupational therapy and physical therapy, as well as major differences. PTs or OTRs will often explain the differences as, "The PT team focuses on improving strength, range of motion, and mobility, whereas the OT team focuses on using that developed strength, range of motion, and mobility to develop skills in activities of daily living (ADLs)."

PTAs complete a 2-year, associate degree program of education in an APTA accredited program. Much of the first year is devoted to general education coursework in humanities, oral and written communication skills, mathematics, natural sciences, biological sciences (especially human anatomy and physiology), and social sciences with emphasis on psychology and sociology. The second year focuses on PTA coursework and laboratory work as well as clinical education experiences.

There are currently about 180 accredited PTA programs in the United States with another 100 being developed (APTA, 1996). An APTA (1994b) survey revealed that 65% of accredited programs are in 2-year community colleges, 8% in universities, 15% in vocational-technical colleges, and 12% in private liberal arts colleges or proprietary institutions. In any given year about 3,000 PTAs graduate nationwide (APTA, 1994b). Most states (41) regulate PTAs through state statute and/or board regulation and credential PTAs through licensing, certification, or registration (APTA, 1995c). The

After successfully completing the physical therapist assistant (PTA) program the student will be able to accomplish the following:

1. Demonstrate a basic understanding of typical human development.

2. Describe the educational service system and the role of the PTA.

3. Assist with administration and clerical functions.

4. Perform written, oral, and nonverbal communication techniques effectively.

5. Perform student services including

   a. instruct student, family, and other personnel in use of assistive and supportive devices that improve mobility;

   b. position/instruct student, family, and other personnel in correct positioning;

   c. perform therapeutic modalities; and

   d. perform and instruct student, family, and other personnel in therapeutic exercise with or without equipment.

6. Perform any lifting and transferring of student with correct body mechanics to ensure the safety of the student and self.

7. Describe typical joint range of motion.

8. Demonstrate ability to implement treatment procedures for rolling, crawling, sitting, standing, and walking; and the movement to get from one position to the next.

9. Demonstrate safety precautions as regards to safety harnesses, walkers, and other adaptive equipment.

Figure 3.5. **Training outcomes for PTAs.** From *Technical Committee Report and Curriculum Guide for Physical Therapy Assistant* (Vocational Education No. 285), by Idaho Board of Vocational Education, 1994, Boise, ID: Author.

APTA accredits PTA programs (APTA, 1994a) and provides guidelines for clinical education (APTA, 1993a) as well as considerations for developing PTA training programs (APTA, 1995a).

Services

The PTA is a qualified paratherapist in the practice of physical therapy who delivers services to students as *delegated* by and under the supervision of the PT (APTA, 1993b, 1991). There is provision for expanded functions through a PTA career ladder (PTA I, II, III) within the PTA category (Carpenter, 1993). PTAs carry out the treatment for the student, as designed by the PT, after the PT has evaluated the student's record, held an interview with the student and family, and completed a physical assessment of the student. The treatment is then delegated to the PTA. The PTA will communicate any observed changes in the student's condition which may require that the PT reassess the student and thus modify the treatment program. PTs and PTAs work in a variety of clinical settings. In the schools, physical therapy services are likely to be delivered through a school contract with a PT. Under these contracts the PTA may be employed by the PT or may be employed by the school and supervised by a PT under contract.

The curriculum for the PTA is designed to prepare the PTA to work under the supervision of a qualified PT who has responsibility for the student's treatment. PTA roles are becoming more defined (Ketter, 1995). Once the student has been evaluated by the PT, he or she delegates specific aspects of treatment to the PTA and the PTA is required to practice only within those prescribed boundaries (APTA, 1995b). Delegation is typically done based on the following factors as noted by Watts (1971): (a) The situation is predictable and the consequences of the treatment are not perilous to the student; (b) the stability of the situation is great and dramatic change is unlikely to occur; (c) the observability of basic indications of problems with the student's treatment is immediately apparent and readily experienced; (d) basic indicators of problems with the student are clear and unambiguous and the indicators are not easily confused with other phenomena; and (e) the consequences of an inappropriate choice by the PTA will not seriously endanger the student. If a student needs both physical and occupational therapy services, and these services are included in his or her plan, these services are often administered in a very collaborative fashion with the PT and OT team working together to meet common educational goals.

CERTIFIED OCCUPATIONAL THERAPY ASSISTANT (COTA)

Training Outcomes

Training outcomes for Idaho COTAs from IBVE (1994a) are shown in Figure 3.6. Competencies for and role delineation between registered occupational therapists (OTRs) and COTAs may be found in AOTA (1990) and AOTA (1994c). The AOTA (1991) also periodically publishes guidelines for accreditation of COTA programs which present in detail the approved training standards for COTAs. The Idaho Occupational Therapy Technical

Committee, commissioned by the IBVE, had little difficulty completing the Technical Committee Report and Curriculum Guide for COTAs—probably because of the long history of successful utilization of paratherapists in occupational therapy. An important clue to the overall role of OTRs and COTAs is found in the AOTA subtitle, *Occupational Therapy: A Vital Link to Productive Living*. The emphasis of occupational therapy is on adapting and improving *activities of daily living* (ADLs).

COTAs complete a 2-year associate degree program of education in an AOTA accredited program or may complete a somewhat shorter training to receive a certificate only. The first year focuses on general education comparable to that of the PTA. The second year is devoted to COTA coursework and laboratory work as well as fieldwork at level I and level II.

After successfully completing the certified occupational therapy assistant (COTA) program the student will be able to accomplish the following:

1. Demonstrate a basic understanding of typical human development.

2. Describe typical fine motor and play development.

3. Describe the educational service system and the role of the COTA.

4. Assist with administration and clerical functions.

5. Effectively perform written, oral, and nonverbal communication techniques.

6. Perform student services including

   a. instruct student, family, and other personnel in use of assistive and supportive devices that improve mobility;

   b. position and instruct student, family, and other personnel in correct positioning;

   c. perform therapeutic activities; and

   d. perform and instruct student, family, and other personnel in therapeutic exercise with or without equipment.

7. Assist in determining effective adapted equipment needs or classroom modifications.

8. Demonstrate ability to execute an oral feeding program.

9. Assess student's progress and effectiveness of treatment plan.

10. Provide psychosocial support to students and families.

Figure 3.6. **Training outcomes for COTAs.** From *Technical Committee Report and Curriculum Guide for Certified Occupational Therapy Assistant* (Vocational Education No. 284), by Idaho Board of Vocational Education, 1994, Boise, ID: Author.

According to the 1994 AOTA Education Data Survey (AOTA, 1994b), there are about 85 accredited or approved technical-level occupational therapy educational programs in the country with about 3 to 5 being added each year. More than half of these programs are housed in 2-year community colleges. About 14% are part of a vocational-technical school, 11% are part of a 2-year junior college, and 3% are housed in 4-year junior colleges. Almost 20% indicate that they are housed in some other type of school such as private liberal arts colleges or proprietary schools (typically hospitals). Capacity for training new COTAs is not increasing as fast as that for PTAs. The available new spaces for students is only increasing at about 3% to 5% per year while the number of qualified applicants per year is increasing by more than 30%. About two thirds of qualified applicants are granted admission each year and almost all actually enroll. Very few programs have unfilled seats and most are reported to be "overenrolled." There are almost 5,000 COTA students enrolled nationwide with about 1,500 graduating each year (AOTA, 1994a). Graduates pass a national examination prior to being certified. COTAs are readily employed, with each graduate receiving three job offers on average and half being employed before being certified (AOTA, 1995b, 1994b). About 12,000 COTAs are working nationwide (AOTA, 1994b).

Services

The COTA is a qualified paratherapist in the practice of occupational therapy who delivers services to students under supervision of the OTR (AOTA, 1995a). OTRs and COTAs work in a variety of settings. Occupational therapy services in the schools are often contracted by the OTR, and the COTA may be an employee of either the school or the OTR. Much like the PTA, a COTA carries out the treatment for the student which has been designed by the OTR after the OTR's evaluation. The occupation of children and youth is playing, being a student and achieving academically, and, as they get older, holding a part-time job. OTRs and COTAs look at the student as a whole person, including their individual lifestyle and interests, and they focus on improving their "occupational" skills. OTRs and COTAs help students attain or regain more independence in their individual activities of daily living. When working with a student with disabilities, the goal is to build on individual strengths to ensure success in all life activities such as education, recreation, and vocation.

The OT team focuses on *sensory processing* (how a student receives and perceives information through a variety of sensory systems), *somatosensory perception* (awareness of sensations from joints, muscle, and skin receptors), and *praxis* (motor planning and smoothly and effortlessly executing motor behaviors during learned tasks). The OT team is especially useful in the schools helping children and youth with visual perceptual and motor problems in reading and writing; those who have hypersensitivity or hyposensitivity to touch; students with concentration, attentional, or hyperactivity problems; students with balance and clumsiness problems; and those with dyspraxia which can negatively impact every aspect of the student's life requiring motor skills.

The OT team typically uses ADLs as the vehicle for their therapy, breaking these activities down into small, manageable steps. Two of the most critical activities are interpersonal communication and feeding/swallowing—activities in which OT and SLP team practices clearly overlap.

SPEECH–LANGUAGE PATHOLOGY ASSISTANT (SLPA)

Training Outcomes

Idaho SLPA training outcomes from the IBVE (1994f) are shown in Figure 3.7. More detailed information regarding speech–language pathology assistants can be found in the technical committee report and curriculum guide for SLPA by the IBVE (1994f), ASHA guidelines for SLPAs (ASHA, 1996), and the consortium guidelines (Council for Exceptional Children [CEC], 1996). The IBVE technical committee report and curriculum guide predates both the ASHA guidelines and consortium guidelines and was used by both organizations as they developed their final guidelines. The consortium guidelines were developed by seven national professional organizations working collaboratively. These consortium members included representatives from ASHA; CEC and three of its subdivisions; the Council of Administrators of Special Education (CASE); Division for Early Childhood (DEC) and the Division for Children's Communication Development (DCCD); Council of Consultants in State Education Language, Speech, Hearing Agencies (CLSHSEA); and the National Association of State Directors of Special Education (NASDE). The issue of support personnel in speech–language pathology has been debated, sometimes very hotly, for more than 25 years. Generally speaking, those who favor their use feel access to services will improve, the specialized skills and time of SLPs will be put to better use, and the best interests of students and families will be served (Paul-Brown, 1995;

After successfully completing the speech–language pathology assistant (SLPA) program the student will be able to accomplish the following:

1. Describe an overview of developmental and acquired disabilities.
2. Demonstrate ethical standards of conduct.
3. Describe the educational and related services delivery system.
4. Demonstrate a knowledge of distinctions of SLP and SLPA roles.
5. Practice effective communications.
6. Practice infection control and safety precautions.
7. Demonstrate phonetics skills.
8. Describe the anatomy and physiology of speech–language production and the impact of various illness, injury, malformation, and surgery.
9. Describe typical processes of speech and language development.
10. Describe typical processes of hearing development and principles of hearing measurement.
11. Demonstrate ability to implement treatment procedures for phonological disorders, delays, and differences.
12. Demonstrate ability to implement treatment procedures for language and communication disorders, delays, and differences.
13. Describe the treatment for hearing disorders and the professions that provide the treatments.
14. Demonstrate ability to implement aural habilitation and rehabilitation treatment procedures.
15. Assist with speech and language screening procedures.
16. Demonstrate behavior management skills.
17. Assist with treatment plan implementation.
18. Observe, record, and report students' specific behaviors.
19. Assist students with hearing aids and other communication devices.
20. Assist with routine maintenance and cleaning of equipment and storage areas.
21. Assist with provision of psychosocial support to students and families.
22. Assist with administrative and clerical duties.

Figure 3.7. **Training outcomes for SLPAs.** From *Technical Committee Report and Curriculum Guide for Speech–Language Pathology Assistant* (Vocational Education No. 292), by Idaho Board of Vocational Education, 1994, Boise, ID: Author.

Spahr, 1995; Werven, 1993a, 1993b). Those that oppose their use feel that quality of services will suffer, services of SLPs will be devalued, and students and families will be misled (Breakey, 1993; Wolf, 1995).

The Idaho SLP Technical Committee also thoroughly discussed the issues as they prepared their curriculum guidelines. These guidelines included the training outcomes (Figure 3.7) for SLPAs as well as student performance standards (competencies), enabling objectives for each of the competencies, specific tasks, scope of practice delineation for SLPAs, and supervision guidelines. Longhurst (in press) describes the development of these guidelines and curriculum in more detail.

There currently are no associate degree programs for SLPAs, but several are in various stages of development (Paul-Brown, 1995). Most of the first year of the SLPA curriculum currently being developed at Idaho State University (ISU) is devoted to general education coursework in oral and written communication skills, biology, psychology, linguistics, mathematics, multicultural and diversity studies (which are also infused in other courses), and introduction to communication disorders. The second year is focused on SLPA coursework and fieldwork. About two thirds of the courses are courses that ISU's juniors in their baccalaureate program are also taking. The other one third are specialized courses designed for SLPAs. All SLPA students are expected to develop and demonstrate computer skills including word processing, data entry and retrieval, records systems, and basic computer applications to clinical intervention.

Services

The SLPA is a qualified paratherapist in the practice of speech–language pathology who delivers services to students as delegated by and under the supervision of the SLP. The SLPA carries out the treatment of the student which has been designed by the SLP after the SLP has assessed the student, developed the treatment plan, and initiated treatment. After treatment is initiated by the SLP and a maintenance and monitoring stage of treatment is reached, the SLPA takes over day-to-day treatment and carefully observes and reports changes that may require modification of the treatment plan by the SLP after further assessment.

The associate degree (or equivalent) in the speech–language pathology curriculum is designed to prepare the SLPA to work only through delegation and under the supervision of a qualified SLP who retains all legal, ethical, and programmatic responsibility for the students' treatment. SLPA roles or scope of practice will become more refined although current guidelines (IBVE 1994f; ASHA, 1996; CEC, 1996) specify these roles reasonably well.

There are only minor differences between the ASHA guidelines (1996) and those referred to as the consortium guidelines (CEC, 1996). ASHA registers SLPAs and approves SLPA training programs. The consortium guidelines suggest that state departments of education credential speech–language paratherapists. ASHA acknowledges the aide level, although guidelines do not include the aide level of paratherapist. Instead they recognize holders of bachelor's degrees as SLPAs with no officially described expanded functions consistent with their higher level of education. The consortium guidelines have a tiered system with different roles at each level. A multitiered system of speech–language paratherapist service delivery is effective and efficient because it delineates tasks that can be performed by basic-, intermediate-, and advanced-level paratherapists (Longhurst, in press-b). ASHA's guidelines suggest generic training and utilization in a variety of work settings, whereas the consortium guidelines focus more on early intervention and school practice. A more basic difference between the two sets of guidelines is that ASHA recognizes only SLPs with a certificate of clinical competence (CCC) from ASHA as supervisors, whereas the consortium guidelines suggest state certification for SLPs who supervise.

PHYSICAL, OCCUPATIONAL, AND SPEECH THERAPY AIDES

Training Outcomes

As much as possible all aides who work with students with disabilities and their families should receive a common core of competency-based values training (see Figure 3.8). In Idaho this is accomplished through a statewide curriculum, Training Providers of Services to Persons with Developmental Disabilities (commonly called DD Aide) (IBVE, 1993). The applied program of this curriculum is *Creating Visions, Direct Care Service Provider Training Manual* by Burton, Gee, and Overholt (1992) and an accompanying instructor's guide (Burton & Seiler, 1992). Other programs (Rast, 1992; Robinson, 1987; Vassiliou, 1991) have been developed to serve similar purposes. This initial training consists of didactic training, in-class activities, and supervised practicum in the schools. The goals of this training are to help the aide understand the characteristics of students with developmental or acquired disabilities and then to demonstrate appropriate skills for working with them and their families during therapeutic interactions. Through this training, aides learn definitions and appropriate use of categorical labels, ethical behavior, how to build positive behaviors, how to implement basic treatment plans, and how to facilitate educational development of students with disabilities. They learn how to provide a clean, safe, and healthy environment and to prepare for emergencies. Finally, they learn the benefits of peer and family support, how to positively involve family members in treatment, and how to communicate effectively with students, their families, and coworkers. This DD Aide training is required as a prerequisite to OT, PT, or SLP aide training in Idaho.

Discipline-specific (OT, PT, or SLP) aide training builds on skills learned in the DD Aide training and then develops additional competencies (see Figure 3.8). Many of the competencies needed by OT, PT, or SLP aides are common to all three disciplines with additional competencies that are discipline specific. They all develop knowledge and skills in describing typical developmental sequences and processes in infants, toddlers, children, and youth. All aides also develop competencies in basically describing developmental and sensory and physical and acquired disabilities such as cerebral palsy, autism, mental retardation, learning and behavioral disabilities, hearing and communication impairment, and traumatic brain injury.

After their introduction to fine motor, gross motor, personal–social, cognitive and language development, and a basic survey of disabilities, training for aides centers on discipline-specific content. For example, OT and PT aides focus on fine and gross motor development such as rolling over, sitting, grasping, crawling, balance, feeding and swallowing, standing, and walking. SLP aides learn more about early language development, auditory discrimination and perception skills, and oral motor skills such as feeding and swallowing as well as communication assistive technologies.

Each aide learns to explain their discipline-specific roles and responsibilities and how to practice ethical standards and effective communication. Although there is some commonality of training across the three disciplines, much of the remaining aide training focuses on the training procedures, materials, equipment, and devices specific to their discipline. In most cases procedures for observations, reporting, and treatment documentation are unique to the discipline. The aide must learn to work alongside and assist the therapist as assigned in individual and group sessions. Typically the therapist is present and providing close supervision when the aides perform their assigned tasks.

Individuals completing initial training for providers of services to persons with disabilities (DD aide) should be able to do the following:

1. Discuss an overview of disabilities.

2. Demonstrate a knowledge of
   a. ethical treatment,
   b. methods of building positive behaviors, and
   c. IFSP/IEP implementation and monitoring.

3. Provide for health and safety needs.

4. Explain roles and needs of family.

Individuals completing discipline-specific aide training should be able to do the following:

1. Describe typical growth and development processes.

2. Describe developmental and acquired disabilities.

3. Explain discipline-specific aide role and responsibilities.

4. Practice ethical and effective communication.

5. Assist with
   a. transport, transfer, and positioning of students,
   b. assistive devices,
   c. maintenance and cleaning,
   d. general treatment procedures,
   e. group sessions,
   f. observation and reporting,
   g. treatment documentation, and
   h. clerical duties.

6. Assist therapist or assistant with discipline-specific treatment/procedures.

7. Observe, document, and report.

8. Apply job keeping skills.

Figure 3.8. **Core competencies for DD aides.** From *Technical Committee Report and Curriculum Guide for Providers of Services to Persons with Developmental Disabilities, Level I.* (Vocational Education No. 269), by Idaho Board of Vocational Education, 1993, Boise, ID: Author.

CAREER PATHWAYS FOR PARATHERAPISTS

All three therapy disciplines utilize a multitiered system. A *career pathway* for paratherapists is a preplanned and articulated system of advancement within or across therapy disciplines. The career pathway for paratherapists in Idaho is shown in Figure 3.9, and is provided as an example of an articulated system that facilitates paratherapist mobility. A career pathway helps to remove barriers for advancement through the discipline levels. The potential

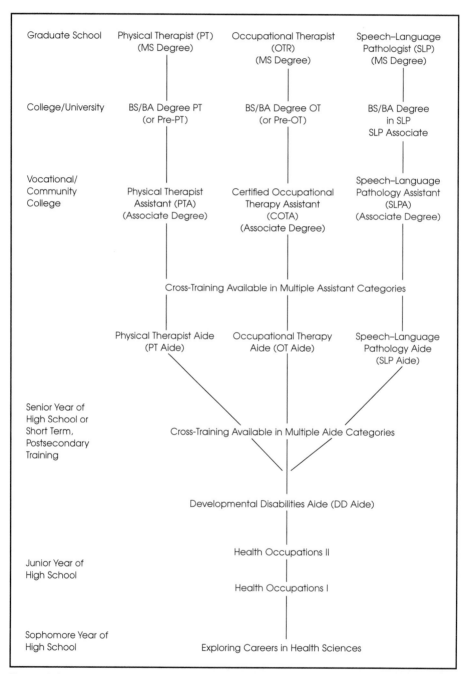

Figure 3.9. **Career pathways for paratherapists.** From "Career pathways for related services paratherapists in early intervention and education," by T. M Longhurst, in press, *Journal of Children's Communication Development*, 18(1).

is that paratherapists are provided opportunities for increased maturity, experience, on-the-job training and continuing education, as well as financial support to move through the career pathway, possibly terminating at the level of therapist within the discipline. Opportunities for training across disciplines are also inherent in a career pathway. For example, for individuals to train as both an OT aide and a PT aide, or as an OT aide and SLP aide, would facilitate the delivery of therapy services.

MANAGING PARATHERAPISTS

In Chapter 4, French provides an excellent overview of how to manage paraeducators that is entirely appropriate in content to managing paratherapists. She has also provided an anecdotal description of supervision of speech–language pathology assistants (French, in press). The *executive functions* of therapists include planning for paratherapist(s), managing schedules, training, assigning or delegating tasks, and creating and maintaining standards of practice. Some specific guidelines go beyond paraeducator supervision and are especially applicable to paratherapists. Therapist licensure standards, national certification standards, formal professional practice statements, and codes of ethics require specific frequency and duration of supervision by therapists (see Table 3.1 for a summary of these requirements). The supervision requirements specified in these documents are typically viewed as *minimum requirements*. They specify that it is the therapist's responsibility to design, provide, and document a supervision scheme that protects the students' rights and maintains the highest standards of quality care. Higher levels of supervision would be required based on the training and experience of the paratherapist, the students served, the specific work setting, and the proximity to the supervisor. For example, more intense, close supervision is required in orientation of a recently hired paratherapist, or during the initiation of a new program or change in student status. The degree of student contact by the paratherapist, the complexity of the task(s), their technical nature, and even the level of interpersonal interaction required may help determine the appropriate level and type (*direct* vs. *indirect*) of supervision (McFarlane & Hagler, 1995). These factors, as well as others, also determine the level of supervision (close, routine, general, or minimal).

There seems to be a general agreement among the different disciplines that a full-time therapist should supervise no more than three full-time equivalent (FTE) paratherapists. More than three part-time paratherapists

Table 3.1
Supervision Requirements for Assistants

Criteria	COTA	PTA	SLPA
Requirements for supervisor	Properly credentialed/ licensed in state	Properly credentialed/ licensed in state	CCC-SLP/licensure 2 years of experience post-CCC Course/CE unit in supervision
Amount/type of supervision	First session and then as needed or conditions dictate (close supervision for inexperienced and then moving progressively to routine, general, or minimal)	First visit and then as needed but at least once a month	30% for first 90 work days (20% direct/ 10% indirect) then adjusted as appropriate but no less than 20%
Off-site assistant contact with therapist	Must be accessible at all times COTA is treating clients/patients	Must be accessible by telecommunication at all times when treating clients/patients	Must be able to be reached by personal contact, phone, pager, or other immediate means during all client/ patient contact time
Therapist/assistant conference	Regularly scheduled and documented	Regularly scheduled and documented	At least every 2 weeks and documented

Note. Supervision requirements may vary from jurisdiction to jurisdiction depending on state rules, regulations, and practice acts. Generally it is assumed that aides work only on site with the supervisor and under close supervision.

could work under a therapist but their cumulative FTE should never exceed three. More than one supervisor may provide supervision of a given paratherapist, but not for the same student, and a single therapist should be assigned as the *supervisor of record* that has responsibility for a given student.

A plan and schedule that summarize the services of the therapist and paratherapist(s) should be used to help organize the team duties. An example of such a plan is shown in Figure 3.10.

The quality of supervision, including on-the-job training and mentoring by the therapist, has a direct impact on the quality of services provided by paratherapists. The higher the quantity and quality of supervision the better the services. School district administrators should be fully aware of the supervision guidelines of the AOTA, APTA, and ASHA and support their therapist(s) in meeting these standards of supervision. Therapists

Student Information		Speech Therapy Schedule			
		School: Edahow Elementary SLP: Diane Franks			
		Week: 12/2/96–12/6/96 SLPA: Terry Madsen			
Name	*Diagnosis & severity*	*SLP/SLPA combined services*[a]	*SLP*	*SLPA alone (with SLP monitoring schedule)*[b]	
T. Smedley	hearing/AR (moderate)	M-W-F Group 1 hr. SLPA AAN SLP F 20 min.			
R. Schow	hearing/AR (moderate)	"			
J. Brockett	hearing/AR (mild)	"			
K. Medley	hearing/AR (moderate)	"			
B. Bain	lang. dis. (severe)		M-F 50 min. (new client)		
L. Kline	lang. delay (mild)			M-W-F 30 min. (maintenance)	1 session/wk. F
K. Lewis	autic (moderate)	M-F Ind. 50 min. SLPA M-Th SLP F			
J. Willes	autic (severe)	M-F Ind. 50 min. SLPA M-Th SLP F			
T. Radford	autic (mod.-severe)	T-Th-F Ind. 50 min. SLPA T-Th SLP F			
D. Sorensen	fluency (severe)		M-W-F 30 min.		
A. Werton	voice (mild)		M-W-F 50 min. (new client)		
P. Boysen	autic (moderate)			T-Th-F 30 min. Group	1 session/wk. F
L. Argyle	autic (mild-mod.)			"	"
J. Batte	autic (moderate)			"	"
S. Robbins	autic (moderate)			"	"
L. Branch	voice (abuse) moderate		M-W-F 50 min. DX-RX/6 wks.		
K. Kangas	TBI (severe)		M-F 50 min.		
J. Pimentel	TBI (moderate)		M-Th 45 min.		
S. Long	autic (moderate)	M-F Ind. 50 min. SLPA M-Th SLP F			
D. Towsley	autic (moderate)	M-F Ind. 45 min. SLPA M-Th SLP F			

[a]The SLP and SLPA are concurrently providing services to the same student.

[b]When the majority of services are provided by the SLPA alone, the supervising SLP must include a schedule of direct student contact to maintain accountability and quality of service.

Figure 3.10. Student review table.

working in the schools are knowledgeable about these standards and would welcome the opportunity to help "educate" their administrators. This will help ensure that the highest quality of services is delivered to infants, toddlers, children, and youth with disabilities in the schools and their families.

SUMMARY

In the therapies there are clear distinctions in the scope of practice between aide and assistant titles in preservice education or training, credentials, scope of practice, amount and type of supervision, and pay and fringe benefits. The scopes of practice for both aides and assistants are subsets of therapists' scopes of practice. When appropriately assigned or delegated, the support that paratherapists provide to therapists can increase the efficiency and effectiveness of the therapy team. All therapists must wrestle with the issue of which therapeutic or educational activities within their scope of responsibility must be performed only by themselves and which can be assigned or delegated to paratherapists under the direction and supervision of the therapist.

Discussion Questions

1. Compare and contrast the credentialing terms *registration, certification,* and *licensure* as used for paratherapists (or for therapists). Do you see any inconsistencies in the different disciplines, say, between OT and SLP?

2. The chapter author feels there are three major determiners of successful paratherapist utilization in the schools. Name them and discuss how, if all three factors are not present, the system would likely have problems.

3. There are many positive aspects of increased utilization of paratherapists in the schools but there are also reasons for concern. List the pros and cons of increased employment of paratherapists.

4. Contrast the terms *aide, assistant,* and *associate* including training, duties, and supervision needs.

5. List the responsibilities of the team that are typically only performed by the therapist. Discuss why it is important that paratherapists not perform these tasks.

Exercises

1. Make arrangements, possibly through your course instructor, to observe and interview a PTA, a COTA, and an SLPA in the schools or early intervention agency. During your interview ask about

   a. their typical day-to-day activities and ask if they have a written schedule you could see

   b. the protocols they work from and ask to see an example

   c. the procedures they use to document progress and ask to see examples of the form(s) they use

2. Make arrangements, again through your course instructor, to observe and interview a PT, OTR, and SLP who is supervising a paratherapist in the schools or early intervention agency. During your interview ask about

   a. their typical weekly schedule and what kinds of activities take up most of their time

   b. how they work with their paratherapist(s)

3. Invite a special educator to talk to your class about utilization of paratherapists in his or her schools or agency.

4. Write to the APTA, AOTA, ASHA, or the licensing board in your state to request guidelines on credentialing for PTAs, COTAs, or SLPAs (select one in which you are most interested).

APTA	AOTA	ASHA
1111 N. Fairfax St.	4720 Montgomery Ln.	10801 Rockville Pike
Alexandria, VA 22314	P.O. Box 31220	Rockville, MD 20852
	Bethesda, MD 20824	

5. Make arrangements, again possibly with the help of your course instructor, to visit a training program in a community college or vocational-technical school for PTAs, COTAs, or SLPAs. Ask an administrator or instructor in the program to give you a tour of their laboratories or other learning environments and request literature they give to prospective students.

6. Compare and contrast the similarities and differences in the roles and responsibilities of paraeducators working in education and vocational programs with the roles and responsibilities of paratherapists aides and assistants.

GLOSSARY OF KEY TERMS

Accreditation (program approval). Process of recognizing educational programs that meet minimum standards of space, faculty, learning resources, and practica for training individuals.

Activities of daily living (ADLs). Everyday activities that persons engage in that require mobility, strength, and range of motion such as walking, writing, keyboarding, speaking, feeding, and swallowing.

Aide. Paratherapist title given to individuals with a minimum level of training (typically in high school or on the job, or short-term vocational training) and a very limited scope of practice in student treatment.

Assigned. A form of direction to aide-level paratherapists by therapists that is more specific and formal than "delegated."

Assistant. Paratherapist title given to individuals with an associate degree (or equivalent) from a physical therapist assistant, certified occupational therapy assistant, or speech–language pathology assistant program. Assistants can work more independently in expanded functions consistent with their more extensive training and experience when compared to the aide.

Associate. Paratherapist title that may be given to individuals with a bachelor's degree such as speech–language pathology associate for a worker with a preprofessional B.S. degree in speech–language pathology.

Career pathway. A preplanned and articulated system of advancement within or across therapy disciplines.

Certification. Typically used to designate that the individual has completed formal training and passed a board examination. Certification may either be administered nationally, by a specific state agency, or even by a training program.

Clinical efficacy. A process of being efficient and effective in clinical treatment and using procedures to document success or the lack thereof (accountability).

Delegated. A form of direction to assistant (or associate) paratherapists by therapists that is less specific and less formal that "assigned." Assumes the assistant has been well trained to perform the duties and needs only general direction to follow the therapist's treatment protocol.

Executive functions. Activities of therapists including student assessment, planning for the paratherapist(s), managing schedules, training, assigning or delegating tasks, adopting and developing treatment protocols, and creating and maintaining standards of practice and supervision.

Expanded functions. Duties and tasks that appropriately exceed the typical scope of practice because the worker has additional training and experience.

Licensure. A credential that legally protects the public from untrained practitioners and prohibits persons using the title or designation without first having met all of the requirements (education, clinical experience, and board examinations).

Minimum supervision requirements. These requirements specify that it is the therapist's responsibility to design, provide, and document a supervision scheme that protects students' and families' rights and maintains the highest standards of quality intervention. These minimum standards should be exceeded with a new paratherapist, initial student interventions, and when problems arise.

Nontreatment duties. These duties are typically viewed as clerical and housekeeping tasks. The aide and assistant perform most of these tasks, leaving time for the therapist to complete those duties that are exclusively his or hers.

Paratherapists. A generic term for aides, assistants, or associates (or those who may have other titles) who work alongside professional level therapists to accomplish common team goals.

Physical therapist (PT). A professional therapist in the schools who helps students develop strength, mobility, and range of motion in joints and muscles to facilitate activities of daily living. They often have at least a bachelor's degree but the master's degree is becoming the minimum practice requirement for new PTs.

Praxis. Motor planning and smoothly and effortlessly executing motor behaviors during learned tasks.

Protocol. A written therapy plan that includes specific instructions to the paratherapist from the therapist.

Registered occupational therapist (OTR). A professional therapist in the schools who works with students to improve skills in activities of daily living such as walking, writing, keyboarding, speaking, eating, and swallowing. They often have a bachelor's degree and the profession is moving to a master's degree as the typical practice requirement for new OTRs.

Registered speech–language pathologist assistant (R-SLPA). A graduate of an ASHA-approved technical training program who has successfully completed a competency evaluation by a qualified supervisor.

Registration. A less stringent form of credentialing than licensure but serves many of the same purposes.

Scope of practice (or scope of responsibility). A delineated set of tasks or responsibilities of a paratherapist or therapist that is consistent with their training, experience, and credential(s).

Sensory processing. How a student receives and perceives information through a variety of sensory systems.

Somatosensory perception. Awareness of sensations from joints, muscles, and skin receptors.

Speech–language pathologist (SLP). A professional therapist in the schools who has the primary responsibility of working with students who have communication problems that adversely affect learning and academic progress. They typically hold a master's degree and many will have a certificate of clinical competence in speech–language pathology (CCC-SLP) from ASHA.

Supervision (close). Requires daily, direct contact at the site of work.

Supervision (direct). The therapist observing and providing directional feedback to the paratherapists with the therapist physically present for all or part of the treatment session.

Supervision (general). Requires at least monthly direct contact, with supervision available as needed by other methods.

Supervision (indirect). The therapist watching videotapes of sessions, reviewing written materials (plans, treatment notes), or communicating with the paratherapist through phone, e-mail, or other means in which directional feedback is provided without the therapist physically present.

Supervision (minimal). Supervision is provided only on a need basis, and may be less than monthly.

Supervision (routine). Requires direct contact at least every 2 weeks at the site of work, with interim supervision occurring by other methods, such as telephonic or written communication.

Supervisor of record. In school or agencies where there may be several SLPs, for example, who provide therapy supervision to a given SLPA, one supervisor is designated as the supervisor of record and accepts responsibility.

Support personnel. A generic term, similar to paratherapist, sometimes given to workers who provide support to professional-level therapists.

Therapists. A generic term to describe professional-level workers in the three therapies within this chapter, which includes physical therapists (PTs), registered occupational therapists (OTRs), and speech–language pathologists (SLPs) (speech therapists).

Treatment duties. Tasks that involve specific intervention with the student or the family such as home programming, exercise, drills, eliciting responses, providing consequences, and charting behaviors that are included in treatment protocols.

Values training. General orientation to disabilities, appropriate reference to and ethical behavior with persons with disabilities and their families.

REFERENCES

American Occupational Therapy Association. (1990). Entry-level role delineation for registered occupational therapists (OTRs) and certified occupational therapy assistants (COTAs). *American Journal of Occupational Therapy, 44*, 1091–1102.

American Occupational Therapy Association. (1991). *Essentials and guidelines for an accredited program for the occupational therapy assistant.* Rockville, MD: Accreditation Department, American Occupational Therapy Association.

American Occupational Therapy Association. (1994a). *1994 education data survey: Final report.* Rockville, MD: Research Information and Evaluation Department, American Occupational Therapy Association.

American Occupational Therapy Association. (1994b). *Occupational therapy manpower: 1994.* Rockville, MD: Research Information and Evaluation Department, American Occupational Therapy Association.

American Occupational Therapy Association. (1994c). Standards of practice for occupational therapy. *American Occupational Therapy, 48*, 1039–1043.

American Occupational Therapy Association. (1995a). Guide for supervision of occupational therapy personnel. *American Journal of Occupational Therapy, 48*, 1045–1046.

American Occupational Therapy Association. (1995b). *Personnel shortages in occupational therapy: Fact sheet.* Rockville, MD: Research Information and Evaluation Department, American Occupational Therapy Association.

American Physical Therapy Association. (1991). *Code of ethics.* Alexandria, VA: Author.

American Physical Therapy Association. (1993a). *Guidelines for clinical education.* Alexandria, VA: Author.

American Physical Therapy Association. (1993b). *Statement defining physical therapy.* Alexandria, VA: Author.

American Physical Therapy Association. (1994a). *Evaluative criteria for accreditation of education programs for the preparation of physical therapy assistants.* Alexandria, VA: Author.

American Physical Therapy Association. (1994b). *PTA fact sheet.* Alexandria, VA: Education Division, American Physical Therapy Association.

American Physical Therapy Association. (1995a). *Considerations: Developing an educational program for the physical therapy assistant.* Alexandria, VA: Author.

American Physical Therapy Association. (1995b). *Guide for professional conduct.* Alexandria, VA: Author.

American Physical Therapy Association. (1995c). *State licensure reference guide.* Alexandria, VA: Author.

American Physical Therapy Association. (1996). *Number of PT and PTA programs as of January 25, 1996.* Alexandria, VA: Author.

American Speech-Language-Hearing Association. (1996). *Guidelines for the training, credentialing, use and supervision of speech-language pathology assistants.* Rockville, MD: Author.

Breakey, L. (1993, May). Support personnel: Times change. *American Journal of Speech–Language Pathology*, 13–16.

Burton, S., Gee, R., & Overholt, J. (1992). *Creating visions, direct care service provider training manual*. Moscow, ID: Curriculum Dissemination Center, University of Idaho.

Burton, S., & Seiler, R. (1992, January). PTA career ladders. *PT Magazine*, 56–61.

Carpenter, C. A. (1993). *Creating visions, direct care service provider training manual*. Moscow, ID: Curriculum Dissemination Center, University of Idaho.

Council for Exceptional Children. (1996). *Consortium guidelines for speech–language paraprofessionals*. Reston, VA: Author.

French, N. K. (in press). A case study of a speech–language pathologist's supervision of assistants in a school setting: Tracy's story. *Journal of Child Communicative Disorders*.

Idaho Board of Vocational Education. (1993). *Technical committee report and curriculum guide for training providers of services to persons with developmental disabilities, level I* (Vocational Education No. 269). Boise: ID: Author.

Idaho Board of Vocational Education. (1994a). *Technical committee report and curriculum guide for certified occupational therapy assistant* (Vocational Education No. 284). Boise: ID: Author.

Idaho Board of Vocational Education. (1994b). *Technical committee report and curriculum guide for occupational therapy aide* (Vocational Education No. 282). Boise, ID: Author.

Idaho Board of Vocational Education. (1994c). *Technical committee report and curriculum guide for physical therapy aide* (Vocational Education No. 293). Boise, ID: Author.

Idaho Board of Vocational Education. (1994d). *Technical committee report and curriculum guide for physical therapy assistant* (Vocational Education No. 285). Boise: ID: Author.

Idaho Board of Vocational Education. (1994e). *Technical committee report and curriculum guide for speech–language pathology aide* (Vocational Education No. 294). Boise, ID: Author.

Idaho Board of Vocational Education. (1994f). *Technical committee report and curriculum guide for speech–language pathology assistant* (Vocational Education No. 292), Boise, ID: Author.

Ketter, P. (1995, March). PTA roles are becoming more defined. *PT Bulletin*, 9.

Longhurst, T. M, & Witmer, D. (1994). Initiating paratherapist training in Idaho. *New Directions, 15*(3), 1–5.

Longhurst, T. M (in press-a). Career pathways for related service paratherapists in early intervention and education. *Journal of Children's Communication Development, 18*(1).

Longhurst, T. M (in press-b). Idaho's three-tiered system for speech–language paratherapist training and utilization. *Journal of Children's Communication Development, 18*(1).

McFarlane, L., & Hagler, P. (1995). *Collaborative service provision by assistants and professionals: A manual for occupational therapists, physical therapists and speech–language pathologists*. Edmonton, Alberta, Canada: Alberta Rehabilitation Coordinating Council.

Minnesota Chapter, American Physical Therapy Association. (1993). *Guidelines for role delineation in physical therapy*. St. Paul: Minnesota Chapter, American Physical Therapy Association.

Paul-Brown, D. (1995, September). Speech–language pathology assistants: A discussion of proposed guidelines. *Asha*, pp. 39–42.

Rast, J. (1992). *Values and visions: An introduction to developmental disabilities*. Parsons: Kansas University, University Affiliated Program–Parsons.

Robinson, C. (1987). *Training direct care workers in non-institutional family scale residential environments for the developmentally disabled/handicapped person*. Cincinnati, OH: Cincinnati University Affiliated Program, Cincinnati Center for Development Disorders Interface Project.

Spahr, F. T. (1995, September). Speech–language pathology assistants. *Asha, 39*.

Vassiliou, D. (1991). *Guidelines and coursework syllabus for the North Dakota statewide MR/DD staff training program*. Minot, ND: Center for Disabilities, Minot State University.

Watts, N. T. (1971). Task analysis and division of responsibility in physical therapy. *Physical Therapy, 51*(1), 23–35.

Werven, G. (1993a, May). Support personnel: An issue for our times. *American Journal of Speech–Language Pathology*, 9–12.

Werven, G. (1993b, May). Support personnel: Werven responds to Breakey. *American Journal of Speech–Language Pathology*, 17–18.

Wolf, K. E. (1995, November/December). Speech–language pathology assistants: Support personnel or lower-level practitioners? *Asha, 45*.

CHAPTER 4

· ·

Management of Paraeducators

· ·

Nancy K. French
University of Colorado at Denver

OVERVIEW

Classrooms are complex and dynamic workplaces that require management by skilled professionals who perform certain well-documented executive functions (Berliner, 1983a, 1983b). Teachers and related services professionals are not commonly thought of as executives, yet the dual metaphors of the classroom as a workplace and the school professional as an executive make particular sense as we explore the role of the school professional with regard to paraeducator/paratherapist supervision.

This chapter first explores the issue of which professional should take on the management role. It then examines each of the first six executive functions of paraeducator/paratherapist supervision listed in Figure 4.1: planning, managing schedules, delegating tasks, providing orientation, on-the-job training, and evaluation. The seventh executive function, managing the work environment, requires such extensive attention that an entire chapter of this text is devoted to that function (see Chapter 5).

Instructional Objectives

After studying this chapter and participating in discussions and exercises, the reader will be able to:

1. Name and define the seven executive functions of paraeducator supervision.

2. Know how to determine which professional plans for the paraeducator, and know the tests of effective plans/planning formats.

1. Plan
   - Set goals
   - Describe activities, methods
   - Set expectations for outcomes
2. Manage schedule
   - Identify task importance/urgency
   - Create schedules
3. Delegate
   - Analyze tasks
   - Determine what to delegate
   - Create work plans
   - Select the right person
   - Direct tasks
   - Monitor performance
4. Orientation
   - Introduce people, policies, procedures, roles, responsibilities
   - Analyze styles, skills
   - Create personalized job descriptions
5. On-the-job training
   - Assess current skills
   - Teach, coach new skills
   - Give feedback on skill performance
6. Evaluate
   - Track performance of duties
   - Provide summative information about job performance
7. Manage the work environment
   - Maintain effective communications
   - Manage conflicts
   - Solve problems

Figure 4.1. **Executive functions associated with paraeducator supervision.**

3. Identify the components of a schedule and differentiate a schedule from a plan.

4. Define delegation, know why and how delegation occurs, and why professionals sometimes fail to delegate.

5. Name and define the steps for delegation.

6. Name and define the components of paraeducator orientation.

7. Describe the purposes of a personalized job description for paraeducators.

8. Name and describe all aspects of planning and providing training to the paraeducator.

9. Understand the role of the professional in the evaluation process.

10. Describe the importance of holding effective meetings with paraeducators.

. . . .

WHO SUPERVISES?

The executive functions of paraeducator/paratherapist supervision are often performed by individual teachers, therapists, school nurses, school psychologists, and/or school counselors. This is most often the case when the paraeducator/paratherapist[1] is assigned directly to a single classroom or specifically to the individual professional. One example of this situation includes a self-contained special education program for children with severe or profound needs where a single special education teacher and several paraeducators work with a group of children who remain in that room for a significant portion of the day, leaving the room only for brief mainstreaming periods. Another example, often found in early childhood education programs, is where a single licensed or certificated professional runs a program in which all the group instruction, supervision of students, personal assistance, and individual help is provided by paraeducator personnel. The key concept is that a single professional holds responsibility for performing all the executive functions associated with paraeducator/paratherapist supervision. Sometimes, however, a paraeducator is employed to support the work of a program that also employs a variety of professionals. In this case, supervision may be provided by professionals who share programmatic responsibility and accountability. The team thus consists of professionals

---

[1]In this chapter, both words—*paraeducator* and *paratherapist*—have been used to convey the concept that the management functions apply to those employees who work alongside professional educators as well as professional therapists in schools. To avoid "wordiness" throughout the rest of the chapter, there are many places where only one of the titles is used.

with similar or different professional roles and skills as well as paraeducators. One example is the instructional team that includes three fifth-grade teachers who share supervision of a single paraeducator. Another example is the special education team that includes professionals with preparation in school psychology, physical therapy, speech–language pathology, and special education who share the supervision of one or more paraeducators/paratherapists. A third example is where the paraeducator, who is paid with special education funds, is assigned to a cluster of classroom teachers for the purpose of supporting inclusion of students with disabilities. In this case, the primary supervision becomes the responsibility of the classroom teachers, but the special educator who provides consultation to the general education team may also share in the planning and monitoring aspects of supervision.

Team assignments tend to confuse the lines of authority and communication that are so readily apparent in one-on-one supervisor–supervisee relationships and, thus, team situations demand greater role clarification. In teams with a designated leader, that person is most likely to perform the executive functions of paraeducator supervision. However, many school teams are leaderless teams in the sense that they do their fundamental work without a designated leader and they share the functions of leadership. When this is the case, teams must also clarify who will perform the executive functions of paraeducator supervision. The following is a list of some of the circumstances in which a team supervises the work of one or more paraeducators:

1. Paraeducators are employed to work in a particular program (e.g., Title I) but move throughout the day to different general education classrooms supporting curricular modifications and adaptations created by professionals.

2. Paraeducators are employed on behalf of a student with intense needs who is included in general education classrooms, and for which several professionals hold ultimate responsibility.

3. Paraeducators are hired in a specific role (e.g., speech–language assistant, occupational therapy assistant) but work intermittently with many children across classrooms or buildings who are served by numerous other providers as well.

4. Paraeducators are assigned other duties (e.g., recess duty) over which the team members have little control, by someone outside of the team (e.g., the principal), yet the team retains responsibility for supervision during that activity.

Each circumstance demands a unique response to the executive functions of paraeducator supervision. The features of team responses to supervision will become apparent in the discussions of the planning, scheduling, delegation, training, monitoring, and evaluation tasks that follow in this chapter.

Summary

Seven executive functions are associated with paraeducator supervision. Whether supervision is performed by an individual or by a team, the executive functions remain the same: planning for the paraeducator, managing the schedule, delegating tasks, orientation, training, evaluating performance, and managing the work environment. When paraeducators are assigned to teams, professional team members must clarify roles with regard to paraeducator supervision and respond in unique ways to variations in paraeducator employment circumstances.

PLANNING

Who plans for the paraeducator? When asked this question, special education teachers, general education teachers, school psychologists, speech–language pathologists, occupational therapists, and physical therapists may all find themselves pointing the finger at one another—or, sadly, at no one at all. Often they say, "I don't need to plan, she/he just knows what to do." Or, they say, "She/he doesn't need a written plan, I just tell her/him what to do on the 'fly'" (French, 1993). Or the paraeducator may speak up in response, saying, "I make my own plans" or "No one plans, I just follow along trying to do what I'm supposed to" (French, 1993). Although these responses may reflect the current state of affairs, none of them exemplifies a legal or ethical position.

Designing instructional environments and making decisions about the goals, objectives, activities, and evaluations of instructional episodes are tasks that are well *outside* the paraeducator's scope of responsibility. As discussed in Chapter 2, it is clearly the responsibility of the teacher or other school professional to provide plans for the paraeducator to follow. Legally and ethically speaking, paraeducators should not make their own plans, nor should they operate without written plans. Specifically, it is not legal or ethical for a special education paraeducator to create or plan modifications or adaptations of lessons that have been designed by general educators. It is the duty of the school professional to plan the lessons, the modifications, and the adaptations with consultation from other appropriate professionals. A general modification plan may be created by a special educator to cover several types of lesson activities and tasks that classroom teachers typically employ. The paraeducator may then apply the general modification plan to the specific instructional activity or task on a day-to-day basis.

So, *Who plans?* is an important question that generates varying responses according to the employment circumstances of the paraeducator. First, if a paraeducator is employed to work under the supervision of a single school professional, then it is obvious who plans—that professional. When a paraeducator is employed to work with a team, it is less obvious, but crucially important, to determine the specific response within the team. *Who* may plan is readily answered. Any of the school professionals may plan, but the team must determine who actually plans by asking themselves the following questions:

1. Who holds ultimate responsibility for the outcome of the instruction?
2. Who will be in the best position, logistically speaking, to direct the performance of the duties?
3. Who is in the best position to provide training for the assigned duties?
4. Who is in the best position to observe and document task performance?

Generally, the response to the first question names the person who plans a particular lesson, unit, or segment of time. However, the responses to questions 2, 3, and 4 contribute important information and may alter the decision about who is the best person to plan a particular segment.

Planning Forms and Formats

Plans do not necessarily adhere to a predetermined format. Many professionals (and teams) use their creative talents to design forms and formats that respond to the unique characteristics of their own situation. Professionals have sufficient latitude to create a planning form or format that pleases them and addresses the combined needs of the team. What is contained in the written plan, the amount of detail, and the specificity of directions are all negotiable. The factors that should be considered include the skills and preferences of the individuals involved, as well as the needs of the program and the student.

Although a paper-based planning form is not necessary and plans may be written on any type of surface (chalkboards, dry-mark boards) or electronic platform (hand-held electronic planner, or centrally located computer), school professionals still tend to rely on paper. Starting each time with blank paper means that the plan-writer will have to write certain pieces of information or structural aspects of the plan over and over again. Forms eliminate the duplication of effort and streamline the planning process.

Paper-based planning forms, like other planning formats, must also meet the dual tests of ease of use and user friendliness. Ease of use means that the plan form or format should be readily available and comprehensive enough to cover all the important topics, yet simple enough that it is easily comprehensible. For example, a template form created and kept on a word processor may be readily available for the professional with a computer on her or his desk to use, while multiple copies of the printed form kept in a nearby file folder may be easier for another. Length of the form is also important. Too many topics and subtopics make it difficult to know what to write in each space. Including too few topics may result in the transmission of too little information or of information that is too general to be useful.

User friendliness of the form or format is best judged by the paraeducator. However, it often means that there is a pleasant use of white space and/or graphics on the page and that the length is sufficient but not overwhelming. A paraeducator, faced with a 2- to 3-page plan, will be less likely to read the plan carefully than he or she would given a single page, neatly written or typed with plenty of white space. The use of terminology and reading level that is consistent with the knowledge and literacy level of the paraeducators is also an important factor in user friendliness. As you begin to design your own planning forms, use the following questions to guide your work:

1. Contents reflect the skills of the paraeducator, the needs of the program, student, or professional, and the preferences of both the professional and the paraeducator.

2. The form is easy to use, readily available, of appropriate length.

3. The form is user friendly. It is easy to read at a glance, uses a reading level that all users enjoy, and uses the fewest words possible to convey necessary information.

Remember that newly created forms should be pilot tested for a period to work out the "kinks" and correct omissions.

Examples of Planning Forms

The examples contained in Figures 4.2, 4.3, and 4.4 have been created by individual teachers and teams of professionals to fit their own circumstances. They each meet the two tests of ease of use and user friendliness. Although the content is unique to those particular teams of people, there are common contents in all the examples. The objective or purpose of the activity, lesson, or adaptation is clearly specified. In each case, the goals of the plans, the specific modifications listed, and the behavioral interventions reflect the decisions made about the needs of students. In special education programs, plans are guided by the Individualized Education Program (IEP). In Title I programs, plans are guided by literacy assessment information. Because so many variations in programs and service delivery approaches are used in schools today, it is impossible to create even a few standard forms that would work for everyone. The executive task of the supervising professional(s) is to create a form or a format that works for the particular professionals and paraeducators involved. The examples of Figures 4.2, 4.3, and 4.4 may serve as guides for your own planning. Figure 4.2 shows a plan form for a situation where the paraeducator is assigned to a series of general education classrooms because students who need curricular and instructional modifications and adaptations are placed in those classrooms. This is a plan that could have been developed by an individual or a team, but is consistent with the situation described previously where the paraeducator moves to different general education classrooms throughout the day.

In this instance, the classroom teacher has prepared a unit for an entire class and has created curricular and instructional modifications and adaptations in collaboration with a special education professional. The paraeducator is assigned to provide support for the modifications or adaptations made for the individual students as well as general instructional support for the class. So, in addition to the lesson plan in the example for Jason, the paraeducator, in this instance, would also be carrying plans for each of the students served in that classroom on a clipboard.

As you examine the contents of this plan, you may notice that there are abbreviations with which you may not be familiar. For example, the term QAR[2] is not familiar to many people. The important factor is that the para-

---

[2]QAR stands for question–answer relationship. It is a way for students to recognize that certain kinds of questions demand certain kinds of answers. The use of QAR helps students know how to formulate answers differently according to the demand of the question and the type of source material they are using to find the answer.

Lesson Plan for Application of Modifications and Adaptations for

Student: _Jason_____ Date of Plan: _____ Duration of Plan: _3 weeks_

1. IEP objectives:
   - J. will attend to tasks for 20 minutes.
   - J. will employ self-monitoring strategies to redirect his own attention to assigned tasks.
   - J. will use knowledge of QARs to find answers in texts and lecture notes.

2. General class topic: *Post-Soviet Eastern Europe*
   General class tasks:
   - Listen to lectures, view video, listen to guest speakers.
   - Read from text, periodicals.
   - Discuss answers to questions in small groups.
   - Write answers to questions on individual papers.

3. Expectations for <u>Jason</u>:
   - Attend to lectures, take notes for 20 minutes, break, return.
   - Use QARs to find answers.
   - Participate in group discussions by finding and contributing answers to group.
   - Write answers to every other question (either even or odd numbers, not both).

4. Paraeducator tasks:
   - Cue Jason with tap on shoulder when he needs to redirect his own attention to task during lectures (note taking), reading, and writing tasks.
   - Provide QAR cue cards for J. to use while looking for answers in text and notes.
   - Remind J. which questions to answer; assist him in QAR.
   - Assist all students in use of QAR as they write answers.

Figure 4.2.   Sample lesson plan.

educator who works from this plan *does* know what QAR is, how to instruct students in the use of QAR, and how to cue students to remember to use QAR. This means that the person who made this plan either taught the paraeducator how to teach QAR or knew that the paraeducator already possessed that skill. Finally, it is important for the responsible professional to monitor periodically to see that the paraeducator is using the cueing systems and QAR appropriately.

Figure 4.3 is a plan form that could be used when the paraeducator is assigned to work with a single student either in an inclusionary situation or in a pull-out situation or resource room. This plan happens to be for a student with severe cognitive needs and limited social functioning. Eric is included in a fifth-grade classroom for much of the day, but is pulled out to the resource room for frequent but short periods to work on various communication and academic skills. In this case, they vary the location of the activity because they want Eric to learn that he can make choices in lots of places

---

Week of: _____

Eric's goal for the week: To understand that he can choose among activities but that once he makes a choice he has to stick with it for a period of time.

Sequence of Activity

1. Eric makes a choice from the choice book.
2. Select the materials he needs for that choice from the shelf.
3. Stick with the choice he made for 10 minutes.
4. Stop the activity when the timer rings.

Time Period(s): Frequently throughout every day—whenever an opportune moment arises.

Location: Vary location daily between Room 17, library, computer lab, and 5th-grade classroom.

Activity Choices

1. Nested boxes
2. Aladdin sticker book
3. Alphabet cards
4. Name game
5. Other choices that other 5th-grade students make

Friends' Goals

1. Observe how to cue Eric to make choices, get materials.
2. Know how to redirect Eric when he gets off task.
3. Know how to cue Eric to stop when bell rings.

Figure 4.3. **Sample lesson plan for Eric.**

throughout the day. This plan is good for a week, but the team will vary the plan just a little in subsequent weeks and thus reuse large portions of this week's plan. For example, the goal statement and the sequence of activity will be the same next week but the activity choices will change. The team finds that using a planning form makes them very efficient. They do not have to rewrite everything every week. This is especially important because it is not the only plan they make for Eric every week. There are also plans for how he will work and what he will do every period of the day. Notice the section in the plan that specifies the objectives for Eric's friends. This is a unique feature of this team's planning format. In this situation, the team is trying to educate students to provide some of the support for Eric so that the adults do not serve to isolate him from his age-peers. The professionals on the special education team negotiated with the fifth-grade teacher to release several designated students to work with Eric as part of a circle of friends. The team added this feature to the planning form when (during the time they monitored the paraeducator's work with Eric) they noticed that the fifth graders were overprotective and tended to do too much for Eric. They realized that to achieve his social goals they had to teach the other students how to work with him. So whenever Eric is pulled out during these periods of the day, certain of his friends are assigned to accompany him and the paraeducator has clear direction on what they are to learn from the experience.

Finally, the form in Figure 4.4 was designed by a special education teacher for a situation where the paraeducator works in small groups with students who are practicing specific skills associated with a particular class. This type of lesson plan format is appropriate for paraeducators who work in resource rooms or in general education classrooms. As in all plans, the paraeducator must understand how to complete all aspects of the lesson. This lesson happens to be about basic vocabulary recognition in ninth-grade biological science for students who have difficulty remembering words and definitions. The teacher who wrote the plan includes a memory device called "Keyword."[3] It is not important for the paraeducator to know or understand the theoretical basis for this technique or for the instructional method used to teach the keyword method to students, as the teacher does, but it is necessary for the paraeducator to know how to explain it to students and to give good examples. Thus, the paraeducator must be trained and coached to deliver this lesson.

---

[3]Keyword is a method where the learner links a word with a definition by constructing a mental image or drawing of a scene that includes the word itself and illustrates the meaning of the word. Like any other skill, students must be taught to understand and use the keyword method.

Vocabulary Drill & Practice

Objective: Students will read and define vocabulary words with 100% accuracy using a keyword device.

Activity:

1. Students sit together at round table.
2. Show one card at a time.
3. Say "What is this word?" and "What does it mean?"
4. If student gives incorrect response, or can't respond, say "This is _____, it means _____." Then help student generate a keyword memory device to recognize and define the word.

Materials: Prepare 3 × 5 file cards with the following words on one side, the definitions on the other (use definitions from Chapter 1 of Bio. Sc. Text): Kingdom, Phyla, Class, Family, Genus, Species

Student Performance:

Record performance

R = reads it correctly   **D** = defines it correctly

	Kingdom	Phyla	Class	Family	Genus	Species
Ana						
Carolo						
David						
Kayla						
Jim						

Figure 4.4.   Sample lesson plan.

Summary

It is legally and ethically correct for professionals who hold responsibility and accountability for the outcomes of an educational program to provide written plans for paraeducators. It is outside the paraeducator's realm of responsibility to create lessons or modifications to lessons. When children are served by a team, or when a paraeducator is assigned to a team, a decision must be made as to who creates the plans. Teams may choose to plan together or to assign a professional team member to plan for a particular segment. When the school professional plans for the paraeducator, numerous decisions about the goals and objectives, the environment, the behavior management, the activities, and the materials are made and then communicated in written form. Planning forms and formats may vary in content and style according to the unique needs of the team members, but should always contain the goal or purpose of the activity and should meet the dual tests of ease of use and user friendliness. Examples of planning forms show how unique circumstances can be addressed through the use of individually created forms and formats.

SCHEDULING

Schedules tell when tasks should be completed, who should do them, and where people are during the day or week. They are often developed simultaneously with lesson or work plans, and provide a graphic display that accompanies the specific information contained in the lesson or work plan. While the lesson plan answers the question "What does the paraeducator do?" the schedule answers the questions "When?" and "Where?"

It is most useful to have schedules that include information about all team members, whether it consists of two members (e.g., teacher and paraeducator) or more. It is also useful to display schedules publicly so that the information is readily available to others. Like plans, schedules can and should reflect the unique needs of the team and the circumstances. The unvarying features include times, locations, and activities of all team members. Figure 4.5 is one example of a schedule form used at a middle school. In this case, the whereabouts of the teacher and the paraeducator are publicly available and a notation telling what they are doing during each time block is included. The schedule does not tell the nature of the activity, the goals, or the materials used in lessons or classes. That information is contained in related plans.

DELEGATING AND DIRECTING

What is delegation? According to Drawbaugh (1984), delegation is the process of getting things done through others who have been trained to handle them.

Daily Schedule		
		for week of: _____
Time	**Paraeducator Activity/Location**	**Teacher Activity/Location**
8:00–8:40	Support Jason, Michele, Taneesha/ Rm 29	Plan with Soc Studies teachers/ SSOffice
8:40–8:50	Accompany Eric to PE/ from Rm 38 to gym	″ ″ ″ ″
8:50–9:20	Support Jason, Michele, Tanya, Roy/ Rm 44	Coteach with Smith/Rm 29
9:20–10:05	7th gr. Lang Arts group/Resource Rm	″ ″ ″ ″
10:05–10:30	Plan time/SPED Office	Plan time/SPED Office
10:30–10:50	Accompany Eric to Health Room for respiration treatment/medication Take Eric to music	Coteach with Jones/Rm 44
10:50–11:25	Lunch	Coteach with Jones/Rm 44
11:25–11:50	Computer lab	Plan with Lang Arts teachers/ LA Ofc.
11:55–12.25	Support Ana, Carolo, David, Kayla, Jim/Rm 44	Testing/consultation/ IEP meetings

Figure 4.5.   Sample daily schedule.

It is the act of entrusting enough authority to another to get the task done without giving up responsibility. As classroom managers, school professionals delegate tasks to paraeducators who are prepared to do the tasks. They monitor how well the task is completed because they retain ultimate responsibility and accountability for the outcomes of instruction. Delegation is an executive function that is fundamentally important to the supervision of paraeducators.

Why Delegate?

There are numerous reasons why school professionals, as managers, delegate tasks to paraeducators. First, it frees the teacher to do work that cannot be delegated, such as assessment, planning, and scheduling. Second, it increases the professional's productivity. By delegating judiciously, a professional doubles the amount of work that is accomplished. Third, judicious delegation emphasizes the management of various aspects of instruction but deemphasizes doing them. Fourth, it provides opportunities for others to develop new skills and initiative. So, not only is delegation a way to achieve increased amounts of attention to students, it is also a way to help paraeducators grow and develop their skills.

How To Delegate

One management expert compared delegation to a legal contract. In a legal contract the parties reach a meeting of the minds as to the content and meaning of the contract's provisions (McConkey, 1974, p. 47). So it is with delegation. The delegatory "contract" between a paraeducator and a school professional includes agreement on (a) the scope of the task, (b) the specific goals or objectives to be reached, (c) the time frame, (d) the authority needed to carry out the task, and (e) the means by which the paraeducator's performance will be monitored and judged.

Sullivan (1980) adds that effective delegation requires that the professional "Focus on results, not the methods, and allow for mistakes" (p. 6). Thus, delegation provides guidance without being overbearing. It must specify the outcomes, the time frame, and the level of authority, but should not demand that the paraeducator perform in exactly the same manner as the professional, nor should it demand perfection.

Time Management

Effective delegation requires effective time management. Effective time management requires the examination of tasks in terms of two factors: the degree to which it is pressing and the consequences (or outcomes) of doing or not doing the task. A task is pressing if someone is urged or pushed to attend to it or to complete it immediately. The pressing nature of a task may be determined by assessing the consequences of not doing the task now, by the absence or presence of a demanding person, or by organizational expectations. For example, the teachers at West Side Middle School generally do not meet with parents during class time, but when an upset parent is standing in the principal's office and demanding to speak to the teacher immediately, that task becomes pressing.

The second factor, consequences of the task, is relative to the contribution it makes to the overall purpose or professional goal of the individual.

Tasks fall somewhere on a continuum between major contributions and minor contributions. Each professional then judges the consequences of each task according to the contribution that the task makes to his or her own goals.

Employing those two factors, school tasks may be placed into one of four quadrants (Figure 4.6). Notice that the tasks located in the upper right-hand quadrant, for the most part, are tasks for which the professional should remember the key word "Do." Tasks in the "Do" quadrant are not appropriately delegated to a paraeducator. For some professionals, such tasks are difficult to get to because they are not so pressing. Yet, each of these tasks makes a major contribution to the professional's goals. Doing these tasks gains major positive consequences for the professional. Deferring and delegating these tasks are both bad choices for the professional who aims to use time well. Although school professionals may also choose to do the tasks that fall into the upper left-hand quadrant themselves, many of them are appropriate for delegation to a paraeducator. School professionals who delegate tasks appropriately take these factors into account along with the skills, preferences, programmatic needs, and job description of the paraeducator.

The lower left-hand quadrant contains tasks that are appropriately delegated to a paraeducator, but may also be deferred until more pressing issues are completed. Mrs. Seidel always kept two baskets on her desk from which Mr. Kelly, the paraeducator assigned to her classroom, drew his assignments. They were labeled "Deadlines" and "No deadlines." Mr. Kelly would go first to the "Deadlines" basket to get information about his assigned tasks, but when he had an odd moment or unexpected downtime, he would go to the "No deadline" basket to draw a task that also needed to be done eventually.

The lower right-hand quadrant contains tasks that are not particularly pressing and that do not result in consequences of major significance. Those tasks may be delegated to a paraeducator, but for the most part, they are tasks that should simply be discarded—not done by anyone. The key-words for the lower right-hand quadrant are "Defer" and "Discard."

Why School Professionals Fail To Delegate

Many school professionals fail to delegate except in limited ways (Drawbaugh, 1984). Figure 4.7 lists many of the documented reasons school professionals fail to delegate. What school professionals do not necessarily articulate clearly is that when they entered their profession they were unprepared to supervise other adults (Vasa, Steckelberg, & Ulrich-Ronning, 1982). Their university programs may not have prepared them to think of themselves as

	Pressing	Not Pressing
Major	• Sudden student behavior crises • Parent conferences/meetings re: crises • Student health crises • Monitoring students in nonclassroom settings • Providing/adapting instruction • Creating adapted instructional materials • Certain documentation/paperwork • Grading some papers (tests) • Taking attendance, lunch counts • Implementing behavior plans, health plans, curricular modifications and adaptations Key "D" Words: Delegate/Do	• Designing individual behavior plans/health plans/curricular modifications/adaptations • Assessment of students' progress • Assessment of students for program eligibility • Long-range planning of instruction • Curriculum development/revision • Building relationships among professionals, paraeducators • Coplanning of behavioral interventions/instruction • Meeting to provide supervision to paraeducators Key "D" Word: Do
Minor	• General office announcements • Some mail, flyers • Some meetings • Interruptions by students, other professionals • Some parent visits • Grading some daily student work Key "D" Words: Delegate/Defer	• Some copy work, filing • Some mail • Some phone calls • Some teachers' lounge conversations • Some classroom decorating activities • Grading some papers • Some record keeping/filing/cleaning up Key "D" Words: Defer/Discard

Figure 4.6.   "D"elegation "D"ecision matrix for school professionals.

managers who fulfilled executive functions. It is likely that they began their careers under the erroneous assumption that they, and they alone, would have to do it all—whatever needed to be done to provide instruction for their students. For years, school professionals have protested that they have little time to plan, to collaborate with others, to co-teach, and to do long-range planning. In spite of the presence of paraeducators in the schools since the 1950s and substantial increases in the numbers of paraeducators since 1973 (Gartner, 1971; Pickett, 1994, 1986), school professionals have continued to believe that they alone must respond to all the urgent tasks of schools.

Steps for Delegation to Paraeducators

Delegation is a process because it consists of a series of steps. The steps to effective delegation can be learned by school professionals even if they did not enter the profession believing that paraeducator supervision was part of their job. Once professionals realize that paraeducator supervision is, indeed,

---

- Believe they can do the job faster and are unwilling to wait.
- Recognize that it takes time to train the paraeducator.
- Lack confidence in the paraeducator's work.
- Cannot tolerate less than perfect results.
- Fear being disliked by someone who may expect them to do the task themselves, or by the person to whom they delegate an unpleasant task.
- Fear that they will lose control.
- Think it is easier to do it themselves than to tell others how to do it.
- Are convinced that delegation burdens the other person more than it benefits him/her.
- Lack the skill to delegate well.
- Lack the skills to work well with adults.
- Fear that delegation reveals incompetence or feel insecure when depending on others.
- Want to account only for themselves and do not want to be indebted to others.
- Believe that "teaching is for teachers" and are unwilling to give the necessary authority.

Figure 4.7. **Some reasons school professionals fail to delegate.** Adapted from *Time and Its Use: A Self-Management Guide for Teachers*, by C. C. Drawbaugh, 1984, New York: Teachers College Press.

an important part of their role, the methods are straightforward. Figure 4.8 provides a list of steps for delegation to paraeducators that are much like the steps identified by Douglass (1979) who worked with corporate executives on similar issues.

The first step, analyze the task, consists of three substeps. The first substep relates to time management considerations. The professional must first assess the task in terms of importance and urgency. Then, the decision of whether it could be done by someone else must be based on legal and ethical

1. Analyze the task
   a. Assess task in terms of urgency and importance.
   b. Decide whether you have to do it or whether it could be performed by someone else.
   c. Identify component parts of the larger task.

2. Decide what to delegate
   a. Consider programmatic and student needs, preferences of professionals and paraeducators, and paraeducator skills.
   b. Decide what training/coaching the paraeducator needs to perform the tasks.

3. Create the plan
   a. Review all essential components of the task.
   b. Clarify appropriate limits of authority.
   c. Establish performance standards.
   d. Determine how you will direct and monitor.
   e. Determine when/how you will train/coach.

4. Select the right person
   a. Consider interests, preferences, and abilities.
   b. Consider the degree of challenge it presents.
   c. Balance and rotate unpleasant tasks.

5. Direct the task
   a. Clarify the objectives and purposes.
   b. Clarify degree of authority.
   c. Clarify the importance/urgency of the task.
   d. Communicate effectively.

6. Monitor performance
   a. Create system for ongoing/timely feedback.
   b. Act promptly/appropriately on feedback.
   c. Insist on achievement of objectives, but not perfection.
   d. Encourage independence.
   e. Tolerate/manage style differences.
   f. Do not short-circuit paraeducator effort by taking tasks back prematurely.
   g. Document and reward good performance.

Figure 4.8.   **Steps for delegation to paraeducators.**

standards. The third part of analyzing the task is the process of breaking the task apart and identifying the components or subtasks. This process is completed with the skills of the person who will perform the task in mind. Thus, the analysis may be more or less detailed depending on the competencies held by the paraeducator.

Deciding what to delegate should be based on three factors: the styles/preferences of the people involved, the student and program needs, and the skills/confidence of the paraeducator. The next step, creating the work plan, was discussed at length in the previous section. The tasks of assessing work styles/preferences, skill levels, and student and program needs and the task of creating a systematic training/coaching plan are discussed in a later section. The quality of a paraeducator's performance is affected significantly by the professional's choice of tasks to delegate.

Selecting the right person is a consideration if multiple paraeducators work in a program or if other human resources are available (e.g., volunteers, peer tutors, peer coaches). For example, at Rampart High School, a schoolwide peer support program prepares typical students to assist special education students. Sometimes the typical peer may take notes for another student. Sometimes a peer may redirect a student who has difficulty attending to tasks. Sometimes peers can be seen helping a student regain composure during a stressful moment. In this situation, the special education teacher on the team makes a decision regarding whether he will delegate a particular task to a peer or to a paraeducator. A situation that developed in music class exemplifies this type of decision. Laura, a special education student, had become infatuated with one of her classmates and insisted on standing next to him in the choir. Ms. Myers, the vocal music teacher, had her hands full with the 105 students in her choir and requested help from the special education team. Mr. Wright, one of the special education teachers, came down to the choir room to assess the situation. After determining the nature of the problem, he decided that he should assign a paraeducator to the situation on a temporary basis rather than trying to employ the services of a peer.

The corollary to selecting the right person is selecting the right task for the person. If a paraeducator is particularly skillful in a particular area, it may make sense to delegate those tasks to the person regularly. For example, Ivory, an experienced paraeducator, is a particularly gifted storyteller. The school professionals with whom she works all recognize and value her accomplishments in storytelling. They frequently find opportunities to take advantage of this unique contribution that Ivory makes to their school.

On the other hand, paraeducators grow and develop as they are assigned challenging work and they learn to do it. Edee was reluctant at first to use the computer in the special education program, but when the team urged her to gradually take on some computer-based record keeping, she found that her fear of the technology dissipated as her skills grew.

Another important consideration in selecting the right person is that some tasks are more unpleasant than others. Even if a person is very good at accomplishing an unpleasant duty, that duty should be rotated and shared by others. For example, in special education and early childhood programs, diaper changing is sometimes necessary. It is a task that no one really likes to do, yet it is important and sometimes urgent. It also has a tremendous impact on the student. The student's privacy is encroached on and his or her dignity is at risk during such an intimate procedure. Thus it is crucial to carefully select (and prepare) the personnel who do the task to maintain the dignity and privacy of the student. Effective managers consider student privacy and dignity while ensuring a fair distribution of unpleasant tasks among all the professionals and paraeducators. Diane, a third-grade teacher at Cherrydale Elementary School, works with Laura, a paraeducator assigned to her classroom. Laura is assigned to the third-grade classroom on behalf of Melinda, a child with significant support needs. Melinda needs "freshening" (as they like to call it) every few hours. Sometimes Diane takes Melinda to the "private corner" to do the "freshening" while Laura continues working with a small group of students on math skills. At other times, Laura takes Melinda while Diane continues with the class. Neither prefers diaper changing but they share it equally.

When school professionals provide good direction, they make the objectives and purposes of the task or lesson clear and they let the paraeducator know how much authority they have to make decisions associated with the task. Explicit information about the extent of authority associated with the task helps paraeducators know how to handle difficult situations. For example, Barbara was given a lesson plan that tells her to work one to one with Javier to reinforce the two-digit multiplication algorithm he learned yesterday. Barbara finds that Javier remembers exactly how to perform the function and is able to complete all the assigned problems in a few minutes. Her supervisor is not immediately available and Javier looks to her for direction. What Barbara needs to know is the level of authority she has to determine whether she proceeds with a more advanced skill, or to make him continue to practice the same skill, or to stop and reward him with a pleasant but unrelated activity.

When professionals clarify the importance and urgency of the task, they help paraeducators know how to make on-the-spot decisions about whether to pursue a task or end it when the student seems uncooperative or when something else interferes with the activity. It also helps when the paraeducator understands how the task at hand fits into the broader goal and how the objective contributes to the end goal or outcome for the student. For example, Eric, a student with severe and multiple disabilities, has been learning to raise and lower his left arm. If Maize, the paraeducator who works with him, understands that Eric is destined for an augmentive communication device that depends on this skill, she will be sure that he practices many times a day and that he practices correctly.

Finally, the need to communicate the plan effectively and clearly is paramount. Unless the plan is communicated in a format that both parties understand in the same way, little will happen for students to ensure the outcomes they deserve. The previous section on planning emphasized ease of use and user friendliness as two criteria for lesson planning. Addressing these two criteria while creating a planning form or format helps the professional communicate well, but it takes one more communicative action to ensure that the plan has actually been received by the paraeducator in the way it was intended. The professional needs also to check for understanding about the plan. Asking "What questions do you have?" is one way to open the opportunity for clarification. Another way might be to ask a specific question like "So, what will you do after Seth completes the alphabetizing task?"

The professional who delegates to a paraeducator must also monitor the performance of the assigned tasks. Of course, the amount and intensity of monitoring depend on the history of the working relationship. Longer histories and high skill levels mean that less direct monitoring is necessary; shorter histories or fewer skills mean that more intensive, direct observation is necessary. According to the demands of the situation, the professional must create a system for ongoing monitoring and timely feedback to paraeducators about their work. Professionals also need to act promptly and appropriately on feedback they receive from paraeducators about the nature of the task or the outcomes. The general rule of thumb is to focus on the objectives, rather than the perfect execution of prescribed actions. However, there are times when precise execution of a technique is necessary. Identifying such times is easier when precision and perfection are not constant demands. Paraeducators are generally quite able to work independently. While monitoring is necessary for ethical practice, it is not necessary to hover over the paraeducator during instructional episodes. In fact, many paraeducators become uncomfortable and find their self-confidence diminished if the professional monitors too closely. Professionals should encourage independence and initiative in getting the goals accomplished and can do so by placing the emphasis on the outcomes rather than the procedures. Communication style and work style differences sometimes result in tasks being performed differently than the planner had envisioned. The professional who delegates tasks should clearly differentiate between idiosyncrasies of style and incorrect performance of a task.

Sometimes professionals who are concerned with perfection err by withdrawing a task from a paraeducator too soon. It is a mistake to short-circuit or diminish paraeducator effort before the paraeducator has a chance to improve his or her skills or understanding of the task. If the delegation was made correctly, the time frame was specified and the expected quality of the performance was stated. Professionals should remind themselves to be patient enough to allow the paraeducator to reach the performance standard. The effective manager provides coaching and feedback on a difficult task rather than removing the task from the paraeducator. Finally, highly effective managers document and reward good performance. Everyone enjoys a bit of praise now and then, but the issue of documenting and rewarding good performance goes beyond the level of "niceness." Documentation of performance should be specific to the objectives of the task and the specifications of the plan. Even when paraeducator performance is not yet perfect, recognition of the good aspects of the performance provides the motivation to continue to grow and improve.

Summary

Delegation is an executive function that is fundamentally important to the supervision of paraeducators. School professionals delegate tasks to paraeducators because, by doing so, they free themselves to do work that cannot be delegated, and thus increase their productivity. They double the amount of work that is accomplished free from the restriction of having to do it all themselves. Through delegation, professionals provide opportunities for paraeducators to develop new skills and initiative. Professionals who manage their time well consider every school task in light of its urgency and its importance. They distinguish among tasks that they must do themselves and those that may be accomplished by someone else. Teachers and other school professionals sometimes fail to delegate appropriately because of time management problems, errors in their thinking, or lack of organization and planning. Effective delegation is a process that consists of a series of steps: analyzing the task, deciding what to delegate, planning, selecting the right person, directing, and monitoring.

PROVIDING ORIENTATION TO NEW PARAEDUCATORS

When people accept employment, they expect to experience an initial orientation to the workplace and the specific job duties. It is also reasonable for new employees to expect to be introduced to their fellow employees. This has not always been the case with paraeducators. For example, Gretchen accepted a position at an elementary school near her home to work 3 hours a day as a paraeducator. The school year had already begun and she was told to report at 8:00 A.M. the following Monday. Gretchen arrived half an hour early. The supervising teacher, Monica, greeted her and took her to the small adjoining room. Monica told Gretchen that she should look at the materials in the top drawer and select some to use with third graders and some others for fourth graders. Gretchen was told that a group of students would arrive at her doorstep about 8:15 and that she would have them for 30 minutes before a new set of students would rotate in, and so on for the entire 3 hours. Gretchen was shocked. She had worked as a high school English teacher before her children were born, but really had no idea how to teach math to third and fourth graders. She spent her entire first day on the job with little adult contact, no information about the layout of the school building, school rules, emergency procedures, other faculty, or appropriate materials or instruction for children this age.

What kind of orientation should Gretchen have received? There are five components of paraeducator orientation: introductions, written information review, orientation interview(s), work style preferences analysis, and needs versus skills analysis. First, common courtesy demands that newly employed paraeducators should be introduced to the other people who work in the school. Second, the paraeducator should be provided with any and all written policies and procedures used in the building. At the minimum such written information should include emergency and safety procedures, school rules, routines, and standard procedures, as well as the school calendar, the building-level schedule, phone numbers and addresses of fellow employees, protocols for reporting absences, requesting substitutes, and getting information about emergency school closures. Many schools have developed a hand-book that contains vital information about safety issues like fire drills, emergency warning systems, playground or assembly rules, and so forth. It may not be necessary to create a separate handbook or packet for paraeducators if a schoolwide handbook already exists. In fact, it makes sense to provide the same written information to paraeducators and professionals. Information about the privacy rights of students, confidentiality of information, and ethical standards should be provided at the same time. Ideally, a building administrator will meet with the newly employed paraeducator to ensure that all the basic information is reviewed and understood.

Then, new paraeducators should have a structured opportunity to get to know the individual and/or team that will provide their supervision. One way for school professionals and newly employed paraeducators to get to know one another is to interview one another. Emery (1991) and Alexander (1987) have each listed questions that may be used and they each recommend that the pair (or the entire team) engage in a systematic interview and that the interviews be documented (Alexander, 1987; Emery, 1991). Some possible interview questions selected from their lists and offered by others are contained in Figure 4.9. Professionals may create other questions that will help them get to know the new person well enough to establish a strong working relationship. This orientation interview is not meant to replace a hiring interview. Rather, it is meant to occur at the beginning of employment to help newly employed paraeducators gain knowledge of the building and of their fellow workers and to help all the team members get to know one another.

1. Where did you grow up?
2. What are your leisure time activities?
3. What was your best memory of school?
4. What teachers had a positive impact on you?
5. What is your understanding of this position?
6. Why are you interested in this kind of work?
7. Describe some skills you have that will help children in the classroom.
8. What are your unique talents and skills?
9. What do you think is the goal of education?
10. What do you think makes a classroom a positive place to learn?

Figure 4.9.   Getting to know one another: paraeducator orientation interview questions.

The third component of orientation includes an introduction to the role of the paraeducator, the schedule, and the specific job duties. This introduction should not be unidirectional. Because paraeducator roles are somewhat negotiable (within certain legal and ethical limits), and because of the possible overlapping of responsibilities, it is most appropriate to gain some additional information about the paraeducator at this stage. Throughout the orientation stage, it is most appropriate to encourage the paraeducator to ask questions or share their concerns about their position or about their assigned duties.

The fourth component of orientation is the work style preferences analysis. It is important to discuss and analyze the paraeducator's and the professional's preferred work styles. Emery (1991) created companion worksheets for use by professionals and paraeducators. Adaptations of those worksheets are provided for use with the exercises at the end of this chapter. The professional version, entitled Professional's Work Style, requires that the professional reflect upon his or her own preferences in order to communicate them to the newly employed paraeducator. The paraeducator version, entitled Paraeducator's Work Style, asks that the paraeducator clarify his or her preferences in order to communicate them.

To begin, the paraeducator and the professional(s) fill out the worksheets individually using the appropriate form. Then, together, the professional(s) and the paraeducator fill in Worksheet 3, the Work Style Score Sheet. The score sheet is intended to be a vehicle for communication about how the two (or the team) will work together. Items where the scores vary by only a point are easy—they automatically become part of the working relationship. Items where the score differences are greater need to be discussed further. Knowing the preferences of a newly employed paraeducator and comparing them to the preferred work style of the professional team members enables the team to start off on the right foot.

Professionals must recognize that style preferences are not inherently good or bad, but that they do exist. The lack of initial recognition of differences often creates a breeding ground for interpersonal problems between paraeducators and professionals. Tolerance and management of differences begins with the recognition of work style preferences. Consider what happens when no discussion about work style preferences occurs at the beginning of the relationship. Gabriella, a paraeducator, upon being closely monitored by the supervising special education teacher, Michelle, filed a grievance with the principal of the school. When the two sat down with the principal to discuss their differences, Gabriella complained that Michelle did not trust her and that she watched over her shoulder too much. Michelle responded that she had no lack of trust for Gabriella and that she thought she was doing her job responsibly. Neither was right or wrong. The only error here was that they had never held a conversation about their stylistic preferences and differences.

The fifth component of orientation, then, is to analyze the needs of the professionals, the program, and the students, then compare the needs to the skills and confidence of the newly employed paraeducator. Although it is not necessary to use forms to do the analysis and comparison, a systematic format, once created, saves time in the future and assures team members that they have addressed all relevant issues. The companion forms titled Professional/Program/Student Needs Inventory and Paraeducator Skills/Confidence Inventory, at the end of this chapter, may be used by professionals and paraeducators respectively to accomplish this comparison. These worksheets will need to be adapted to fit the specific characteristics of individual programs and professionals. For example, professionals in a preschool program might eliminate some tasks (e.g., helping with workbooks) and keep others (e.g., self-help, read to students). They might add tasks that are specific to a program (e.g., work on articulation skills with children). Professionals in a vocational preparation program, on the other hand, might eliminate some tasks, add others, and reword tasks like "Help students in drill and practice lessons" to something like "Help students apply basic computational skills on the job" to reflect the differences in programmatic emphasis, as well as the age and needs of students. Again, the wide variety of programs, professionals, and student needs precludes the possibility of creating a single form that is entirely useful in all situations. The examples presented in this text are intended to be used as formats or guidelines from which professionals can create unique devices that address specific program characteristics.

After the inventories are completed a "needs versus preferences" analysis occurs. To do so, the Professional/Program/Student Needs Inventory and the Paraeducator Skills/Confidence Inventory should be examined side by side to determine which tasks will become an immediate part of the personalized job description and which tasks will be listed but for which training must precede performance. Items on which there is a scoring match (i.e., the professional needs the task done and the paraeducator agrees that he/she can do it now) automatically become part of the PJD. Items for which the need exists, but the skills and confidence are lacking, must be discussed and evaluated individually. The inventories become the vehicle by which these important negotiations are structured. Tasks which the professional needs, but are not matched by paraeducator skill or confidence, may be treated in one of two ways. They may be listed as future tasks, following appropriate preparation. Or they may be transferred to a growth and development plan, as discussed in the next section.

Summary

Paraeducators should receive an initial orientation to the workplace and to their job duties as well as an introduction to other staff and faculty. Once paraeducators have had the opportunity to become acquainted with their supervisor(s) they should receive written information regarding the policies, procedures, rules, and regulations that govern the district or agency. During the orientation phase, the work style preferences of paraeducator and supervising professional(s) should be compared. Then a needs versus skills analysis should be conducted to determine the match between the needs of the program or the professional and the paraeducator's current skill level.

PERSONALIZING JOB DESCRIPTIONS

The need for job descriptions for paraeducators is well documented (Pickett, Vasa, & Steckelberg, 1993). The personalized job description (PJD) serves as an addendum to the general job description that school districts use to hire paraeducators. The PJD delineates the specific duties for which a particular paraeducator will be held responsible and it clarifies the need for the training and coaching necessary to equip the paraeducator to perform all of the tasks needed by the professional, the program, or the team on behalf of the students. The form included at the end of the chapter titled Personalized Job Description for Paraeducators provides a skeletal structure for creating a PJD for each newly employed paraeducator.

Providing a personalized job description for a newly employed paraeducator creates a common basis of understanding about the nature of the job and about the circumstances that exist in the particular workplace. It allows the newly employed paraeducator a glimpse into the future. It also opens the door for the person who is not well suited to the position to make a move quickly. As difficult as it may seem, it is better for everyone to recognize a poor fit early.

Consider the situation of Madison, a newly employed speech–language therapy assistant. Madison accepted employment as a paraeducator after reading about the position in the newspaper. She had taken some college courses toward a degree in speech communication and thought the position sounded interesting. She interviewed well and appeared to have a good understanding of the position. Tracy, the speech–language pathologist, provided Madison with orientation information and they completed the companion needs and skills inventories the second day on the job. Madison realized right away that this job was not what she thought it would be. She found herself in the awkward position of having accepted a position that she did not really want. Madison tried to be honest with Tracy but Tracy begged Madison to stay and give it a try. Four months later, Madison resigned. Only then did Tracy realize that she had just expended tremendous effort training and coaching a person who was not well suited to the position in the first place. She regretted that she had not heeded Madison's initial concerns.

Finally, a PJD provides the professional a glimpse into the paraeducator's immediate and long-range training needs. Training plans can be created and the process can begin soon after employment. Meanwhile, delegated tasks can be selected or modified to match the present skill level of the paraeducator.

Summary

Personalized job descriptions may be created from the information accumulated in the preferred work style inventories and the needs versus skills analysis. The PJD should include space to document the dates on which performance feedback was provided to the paraeducator. When developed during the orientation phase of employment, PJDs may serve as an introduction to the roles and responsibilities of the position and may have the side effect of ending the employment of a person who is not well suited to the position.

PLANNING/PROVIDING/DOCUMENTING PARAEDUCATOR GROWTH AND DEVELOPMENT

Planning

There are two key reasons for creating a paraeducator growth and development plan and two corresponding plan components. When a self-identified gap exists between the programmatic and professional needs and the skills or levels of confidence of the paraeducator, the first reason is readily apparent. Training is needed. Yet, due to the many constraints inherent in bureaucratic systems like schools, training is unlikely to occur incidentally. It must be conscientiously planned if it is to occur at all.

The second reason, although less obvious, is just as important. Paraeducators, like everyone else in schools, are lifelong learners. They need to strive continually for renewal and refinement of their skills and to maintain current knowledge. Areas in which skill refinements are needed are often noted during observations and monitoring of task completion by professionals. In addition, schoolwide initiatives as well as the paraeducator's personal interests often provide the substance of other growth and development areas. For example, Ophelia, a paraeducator in a Title I reading program, had a growth and development plan that included training in the district's new communication skills curriculum. She participated in the training alongside many Title I teachers who were also becoming acquainted with the new curricular format and objectives.

Professionals who supervise paraeducators should lead the work of creating a growth and development plan that specifies the training that is needed or desired, the person responsible for securing or arranging the training, the date by which it will be accomplished, and the accountability measures that will ensure application of the training to the job duties. The sample Growth and Development Plan form, also adapted from the work of Emery (1991) and contained with the forms at the end of this chapter, consists of two sections. The first page provides space to list training areas identified through the needs versus skills analysis and the second page provides space to list training areas identified in other ways—either through on-the-job monitoring, personal interest, or schoolwide initiative.

Providing Training

Providing training activities may be accomplished in numerous ways. Some training may occur on the job, incidentally throughout the day or week, or during team meetings. Other knowledge and skills demand a more formal setting—perhaps a workshop, a course, or a seminar held either outside of the school day or away from the school setting. To be most effective, training should include theory, demonstration, practice, feedback, and coaching for application (Joyce & Showers, 1980). Theory means that the skill, strategy, or concept is clearly explained or described. Demonstration describes or shows how the skill, strategy, or concept is applied in realistic situations. Practice means that the paraeducator actually tries out the skill or applies the concept in carefully controlled and safe circumstances, either through role play, small group discussion, or actual student interaction.

Feedback is then provided to the paraeducator regarding her performance so that, in this safe situation, the paraeducator can continue to practice until the skill is developed well enough to use on the job. Feedback is a communication to a person that gives the person information about how he or she performs. It should help paraeducators consider and alter their performance and thus better achieve the goal. Feedback is most effective when it meets the following criteria (Pfeiffer & Jones, 1987):

- Descriptive rather than judgmental
- Specific rather than general
- Considerate of the needs of the paraeducator
- Directed toward performance rather than personal characteristics
- Well timed
- Accurate transmission of the message (check with the paraeducator)

Finally, coaching occurs on the job while the paraeducator works with students. Coaching is the most significant of all training practices because it allows for fine tuning of newly acquired skills until the skill becomes solidly cemented into the repertoire of the paraeducator. Without coaching, newly acquired skills also become habitual but may not be correct. When supervisors take on the coaching role, they must take care to separate the coaching functions from the evaluative aspect of their jobs. Paraeducators do not thrive in situations where the coaching actions of their supervisor make them feel as though they are being "called on the carpet." Just as coaching of Olympic athletes consists of giving/getting feedback about athletic performance, the coaching of paraeducators consists of giving/getting feedback about performance of essential instructional and other job duties. Coaching may be perceived as threatening to the paraeducator, but a supervisor who takes care to adhere to the feedback criteria diminishes the threat.

Documenting Training

Documenting the training episodes and the skill acquisition of the paraeducators helps to establish the importance of the training in the culture of the team. It also provides a safeguard in three situations: (a) working with a paraeducator who does not meet the employment standards, (b) protecting the safety and welfare of students, and (c) providing a basis for legal defense if necessary.

In the first situation, where a paraeducator is unable or unwilling to do the work, it is important that the professional provide the paraeducator every opportunity to improve the knowledge, skills, or dispositions necessary to be able to do the job. The opportunities should be documented along with the resulting performances. If performance remains substandard after training, feedback, and coaching have been provided then, and only then, should dismissal proceedings be enacted.

The second consideration, protecting the safety and welfare of students, is especially relevant in programs that include students with health needs. Some health needs are so significant that the lack of proper attention to the task could result in serious injury or health risk to the student. Documentation of specific training regarding health care functions helps the professional remember who is qualified to perform certain tasks and who is not. It also helps the professional remember to provide the same training for newly hired paraeducators who start midyear that they provided at the beginning of the year.

For example, Alice, a teacher of students with significant cognitive and physical needs, hired three paraeducators when her program moved to a new school building. The school nurse, who held ultimate responsibility for the Individualized Health Plans for these students, trained everyone to perform all the necessary health care tasks during the first week of school. Alice showed the new paraeducators some of the video clips she had filmed of herself working with the students during the previous school year. The paraeducators could see exactly how these students needed to be positioned and transferred and how Alice protected her back while lifting or moving the students. Alice worked with the group to demonstrate several instructional methods that were useful with the students. In spite of all the effort Alice spent on appropriate training, within the month one paraeducator left because she decided this job was not right for her. Only 3 weeks later another paraeducator left her position to take a higher paying clerical position in the district's administration building. The third paraeducator left just before Thanksgiving when her husband lost his job and they had to move. Alice found herself engaged in the hiring process for an entire semester and each time she hired another paraeducator, she had to remember the list of skills on which to provide training and gather the resources to do the training. She knew better than to try to hold all this information in memory. She kept copies of the *Growth and Development Plans* for each paraeducator inside her lesson plan book for handy reference. As she taught each skill to each person, she noted the date and time of day on the plan. Thus, she did not forget any of the procedures and the physical well-being of her students was assured.

The third consideration is a frightening one for school professionals. Sometimes parents sue the school or certain school professionals when they believe their son or daughter has been placed at risk or, in special education, when he or she has failed to acquire the outcomes documented on the IEP. The Individuals with Disabilities Education Act (IDEA) reauthorization of 1990 specifically requires that all personnel who work with students who have disability labels have the skills required for the position. Although there is only a relatively small precedent, professionals and paraeducators are somewhat at risk of being sued if the paraeducator is not adequately prepared to perform the instructional duties assigned. If, on the other hand, training is provided and supervision occurs as it should, then each of those activities should be fully documented to protect against the risk.

Summary

Planning for paraeducator training is important because it is unlikely to occur incidentally and because paraeducators should be lifelong learners. Training should include theory, demonstration, practice, feedback, and coaching for application. Feedback is most effective when it is descriptive, specific, considerate, directed toward performance, well timed, and checked with the recipient. Coaching involves giving feedback to the paraeducator to improve skill performance. Documentation of training activities is necessary to protect the safety of students and the welfare of paraeducators and programs.

EVALUATING

Frequently, school professionals play a substantial role in the evaluation of paraeducator performance. Even when their professional contracts preclude direct evaluative responsibility, school professionals often are asked to contribute information that will assist in summative evaluation processes required by the district or agency. The professional's interest in evaluation should go beyond the district's or agency's formal evaluation procedure, however, to promote the growth and development of the paraeducator (Pickett et al., 1993). Evaluating the paraeducator's performance may highlight the need for additional training or coaching or may identify high-quality work. Summative performance evaluations may occur at designated times such as the end of a semester or year, but should reflect multiple reviews of performance rather than the review of a single episode.

Evaluation requires judgment. Fair evaluation is based on a comparison of performance to a standard, on facts rather than opinions, and on first-hand knowledge rather than hearsay. As mentioned previously, the characteristics of fair evaluation include the following:

- *Frequency:* Frequent performance observations yield fairer ratings because they sample multiple opportunities to perform duties.

- *Specificity:* Generalities rarely help performance; people can only improve their skills if they know what specific behaviors to work on.

- *Honesty:* Be straightforward, tell it like it is, yet be tactful, respectful, and dignity preserving.

- *Consistency:* Professional team members have to get their "acts" together and provide information that does not conflict.

Frequent performance ratings yield fairer overall ratings because they document multiple performances of the same or similar tasks and conditions. From the paraeducator's point of view, multiple ratings also help reduce the amount of anxiety or nervousness associated with being evaluated. When Eileen was observed for the first time by her supervising school professional, she was extremely nervous and noticed that her hands were shaking. Now, she is more at ease with the process because it has occurred so often.

The next characteristic, specificity, means that the information contained in the performance rating describes, in behavioral terms, exactly what behavior the paraeducator does or does not display and the judgment regarding that behavior. When a paraeducator receives specific information about poor performance she knows exactly what behavior to avoid in the future. Specificity also means that good performance is recognized and named. For example, after Peggy, a special education teacher, observed Elodia assisting James to eat his lunch, she commented, "Elodia, I noticed that James showed greater interest in eating when you gave him the choice of which food to eat first. That is a good thing to do because it helps him understand that he can make choices."

Honesty in evaluation is crucial. Supervisors who try to be "nice" by telling the paraeducator that she is doing fine, or by saying nothing at all, often find that they have deluded themselves into believing that things will be okay. Eventually, poor performance of tasks or unsatisfactory knowledge, skills, or attitudes will hurt the quality of services to students or may damage the work of the entire team. Honesty means that the supervisor must know and be able to articulate the expected performance as well as the discrepancy that exists. On the other hand, some supervisors make the mistake of believing that the paraeducator "already knows" that he or she is doing well and, thus, fail to honestly appraise good performance. Honestly identifying and recognizing good performance is as important as honestly confronting poor performance.

Finally, consistency means that multiple professional team members should either work together to provide performance evaluation information or they should designate a single team member to do so. Because judgment is idiosyncratic, different evaluators are likely to describe the same performance in different ways unless they discuss and come to consensus on the descriptors that apply.

Performance Standards

One basis for fair evaluation is the establishment of performance standards. Performance standards that foster growth and development emerge from the PJDs that were discussed in the orientation section. Once a PJD is created, then each duty may be transferred to the Paraeducator Performance Rating form (see Worksheet 8 at the end of the chapter) and used to rate the performance of each duty. The rating scale for items on this rating form reflects the developmental nature of learning how to teach and participate as a team member. No one learns to perform job duties instantly and no one is born knowing how to teach well. It takes time and practice to acquire sophisticated levels of skill. Skill level markers such as "independent," "developing," "emerging," or "unable to perform" recognize teaching as a developmental sequence of skills that improve with time and practice. Suggested operational definitions of the markers are as follows:

- *Independent:* Paraeducator is able to perform task, as taught, without guidance.

- *Developing:* Paraeducator can perform task, as taught, but relies on cues or prompts as guidance for portions of the performance.

- *Emerging:* Paraeducator performs parts of task or tries to perform but requires substantial guidance/assistance to complete all aspects.

- *Unable to perform:* Paraeducator does not know how to perform the task.

Ratings of this type may be used to determine the need for further training and coaching or a change of assigned responsibilities. Judgments about whether a paraeducator can reasonably be expected to perform at a given level should be specified in advance. For example, when Audrey, a newly employed paraeducator, started to work, her supervisor, Ed, specified that she would be expected to teach groups of students to use QAR and the keyword method. Ed expected that, prior to training, Audrey would be unable to perform the task but that immediately following training, Audrey would perform at an emerging level of performance. He specified that by the end of the first quarter Audrey should be able to provide instruction in both these learning strategies at an independent level.

Observations

The supervisory function of monitoring performance is best accomplished through first-hand observations of task performance. The most fruitful observations involve written data (Goldhammer, Anderson, & Krajewski, 1980). The data that may be collected during observations vary with the type of observation. The following is a list of several types of data that are useful in unfocused observations—those observations that have no particular skill or duty as the central feature (French, Kozleski, & Sands, 1992):

- *Audio, video recording:* Observer captures all events within visual, auditory range.
- *Scripting:* Observer writes down everything he/she hears.
- *Notes on significant instructional events:* Observer writes down instructional events he/she interprets as related to the target skill or behavior.
- *Notes on significant interpersonal events:* Observer writes down interpersonal events he/she interprets as related to the target skill or behavior.

The decision to conduct a focused versus an unfocused observation depends on the anticipated outcome. If the goal is to gather general performance information, then an unfocused observation may be appropriate (French et al., 1992). Some potential applications of unfocused observation methods include:

- Personal style components
- Voice, gestures, delivery

- Content of lesson

- Interactions with students/adults

- Organization of lesson or materials

- Time use

- Overall behavior or group management

For example, Martha, a special educator at Blue Ridge High School, wants to monitor the work of the paraeducator, Jose, in general education classes. They meet to plan the observations and Jose indicates that he just wants general feedback on how he moves in and out of classes, how he relates to students, and how he fits in with the flow of the classroom teacher. This calls for data collected by video camera, audio recorder, or scripting. Later, after the observation, Martha and Jose can meet to analyze the data and make evaluative judgments about Jose's performance based on those data.

On the other hand, the supervisor may need specific information about a certain skill or the performance of a particular duty. Or the paraeducator may be working on a certain skill and requesting feedback in that area. In either case, a focused observation is in order. The following is a list of some focused observational methods:

- *Checklist:* Identifies or tallies the presence, absence, or frequency of specific behaviors.

- *Selective verbatim:* Captures word for word certain, preselected events.

- *Timeline coding:* Tracks the behaviors of either the paraeducator or the students at frequent intervals during an observation period.

- *Seating chart observation records:* Identifies or tallies the specified behaviors of individual students during instruction.

Some of the possible specific target behaviors for which focused methods are best used include:

- Rephrasing or restating questions

- Touching, courtesy, listening

- Frequency of questions

- Types of questions (open versus closed, factual versus higher order thinking)

- Amount/type of "teacher" talk (giving directions, pertinent examples, talking about tangential topics)

- Number of directions

- Student at-task behavior

- Student or paraeducator movement through the room

The specific target behavior, skill, or duty dictates the type of data to be collected. For instance, when Jose learned the skill of teaching students to use the keyword method discussed previously, he was concerned that he had difficulty guiding students to use it properly. He asked Martha to observe and take data. They decided that the most useful information would result from the selective verbatim method. Selective verbatim is a technique in which the observer writes down all instances of a certain type of interaction or communication (Acheson & Gall, 1980). In this case, Jose wanted to know if his directions to students about how to use the keyword method were clear and sequential. Martha observed and recorded all the directions that Jose gave to his group of students. Later, they examined the written record together. Together, they analyzed the directions for clarity and sequence. Jose was able to see what he needed to do by studying the data from his own instructional episode. This type of monitoring of job performance honors the dignity of the paraeducator and promotes continual growth and development.

Documenting Performance Ratings

Earlier, the documentation of training episodes was discussed. Documenting training episodes is important because it protects the professional, the student, and the program from various risks, and helps ensure that the training actually takes place. Likewise, documenting performance ratings protects all parties against risk and reminds team members about the need for training. Documentation is most easily and readily accomplished when the Paraeducator Performance Rating form is used to write the date that oral feedback regarding performance of duties was given and to indicate the skill marker that applies on that date.

Summary

Evaluation of paraeducator performance is also included in the list of executive functions of paraeducator supervision. Paraeducator skill development in instructional methods is a developmental process. Different levels of development are expected at different stages of paraeducator employment. Evaluation of paraeducator job performance requires judgment and should be based on fair performance standards, first-hand observations, written data, and appropriate documentation of performance.

CONDUCTING MEETINGS

By now it should be obvious that meetings between the supervisor(s) and the paraeducator(s) are fundamental to ethical supervisory behavior. Many of the executive functions of paraeducator supervision can only be accomplished during meetings. Giving directions, providing on-the-job training, providing feedback on performance, solving problems, managing conflicts, communicating about goals, and evaluation are functions that are primarily accomplished when sitting face to face. Yet, in one study, about 25% of the special education teachers who supervised paraeducators admitted that they never held formalized, sit-down meetings; another 25% said that such meetings were rare (French, 1994). Meetings must be frequent enough to ensure legal and ethical completion of educational tasks and to ensure smooth operation of the team. Meetings must also be of significant enough duration to get the agenda accomplished, and they must include the right people. Whether the team consists of two people—teacher and paraeducator—or of a multidisciplinary group of people, the considerations are the same. Considerations include when to meet, establishing group norms, establishing a functional meeting location, using an agenda, documenting the group's decisions, and reviewing the effectiveness of the meetings.

When To Meet

One of the most frequent laments of teachers is "There's no time to meet with the paraeducator!" In reality, we all have the same amount of time. We just allocate it differently according to our perceived purposes and priorities. Finding time to meet is important even when it is not urgent. Like many other tasks, meetings between paraeducators and professionals are upper right-hand quadrant activities on the time management matrix presented earlier in Figure 4.6. These activities tend to be among the most important activities of any profession, yet they are the most difficult to attend to because they lack the adrenaline-producing characteristic of urgency. When professionals begin to recognize that paraeducator supervision is, indeed, an important part of their jobs, then they can begin solving the problem of when to meet.

Finding a consistent meeting time may require some creativity. Some teams have requested and received permission to pay paraeducators for meeting time outside of student contact time. In other schools and agencies that solution is not possible. Some teams have relied on a flexible schedule, where some paraeducators come early or stay late 1 day of the week but leave earlier or later on another day to compensate.

Consider how the team in the Ames Elementary special education program for primary-aged children with severe cognitive, affective, language, and physical needs used a "flex" schedule to address the dilemma. The program team consists of a special education teacher, a speech–language pathologist, four paraeducators, a school nurse one morning a week, and a physical therapist one morning a week. They also worked with an occupational therapist who consulted with them on a periodic basis. Establishing team meetings where all the members could be present was no small task. After much consideration, Nancy, the team leader, set Thursday mornings at 7:15 as the team meeting time. The usual start time for the paraeducators was 8:15; students arrived at 8:25 and the paraeducators had to greet the buses. This gave the team 1 hour and 10 minutes a week of uninterrupted time to meet, but required the paraeducators to arrive 1 hour earlier than their usual start time. In trade, each of the four paraeducators selected 1 day of the week to leave 1 hour early. It worked for them because it gave them a predictable extra hour one afternoon a week to do errands or make special appointments. When the team took their plan to Mr. Colin, the principal, he wanted to know how they had planned to cover the duties of each paraeducator for that hour. Nancy's job as team leader and schedule-maker was to create a schedule that ensured the ongoing education of all the students while the team operated short-handed. The Ames Elementary solution may not be the right one for all situations, but the use of flex time makes sense for many types of programs.

Other possible solutions include the creation of a master schedule that permits all team members a common planning time during the school week. After school, lunchtime, and school time meetings are possible in some cases and places. No solution is likely to happen without negotiation and careful planning.

Establishing Meeting Norms

Meeting times, once established, are preciously short. Short meetings generally suit most people, but getting the job done is paramount. To maintain short meetings that get the job done requires several organizational conditions. The first is to establish meeting norms and discuss them early in the team's relationship. Norms may be reviewed or changed when needed. Some teams set norms that include considerations such as how decisions are made, what problem-solving process they will use when a tough challenge presents itself, punctuality, who will record meeting notes, who will facilitate the conversation, whether there will be snacks, and, if so, who will bring them. Teams that have established norms spend less time arguing or rehashing old subjects and get more work done in shorter amounts of time. Teams that fail to establish norms often find themselves wrestling with the same difficult problems over and over again. For example, in one team, members used to drift into the meeting one at a time so that no quorum existed for the first half of the meeting. Those who were punctual sat and discussed the issues but were unable to make final decisions without all the players. By the time the quorum was established, the team had only half the time to do the complete agenda. Items were delayed until the next meeting and the cycle continued. What did they do? One displeased team member took it on herself to lead a discussion about the way their team functioned. They spent what was left of a meeting one day talking about their lack of effectiveness and how it was caused by the lack of a norm about punctuality. They made a decision to correct the situation and to self-review at the end of each meeting to decide how they had done. The stress was alleviated and the team functioning improved.

Meeting Location, Setup, and Atmosphere

Another meeting consideration includes setting a consistent place, away from distractions, and establishing a norm that no one leaves the meeting or accepts outside interruptions. Seating arrangements should also be considered. Teams that get work done at short meetings sit face to face at a table where everyone can see the materials. Some teams have food at meetings either to establish a pleasant atmosphere or because the meeting occurs during lunchtime. Food, however, can become a distraction. If food is present and it causes distraction from the business at hand, it should either be eliminated or a team norm should be established to preserve the business-like atmosphere.

Facilitating the Discussion

In smoothly functioning meetings, one person is designated as the meeting facilitator. A facilitator makes sure that each person has a chance to talk and that the talk is not monopolized by a few members. Facilitators also ensure that each topic is discussed to closure and that the topic is either tabled or terminated. The role of facilitator may be assigned to one team member or rotated among team members.

Agendas

The use of an agenda (Figure 4.10) characterizes effective task-oriented meetings. Agendas may be created in advance by a team leader or by members of the group. Some teams post the blank agenda form in a common location so that all team members can post items that need to be discussed. This system has the advantage of alerting everyone to the topics in advance so that individuals can prepare for the discussion or bring relevant materials. Another approach to agenda-making is to begin each meeting with a statement of the anticipated agenda and allow participants to add items that also should be added. If the number or complexity of topics will exceed the time limit, the group must then prioritize the topics to determine those that must be discussed immediately and those that can be delayed.

Documenting Accomplishments

The decisions made or actions taken at a meeting are irrelevant if no one can remember what they were 2 months later. Documentation is essential to help individuals remember decisions and actions and to establish a written record of plans, training topics, coaching episodes, schedule changes, as well as decisions about behavioral and instructional interventions for students. An easy way to document meetings is to have a recorder write directly on the agenda form, then make copies for participants. Another way is to have a "Meeting Memo" format that includes topics such as discussions, decisions, and next steps. The sample agenda shown in Figure 4.10 is a combination agenda/ meeting record form that can be adapted to fit many specific needs.

Assessing the Meeting Effectiveness

Periodically, teams must invest a little time in self-reflection and review to assess the value and effectiveness of their meetings. Through periodic self-assessment, teams may minimize wasted meeting time, distinguish the tasks

---

Agenda

Date: _____

In attendance: _____

Topics:	Action Needed	Time Allotment
1.		
2.		
3.		
4.		
5.		

Meeting Record

Action/Decision	Person Responsible	Target Date

Figure 4.10.   Sample agenda form.

they must do together from those that could be done apart, and evaluate the quality of their interactions. It is most useful to monitor meeting components that frequently cause problems. Frequently reported problems include participant notification, perceived importance of the meeting, expectations of participants, agenda, punctuality of participants, time flow and management, listening, problem management, and overall satisfaction with the outcomes.

Summary

Meetings are important because many of the executive functions of para-educator supervision are accomplished during meetings. Finding a place in the schedule, appropriate locations, and sufficient time challenge the super-vising professional. Precious meeting time should be managed by establishing meeting norms, using agendas, facilitating the discussion, and documenting the work of the meeting. Finally, maximum meeting effectiveness is maintained by periodic review of problem areas.

Discussion Questions

1. Discuss how the job of the school professional is like that of an executive or a manager in a corporation.

2. Stop and think about a school situation—either where you work or where you have observed. Briefly describe the way paraeducators are deployed in the school. Where are they located throughout the day? Who are they with? What effect does that have on the supervision provided to them? Who supervises?

3. Think about jobs you have held. What steps did the employer or the supervisor take to make sure that you were oriented to the job? Now discuss what you could do to orient new paraeducators to their jobs.

4. Think about the best and the worst working relationships you've had with other people. To what extent were the working relationships affected by similarities and differences in your work styles and preferences?

5. Think about the major tasks required of you (or someone else) each week or month. How do you decide what you do and what the other people do?

(Continues)

Discussion Questions (*Continued*)

6. Think about the types of tasks you might assign to a paraeducator. For each task, think about the particular skills the paraeducator would need to possess.

7. Think about times that you have failed to delegate a task to another person. Tell why. Then reread the section on delegation and see where your reasons fit.

Exercises

(Worksheets appear after the Case Study.)

1. Complete the Professional's Work Style form (Worksheet 1) for yourself. Compare your answers to those that you think the paraeducator(s) you might supervise will give to the corollary questions. *OR*, if you work with a paraeducator, have the paraeducator complete the Paraeducator's Work Style form (Worksheet 2). Then sit down together to compare scores using the Work Style Score Sheet (Worksheet 3).

2. First modify, then use the Professional/Program/Student Needs Inventory (Worksheet 4) to analyze the need for paraeducator support. Cross off any items that do not pertain to your program or personal needs. Add any missing items.

3. Examine and modify the Paraeducator Skills/Confidence Inventory (Worksheet 5) to match the Professional/Program/Student Needs Inventory as you've modified it (in Exercise 2). If you work with a paraeducator, ask the paraeducator you supervise to complete the Paraeducator Skills/Confidence Inventory then sit down together and complete the Personalized Job Description for Paraeducators (Worksheet 6).

4. Go back to the instruments you have used to identify the programmatic needs and the paraeducator's skills and/or confidence in performing those tasks. Think about where there is a good match between what needs to be done by the paraeducator and the paraeducator's skills and/or confidence. Now think about the places in which a gap exists between the two. Are there places where some kind of training would help? If so, list these items on page 1 of the paraeducator Growth and Development Plan (Worksheet 7).

(*Continues*)

Exercises (Continued)

5. Examine and modify the meeting agenda/documentation form (Figure 4.10) to suit your own needs and preferences. Create a form that you can copy to use again and again. Share it with the other people you meet with to get their feedback before finalizing your form.

6. In a small group, discuss the situation Alice experienced (see the section on Documenting Training) and compare how you currently keep track of the training a paraeducator receives. Examine and discuss how you might use the paraeducator Growth and Development Plan form (Worksheet 7) to document paraeducator training.

7. Think about the components of fair performance ratings or evaluations. If you were being evaluated on your work performance, which of these practices would you want to apply to your situation? What basis should your supervisor use to judge your work?

8. Describe your experiences with meetings of various types. Are there differences in the ways that you participate in and feel about different meetings? What makes a meeting effective? What makes a meeting ineffective?

Case Study

Read the following vignette about Chris and Mrs. Merman. Then meet with others to discuss the case discussion questions that follow the vignette.

Chris and Mrs. Merman

Chris is a special education paraeducator assigned to Mrs. Merman's fifth-grade classroom because there are three special education students who need additional behavioral and academic support to be able to succeed in her class. Mrs. Merman asked Chris to lead a small group reading activity with those students and two others while she observed unobtrusively from a nearby table. She noticed that Chris was slipping into some biased interactions with the students; he was calling on the boys more often than girls, giving boys additional probes, and delving more deeply into their thinking to help them answer correctly, while giving girls only one chance

(Continues)

Case Study (Continued)

before moving on, and was avoiding calling on the poorer readers at the table. During the lunch break, she spent a few moments talking about the lesson with Chris. When she began to point out the mistakes, he became defensive, turned away, and muttered loudly enough for her to just barely hear, "You didn't see much of the lesson. You were busy catching up on your paperwork."

Case Discussion Questions

1. What executive functions of supervision does Mrs. Merman need to consider here?

2. Whose responsibility is it to provide supervision to Chris?

3. What is the problem? Could it have been avoided?

   a. Could Mrs. Merman have foreseen that this problem was coming?

   b. Should Chris have received prior training on how to distribute response opportunities equitably? Who is responsible for such training?

   c. Should Mrs. Merman confront Chris or let it go?

   d. Was Mrs. Merman correct to assign Chris such a task?

4. What do you think about the circumstances under which Mrs. Merman began to discuss the lesson with Chris?

Worksheet 1
Professional's Work Style

Directions: Circle the number that indicates your level of agreement/disagreement with each statement.

	Disagree			Agree	
1. I like to supervise closely.	1	2	3	4	5
2. I like a flexible work schedule.	1	2	3	4	5
3. I like to let team members know exactly what is expected.	1	2	3	4	5
4. I like to provide (or at least determine) all the materials that will be used.	1	2	3	4	5
5. I like to have a written work schedule.	1	2	3	4	5
6. I need time to think ahead about the next task.	1	2	3	4	5
7. I like to determine the instructional methods that will be used.	1	2	3	4	5
8. I like for the paraeducator to try new activities independently.	1	2	3	4	5
9. I like to give explicit directions for each task.	1	2	3	4	5
10. I like to do several things at one time.	1	2	3	4	5
11. I like to work with teams that take on challenges.	1	2	3	4	5
12. I like taking care of details.	1	2	3	4	5
13. I like to be very punctual.	1	2	3	4	5
14. I like to get frequent feedback on how I can improve as a supervisor.	1	2	3	4	5
15. I like to bring problems out in the open.	1	2	3	4	5
16. I like to give frequent performance feedback to the paraeducator.	1	2	3	4	5
17. I like to discuss when activities do not go well.	1	2	3	4	5
18. I like working with other adults.	1	2	3	4	5
19. I like to encourage others to think for themselves.	1	2	3	4	5
20. I am a morning person.	1	2	3	4	5

Page 1   (*Continues*)

Note. Adapted from *Building Team Pride: Teachers and Paraeducators Working Together,* by M. J. Emery, 1991, Columbus: University of Missouri.

Worksheet 1 (*Continued*)

	Disagree				Agree
21. I like to speak slowly and softly.	1	2	3	4	5
22. I like to work alone with little immediate interaction.	1	2	3	4	5
23. I need a quiet place to work without distractions.	1	2	3	4	5
24. I prefer that no one else touches my things.	1	2	3	4	5
25. I prefer to work from a written plan.	1	2	3	4	5

Page 2

Worksheet 2
Paraeducator's Work Style

Directions: Circle the number that indicates your level of agreement/disagreement with each statement.

	Disagree				Agree
1. I like to be supervised closely.	1	2	3	4	5
2. I like a flexible work schedule.	1	2	3	4	5
3. I like to know exactly what is expected.	1	2	3	4	5
4. I like to decide which materials to use.	1	2	3	4	5
5. I like to have a written work schedule.	1	2	3	4	5
6. I need time to think ahead about the next task.	1	2	3	4	5
7. I like to determine the instructional methods that I use.	1	2	3	4	5
8. I like to try new activities independently.	1	2	3	4	5
9. I like to be told how to do each task.	1	2	3	4	5
10. I like to do several things at one time.	1	2	3	4	5
11. I like to take on challenges.	1	2	3	4	5
12. I like taking care of details.	1	2	3	4	5
13. I like to be very punctual.	1	2	3	4	5
14. I like to give frequent feedback on how I prefer to be supervised.	1	2	3	4	5
15. I like to bring problems out in the open.	1	2	3	4	5
16. I like to get frequent feedback on my performance.	1	2	3	4	5
17. I like to discuss when activities do not go well.	1	2	3	4	5
18. I like working with other adults.	1	2	3	4	5
19. I like to think things through for myself.	1	2	3	4	5
20. I am a morning person.	1	2	3	4	5
21. I like to speak slowly and softly.	1	2	3	4	5
22. I like to work alone with little immediate interaction.	1	2	3	4	5
23. I need a quiet place to work without distractions.	1	2	3	4	5
24. I prefer that no one else touches my things.	1	2	3	4	5
25. I prefer to work from a written plan.	1	2	3	4	5

Note. Adapted from *Building Team Pride: Teachers and Paraeducators Working Together,* by M. J. Emery, 1991, Columbus: University of Missouri.

Worksheet 3
Work Style Score Sheet

Directions: Transfer scores from Worksheets 1 and 2 to this form. Examine areas of agreement and disagreement. Your combined profile is unique: There are no "correct" scores or combinations. Decide whether your combinations are okay or not. Have a conversation in which you strive to determine how you will proceed to work together in light of your areas of agreement and disagreement.

Disagree	Agree	General Content of Item	Disagree	Agree
1 2 3	4 5	1. Closeness of supervision	1 2 3	4 5
1 2 3	4 5	2. Flexibility of work schedule	1 2 3	4 5
1 2 3	4 5	3. Preciseness of expectations	1 2 3	4 5
1 2 3	4 5	4. Decisions on which materials to use	1 2 3	4 5
1 2 3	4 5	5. Written work schedule	1 2 3	4 5
1 2 3	4 5	6. Time to think ahead about the next task	1 2 3	4 5
1 2 3	4 5	7. Decisions on instructional methods	1 2 3	4 5
1 2 3	4 5	8. Trying new activities independently	1 2 3	4 5
1 2 3	4 5	9. Specifying how to do each task	1 2 3	4 5
1 2 3	4 5	10. Doing several things at one time	1 2 3	4 5
1 2 3	4 5	11. Taking on challenges	1 2 3	4 5
1 2 3	4 5	12. Taking care of details	1 2 3	4 5
1 2 3	4 5	13. Punctuality	1 2 3	4 5
1 2 3	4 5	14. Giving/getting feedback on supervision	1 2 3	4 5
1 2 3	4 5	15. Dealing with problems out in the open	1 2 3	4 5
1 2 3	4 5	16. Giving/getting frequent feedback	1 2 3	4 5
1 2 3	4 5	17. Discussing activities that do not go well	1 2 3	4 5

Page 1 (*Continues*)

Note. Adapted from *Building Team Pride: Teachers and Paraeducators Working Together,* by M. J. Emery, 1991, Columbus: University of Missouri.

Worksheet 3 *(Continued)*

Disagree	Agree	General Content of Item	Disagree	Agree
1 2 3 4 5		18. Working with other adults	1 2 3 4 5	
1 2 3 4 5		19. Thinking things through for myself	1 2 3 4 5	
1 2 3 4 5		20. I am a morning person	1 2 3 4 5	
1 2 3 4 5		21. Speak slowly and softly	1 2 3 4 5	
1 2 3 4 5		22. Working alone—little interaction	1 2 3 4 5	
1 2 3 4 5		23. Quiet place to work/ no distractions	1 2 3 4 5	
1 2 3 4 5		24. Touching others' things	1 2 3 4 5	
1 2 3 4 5		25. Working from a written plan	1 2 3 4 5	

Page 2

Worksheet 4
Professional/Program/Student Needs Inventory

Directions: Consider the needs of students, the team, and the program as a whole. Decide which of the tasks/duties could be completed by a paraeducator. Teams may individualize this inventory by changing items that are not applicable as stated, or by replacing items with more appropriate tasks or duties. Specify details as needed for clarity. Circle yes to mean that the item is a program need or no to show that the team does not need the paraeducator to perform the task/duty.

Delivery of Instruction

1. Observe and record student progress in academic areas — Yes No
2. Help students in drill and practice lessons (e.g., vocabulary, math facts) — Yes No
3. Read/repeat tests or directions to students — Yes No
4. Listen to students read orally — Yes No
5. Help students with workbooks/other written assignments — Yes No
6. Assist students to compose original work (e.g., stories, essays, reports) — Yes No
7. Tape-record stories, lessons, assignments — Yes No
8. Modify instructional materials according to directions (e.g., lesson plans, IEPs) — Yes No
9. Read to students (specify _____ (e.g., text material, stories)) — Yes No
10. Help students work on individual projects — Yes No
11. Facilitate students' active participation in cooperative groups — Yes No
12. Helps students select library books/reference materials — Yes No
13. Help students use computers (specify purpose _____) — Yes No
14. Translate instruction/student responses (e.g., sign or other language) — Yes No
15. Translate teacher-made materials/text materials into another language — Yes No
16. Explain/reteach concepts to students in other language (e.g., sign, Spanish) — Yes No
17. Carry out lessons in community-based settings (e.g., travel training, job shadowing) — Yes No
18. Monitor student performance in community-based settings — Yes No

Page 1   (*Continues*)

Note. Adapted from *Building Team Pride: Teachers and Paraeducators Working Together,* by M. J. Emery, 1991, Columbus: University of Missouri.

Worksheet 4 (*Continued*)

19.

20.

21.

22.

23.

Activity Preparation/Follow-up

1. Find/arrange materials/equipment (e.g., mix paints, set up lab materials)	Yes	No
2. Modify or adapt materials/equipment for particular student	Yes	No
3. Construct learning materials	Yes	No
4. Prepare classroom displays	Yes	No
5. Order materials and supplies	Yes	No
6. Organize classroom supplies/materials	Yes	No
7. Operate equipment (e.g., tape recorders, VCRs, overhead projectors)	Yes	No
8. Make audio and/or visual aids (transparencies, written notes, voice notes, etc.)	Yes	No
9. Schedule guest speakers/visitors as directed	Yes	No
10. Help prepare and clean up snacks	Yes	No
11. Help students clean up after activities	Yes	No
12. Distribute supplies/materials/books to students	Yes	No
13. Collect completed work from students	Yes	No

14.

15.

16.

Supervision of Groups of Students

1. Supervise groups of students on arrival or departure	Yes	No
2. Supervise groups of students during lunch	Yes	No
3. Supervise groups of students during recess	Yes	No
4. Supervise groups of students loading/unloading buses	Yes	No
5. Monitor students during all passing periods	Yes	No
6. Escort groups of students to bathroom, library, gym, etc.	Yes	No

(*Continues*)

Worksheet 4 (*Continued*)

7. Accompany students to therapy sessions, individual   Yes   No
   appointments

8.

9.

10.

11.

12.

13.

Behavior Management

1. Supervise time-out/in-school suspension room	Yes	No
2. Observe and chart individual student behavior	Yes	No
3. Give positive reinforcement and supports as directed by plans/IEPs	Yes	No
4. Mediate interpersonal conflicts between students	Yes	No
5. Provide instruction to students on how to mediate their own conflicts	Yes	No
6. Provide cues, prompts to students who are mediating conflicts	Yes	No
7. Provide physical proximity for students with behavior problems	Yes	No
8. Circulate in classroom to provide behavioral supports where needed	Yes	No
9. Enforce class and school rules	Yes	No
10. Assist students who are self-managing behavior (e.g., provide cues, prompts)	Yes	No
11. Help students develop/self-monitor organizational skills	Yes	No
12. Provide cues, prompts to students to use impulse/anger control strategies	Yes	No
13. Provide cues, prompts to students to employ specific prosocial skills	Yes	No
14. Teach prosocial skill lessons	Yes	No
15. Facilitate appropriate social interactions among students	Yes	No
16. Assist other students in coping with the behaviors of specific students	Yes	No

17.

18.

         (*Continues*)

Worksheet 4 *(Continued)*

Personal Attention to Student(s)

1. Help student(s) get dressed/undressed	Yes	No
2. Help a student eat/obtain nourishment	Yes	No
3. Help a student with toileting/change diapers	Yes	No
4. Help a student physically get to other locations	Yes	No
5. Assist a student with grooming, cleanliness	Yes	No
6. Provide health-related needs (e.g., suction trach tube, empty colostomy bags, regulate/monitor oxygen) as delegated by a nurse	Yes	No
7. Administer medications as prescribed by doctor and delegated by nurse	Yes	No
8.		
9.		

Ethics

1. Maintain confidentiality of all information regarding students	Yes	No
2. Protect the privacy of students during personal care	Yes	No
3. Respect the dignity and rights of every child at all times	Yes	No
4. Report suspected child abuse according to the law, local policies, procedures	Yes	No
5. Abide by school district policies, school rules, and team standards in all areas	Yes	No
6. Communicate with parents and families to the extent indicated by the team	Yes	No
7. Provide accurate information about the student with all those who have the right to know (e.g., team members)	Yes	No
8. Carry out all assigned duties responsibly, in a timely manner	Yes	No
9. Protect the welfare and safety of students at all times	Yes	No
10. Maintain composure/emotional control while working with students	Yes	No
11. Demonstrate punctuality and good attendance, handle absences appropriately	Yes	No
12.		
13.		

Page 4 *(Continues)*

Worksheet 4 (*Continued*)

14.

15.

Team Participation/Membership

1	Meet with team as scheduled/directed	Yes	No
2.	Participate in team meetings by contributing information, ideas, and assistance	Yes	No
3.	Participate in team meetings by listening carefully to the ideas of others	Yes	No
4.	Engage in appropriate problem-solving steps to resolve problems	Yes	No
5.	Engage in mature conflict management steps/processes	Yes	No
6.	Use appropriate communicative actions in adult–adult interactions	Yes	No
7.	Respect the privacy/dignity of other adults	Yes	No
8.			
9.			
10.			
11.			

Clerical Work

1.	Take attendance	Yes	No
2.	Type reports, tests, seat work, IEPs, assessment reports	Yes	No
3.	Make copies	Yes	No
4.	Sort and file student papers	Yes	No
5.	Record grades	Yes	No
6.	Collect fees (i.e., lab, book, milk, activity, etc.)	Yes	No
7.	Correct assigned student-lessons/homework	Yes	No
8.	Grade tests	Yes	No
9.	Help with paperwork to facilitate parent–teacher appointments	Yes	No
10.	Inventory materials and fill out routine forms	Yes	No
11.	Make arrangements for field trips	Yes	No
12.	Maintain files for IEPs, assessment reports, other program reports	Yes	No
13.	Maintain databases of student information	Yes	No

(*Continues*)

Worksheet 4 *(Continued)*

14.

15.

Other

1. Attend IEP meetings	Yes	No
2. Attend parent–teacher conferences	Yes	No
3. Communication with families (specify)	Yes	No
4. Contribute unique skills and talents (specify)	Yes	No

5.

6.

7.

8.

Page 6

Worksheet 5
Paraeducator Skills/Confidence Inventory

Directions for the Paraeducator: Complete this form by considering your own skills and confidence to perform each task. Decide how well-prepared and confident you feel on each of the tasks/duties. Scores may range from 1 to 5. Circle 1 if you are unprepared to do the task and want/need training in order to begin. Circling 2 indicates that you may begin doing the task but need further instruction on how to do it well. Circling 3 or 4 indicates that you are confident enough to do the task but want to improve your skills. Circle 5 if you feel well-prepared and highly skilled to perform that task.

Delivery of Instruction	Unprepared				Highly Skilled
1. Observe and record student progress in academic areas	1	2	3	4	5
2. Help students in drill and practice lessons (e.g., vocabulary, math facts)	1	2	3	4	5
3. Read/repeat tests or directions to students	1	2	3	4	5
4. Listen to students read orally	1	2	3	4	5
5. Help students with workbooks/other written assignments	1	2	3	4	5
6. Assist students to compose original work (e.g., stories, essays, reports)	1	2	3	4	5
7. Tape-record stories, lessons, assignments	1	2	3	4	5
8. Modify instructional materials according to directions (e.g., lesson plans, IEPs)	1	2	3	4	5
9. Read to students (specify _____ (e.g., text material, stories))	1	2	3	4	5
10. Help students work on individual projects	1	2	3	4	5
11. Facilitate students' active participation in cooperative groups	1	2	3	4	5
12. Help students select library books/reference materials	1	2	3	4	5
13. Help students use computers (specify purpose _____)	1	2	3	4	5
14. Translate instruction/student responses (e.g., sign or other language)	1	2	3	4	5

Page 1   (*Continues*)

Note. Adapted from *Building Team Pride: Teachers and Paraeducators Working Together,* by M. J. Emery, 1991, Columbus: University of Missouri.

Worksheet 5 (*Continued*)

Delivery of Instruction	Unprepared				Highly Skilled
15. Translate teacher-made materials/text materials into another language	1	2	3	4	5
16. Explain/reteach concepts to students in other language	1	2	3	4	5
17. Carry out lessons in community-based settings (travel training, job shadowing)	1	2	3	4	5
18. Monitor student performance in community-based settings	1	2	3	4	5
19.					
20.					
21.					
22.					
23.					

Activity Preparation/Follow-up	Unprepared				Highly Skilled
1. Find/arrange materials/equipment (e.g., mix paints, lab materials)	1	2	3	4	5
2. Modify or adapt materials/equipment for particular student	1	2	3	4	5
3. Construct learning materials	1	2	3	4	5
4. Prepare classroom displays	1	2	3	4	5
5. Order materials and supplies	1	2	3	4	5
6. Organize classroom supplies/materials	1	2	3	4	5
7. Operate equipment (e.g., tape recorders, VCRs, overhead projectors)	1	2	3	4	5
8. Make audio and/or visual aids (transparencies, written notes, voice notes, etc.)	1	2	3	4	5
9. Schedule guest speakers/visitors as directed	1	2	3	4	5
10. Help prepare and clean up snacks	1	2	3	4	5
11. Help students clean up after activities	1	2	3	4	5
12. Distribute supplies/materials/books to students	1	2	3	4	5
13. Collect completed work from students	1	2	3	4	5

Page 2 (*Continues*)

Worksheet 5 *(Continued)*

Activity Preparation/Follow-up	Unprepared			Highly Skilled	
14.					
15.					
16.					

Supervision of Groups of Students	Unprepared			Highly Skilled	
1. Supervise groups of students on arrival or departure	1	2	3	4	5
2. Supervise groups of students during lunch	1	2	3	4	5
3. Supervise groups of students during recess	1	2	3	4	5
4. Supervise groups of students loading/ unloading buses	1	2	3	4	5
5. Monitor students during all passing periods	1	2	3	4	5
6. Escort groups of students to bathroom, library, gym, etc.	1	2	3	4	5
7. Accompany students to therapy sessions, individual appointments	1	2	3	4	5
8.					
9.					
10.					
11.					
12.					
13.					

Behavior Management	Unprepared			Highly Skilled	
1. Supervise time-out/in-school suspension room	1	2	3	4	5
2. Observe and chart individual student behavior	1	2	3	4	5
3. Give positive reinforcement and support as directed by plans/IEPs	1	2	3	4	5
4. Mediate interpersonal conflicts between students	1	2	3	4	5
5. Provide instruction to students on how to mediate their own conflicts	1	2	3	4	5

(Continues)

Worksheet 5 *(Continued)*

Behavior Management	Unprepared			Highly Skilled	
6. Provide cues, prompts to students who are mediating conflicts	1	2	3	4	5
7. Provide physical proximity for students with behavior problems	1	2	3	4	5
8. Circulate in classroom to provide behavioral supports where needed	1	2	3	4	5
9. Enforce class and school rules					
10. Assist students who are self-managing behavior (e.g., provide cues, prompts)	1	2	3	4	5
11. Help students develop/self-monitor organizational skills	1	2	3	4	5
12. Provide cues, prompts to students to use impulse/anger control strategies	1	2	3	4	5
13. Provide cues, prompts to students to employ specific prosocial skills	1	2	3	4	5
14. Teach prosocial skill lessons					
15. Facilitate appropriate social interactions among students	1	2	3	4	5
16. Assist other students in coping with the behaviors of specific students	1	2	3	4	5
17.					
18.					

Personal Attention to Student(s)	Unprepared			Highly Skilled	
1. Help student(s) get dressed/undressed	1	2	3	4	5
2. Help a student eat/obtain nourishment	1	2	3	4	5
3. Help a student with toileting/change diapers	1	2	3	4	5
4. Help a student physically get to other locations	1	2	3	4	5
5. Assist a student with grooming, cleanliness	1	2	3	4	5
6. Provide health-related needs (e.g., suction trach tube, empty colostomy bags, regulate/monitor oxygen) as delegated by a nurse	1	2	3	4	5

(Continues)

Worksheet 5 *(Continued)*

Personal Attention to Student(s)	Unprepared		Highly Skilled		
7. Administer medications as prescribed by doctor and delegated by nurse	1	2	3	4	5
8.					
9.					

Ethics	Unprepared		Highly Skilled		
1. Maintain confidentiality of all information regarding students	1	2	3	4	5
2. Protect the privacy of students during personal care	1	2	3	4	5
3. Respect the dignity and rights of every child at all times	1	2	3	4	5
4. Report suspected child abuse according to the law, policies, procedures	1	2	3	4	5
5. Abide by school district policies, school rules, and standards in all areas	1	2	3	4	5
6. Communicate with parents and families as indicated by the team	1	2	3	4	5
7. Provide accurate information about the student with all those who have the right to know (e.g., team members)	1	2	3	4	5
8. Carry out all assigned duties responsibly, in a timely manner	1	2	3	4	5
9. Protect the welfare and safety of students at all times	1	2	3	4	5
10. Maintain composure/emotional control while working with students	1	2	3	4	5
11. Demonstrate punctuality, good attendance, handle absences appropriately	1	2	3	4	5
12.					
13.					
14.					
15.					

(Continues)

Worksheet 5 *(Continued)*

Team Participation/Membership	Unprepared		Highly Skilled		
1. Meet with team as scheduled/directed	1	2	3	4	5
2. Participate in team meetings by contributing appropriate information, ideas, and assistance	1	2	3	4	5
3. Participate in team meetings by listening carefully to the ideas of others	1	2	3	4	5
4. Engage in appropriate problem-solving steps to resolve problems	1	2	3	4	5
5. Engage in mature conflict management steps/processes	1	2	3	4	5
6. Use appropriate communicative actions in adult–adult interactions	1	2	3	4	5
7. Respect the privacy/dignity of other adults	1	2	3	4	5
8.					
9.					
10.					
11.					

Clerical Work	Unprepared		Highly Skilled		
1. Take attendance	1	2	3	4	5
2. Type reports, tests, seat work, IEPs, assessment reports	1	2	3	4	5
3. Make copies	1	2	3	4	5
4. Sort and file student papers	1	2	3	4	5
5. Record grades	1	2	3	4	5
6. Collect fees (i.e., lab, book, milk, activity, etc.)	1	2	3	4	5
7. Correct assigned student-lessons/homework	1	2	3	4	5
8. Grade tests	1	2	3	4	5
9. Help with paperwork to facilitate parent–teacher appointments	1	2	3	4	5
10. Inventory materials and fill out routine forms	1	2	3	4	5
11. Make arrangements for field trips	1	2	3	4	5

Page 6

(Continues)

Worksheet 5 (*Continued*)

Clerical Work	**Unprepared**			**Highly Skilled**	
12. Maintain files for IEPs, assessment reports, other program reports	1	2	3	4	5
13. Maintain databases of student information	1	2	3	4	5
14.					
15.					

Other	**Unprepared**			**Highly Skilled**	
1. Attend IEP meetings	1	2	3	4	5
2. Attend parent–teacher conferences	1	2	3	4	5
3. Communication with families (specify _____)	1	2	3	4	5
4. Contribute unique skills and talents (specify _____)	1	2	3	4	5
5.					
6.					
7.					
8.					

Page 7

Worksheet 6
Personalized Job Description for Paraeducators

_____
(Name)

Directions: Complete this form by considering the work style preferences of team members, the programmatic and student needs, the skills and confidence of the individual paraeducator. List only those tasks/duties that are to be completed by the paraeducator named above (even if the paraeducator has not yet received required training for the duties or tasks listed). Use Worksheet 7 as a companion sheet to document tasks for which further training is necessary. Remember: On a team that includes multiple paraeducators, the Personalized Job Descriptions may be different for each one.

Delivery of Instruction

1.
2.
3.
4.
5.
6.
7.
8.
9.
10.
11.
12.
13.
14.
15.
16.
17.
18.
19.

Page 1   (_Continues_)

Note. Adapted from _Building Team Pride: Teachers and Paraeducators Working Together,_ by M. J. Emery, 1991, Columbus: University of Missouri.

Worksheet 6 *(Continued)*

Activity Preparation/Follow-up

1.
2.
3.
4.
5.
6.
7.
8.
9.
10.
11.
12.
13.
14.
15.
16.

Supervision of Groups of Students

1.
2.
3.
4.
5.
6.
7.
8.
9.
10.
11.
12.
13.

(Continues)

Worksheet 6 *(Continued)*

Behavior Management

1.
2.
3.
4.
5.
6.
7.
8.
9.
10.
11.
12.
13.
14.
15.
16.
17.
18.

Personal Attention to Student(s)

1.
2.
3.
4.
5.
6.
7.
8.
9.

Worksheet 6 *(Continued)*

Ethics

1.
2.
3.
4.
5.
6.
7.
8.
9.
10.
11.
12.
13.
14.
15.
16.

Team Participation/Membership

1.
2.
3.
4.
5.
6.
7.
8.
9.
10.
11.

Worksheet 6 *(Continued)*

Clerical Work

1.
2.
3.
4.
5.
6.
7.
8.
9.
10.
11.
12.
13.
14.
15.

Other

1.
2.
3.
4.
5.
6.
7.
8.

Worksheet 7
Growth and Development Plan
for

_____
(Paraeducator Name)

Skills Inventory Training Areas	Training Activity	Person Responsible	Start Date	Completion Date

Page 1

(*Continues*)

Note. Adapted from *Building Team Pride: Teachers and Paraeducators Working Together*, by M. J. Emery, 1991, Columbus: University of Missouri.

Worksheet 7
Growth and Development Plan
for

_____
(Paraeducator Name)

Other Training Areas (Identified through observation, interest, or school initiative)	Training Activity	Person Responsible	Start Date	Completion Date

Worksheet 8
Paraeducator Performance Rating

Directions: To use this form, first transfer each of the tasks/duties from the Personalized Job Description to the corresponding blanks. Document the performance of each task/duty by indicating the assessed performance level on each date. It is appropriate to hold a feedback conference for each date listed.

Ratings: I = Independent—paraeducator performs this task with no guidance
D = Developing—paraeducator performs this task with some cues, prompts, guidance
E = Emerging—paraeducator performs this task with significant guidance, assistance
U = Unable to Perform—paraeducator does not perform this task, even with guidance, assistance

	Performance Rating			
Delivery of Instruction	**Date**	**Date**	**Date**	**Date**
1.	_____	_____	_____	_____
2.	_____	_____	_____	_____
3.	_____	_____	_____	_____
4.	_____	_____	_____	_____
5.	_____	_____	_____	_____
6.	_____	_____	_____	_____
7.	_____	_____	_____	_____
8.	_____	_____	_____	_____
9.	_____	_____	_____	_____
10.	_____	_____	_____	_____
11.	_____	_____	_____	_____
12.	_____	_____	_____	_____
13.	_____	_____	_____	_____
14.	_____	_____	_____	_____
15.	_____	_____	_____	_____
16.	_____	_____	_____	_____
17.	_____	_____	_____	_____
18.	_____	_____	_____	_____

Worksheet 8 *(Continued)*

Activity Preparation/Follow Up	Performance Rating			
	Date	Date	Date	Date
1.	——	——	——	——
2.	——	——	——	——
3.	——	——	——	——
4.	——	——	——	——
5.	——	——	——	——
6.	——	——	——	——
7.	——	——	——	——
8.	——	——	——	——
9.	——	——	——	——
10.	——	——	——	——
11.	——	——	——	——
12.	——	——	——	——
13.	——	——	——	——
14.	——	——	——	——
15.	——	——	——	——
16.	——	——	——	——

Supervision of Groups of Students	Performance Rating			
	Date	Date	Date	Date
1.	——	——	——	——
2.	——	——	——	——
3.	——	——	——	——
4.	——	——	——	——
5.	——	——	——	——
6.	——	——	——	——
7.	——	——	——	——
8.	——	——	——	——
9.	——	——	——	——
10.	——	——	——	——

(Continues)

Worksheet 8 *(Continued)*

Supervision of Groups of Students	Performance Rating			
	Date	Date	Date	Date
11.	——	——	——	——
12.	——	——	——	——
13.	——	——	——	——

Behavior Management	Performance Rating			
	Date	Date	Date	Date
1.	——	——	——	——
2.	——	——	——	——
3.	——	——	——	——
4.	——	——	——	——
5.	——	——	——	——
6.	——	——	——	——
7.	——	——	——	——
8.	——	——	——	——
9.	——	——	——	——
10.	——	——	——	——
11.	——	——	——	——
12.	——	——	——	——
13.	——	——	——	——
14.	——	——	——	——
15.	——	——	——	——
16.	——	——	——	——
17.	——	——	——	——
18.	——	——	——	——

Personal Attention to Students	Performance Rating			
	Date	Date	Date	Date
1.	——	——	——	——
2.	——	——	——	——
3.	——	——	——	——

Worksheet 8 (Continued)

Personal Attention to Students	Performance Rating			
	Date	Date	Date	Date
4.	___	___	___	___
5.	___	___	___	___
6.	___	___	___	___
7.	___	___	___	___
8.	___	___	___	___
9.	___	___	___	___

Ethics	Performance Rating			
	Date	Date	Date	Date
1.	___	___	___	___
2.	___	___	___	___
3.	___	___	___	___
4.	___	___	___	___
5.	___	___	___	___
6.	___	___	___	___
7.	___	___	___	___
8.	___	___	___	___
9.	___	___	___	___
10.	___	___	___	___
11.	___	___	___	___
12.	___	___	___	___
13.	___	___	___	___
14.	___	___	___	___
15.	___	___	___	___
16.	___	___	___	___

Team Participation/Membership	Performance Rating			
	Date	Date	Date	Date
1.	___	___	___	___
2.	___	___	___	___
3.	___	___	___	___
4.	___	___	___	___
5.	___	___	___	___
6.	___	___	___	___

(*Continues*)

Worksheet 8 *(Continued)*

Team Participation/Membership	Performance Rating			
	Date	Date	Date	Date
7.	____	____	____	____
8.	____	____	____	____
9.	____	____	____	____
10.	____	____	____	____
11.	____	____	____	____

Clerical Work	Performance Rating			
	Date	Date	Date	Date
1.	____	____	____	____
2.	____	____	____	____
3.	____	____	____	____
4.	____	____	____	____
5.	____	____	____	____
6.	____	____	____	____
7.	____	____	____	____
8.	____	____	____	____
9.	____	____	____	____
10.	____	____	____	____
11.	____	____	____	____
12.	____	____	____	____
13.	____	____	____	____
14.	____	____	____	____
15.	____	____	____	____

Other	Performance Rating			
	Date	Date	Date	Date
1.	____	____	____	____
2.	____	____	____	____
3.	____	____	____	____
4.	____	____	____	____
5.	____	____	____	____
6.	____	____	____	____
7.	____	____	____	____
8.	____	____	____	____

Page 5

REFERENCES

Acheson, K. A., & Gall, M. D. (1980). *Techniques in the clinical supervision of teachers: Preservice and inservice applications.* New York: Longman.

Alexander, H. L. (1987). *Developing a working relationship with teachers and paraeducators.* Topeka: Kansas State Department of Education.

Berliner, D. (1983a). The executive functions of teaching. *Instructor, 93*(2), 28–33, 36, 38, 40.

Berliner, D. C. (1983b). *If teachers were thought of as executives: Implications for teacher preparation and certification.* Paper prepared for the national Institute of Education conference on State and Local Policy Implications of Effective School Research. (EDRS Document No. 245357)

Douglass, M. E. (1979). *The time management workbook.* Grandville, MI: Time Management Center.

Drawbaugh, C. C. (1984). *Time and its use: A self-management guide for teachers.* New York: Teachers College Press.

Emery, M. J. (1991). *Building team pride: Teachers and paraeducators working together.* Columbus: University of Missouri.

French, N. K. (1993). *Teachers and paraeducators: How they work together.* Unpublished manuscript, University of Colorado at Denver.

French, N. K. (1994). *Teachers as supervisors: What they know and what they do.* Unpublished manuscript, University of Colorado at Denver.

French, N. K., Kozleski, E. B., & Sands, D. S. (1992). *Practicum experiences for special education teachers: A handbook for teachers who supervise special education practicum students.* Resources in Education, December. (EDRS Document No. 334 778)

French, N. K., & Pickett, A. L. (1995). Paraeducators in special education: Issues for teacher educators. Manuscript submitted for publication.

Gartner, A. (1971). *Paraeducators and their performance: A survey of education, health and social services programs.* New York: Praeger.

Goldhammer, R., Anderson, R. H., & Krajewski, R. J. (1980). *Clinical supervision: Special methods for the supervision of teachers* (2nd ed.). New York: Holt, Rinehart and Winston.

Joyce, B., & Showers, B. (1980). Improving inservice training: The messages of research. *Educational Leadership, 37,* 379–385.

McConkey, D. D. (1974). *No-nonsense delegation.* New York: AMACOM.

Pfeiffer, J. W., & Jones, J. E. (1987). *A handbook of structured experiences for human relations training* (Vol. III). San Diego, CA: University Associates.

Pickett, A. L. (1986). Certified partners: Four good reasons for certification of paraeducators. *American Educator, 10*(3).

Pickett, A. L. (1994). *Paraeducators in the education workforce.* Washington, DC: National Education Association.

Pickett, A. L., Vasa, S. F., & Steckelberg, A. L. (1993). *Using paraeducators effectively in the classroom.* Fastback 358. Bloomington, IN: Phi Delta Kappa Educational Foundation.

Sullivan, M. (1980). *Managing your time and money: Strategies for success*. New York: American Express Co.

Vasa, S. F., Steckelberg, A. L., & Ulrich-Ronning, L. (1982). *A state of the art assessment of paraeducator use in special education in the state of Nebraska*. Lincoln: Department of Special Education and Communication Disorders, University of Nebraska–Lincoln.

CHAPTER 5

· ·

Team Building: Communication and Problem Solving

· ·

Kent Gerlach
Pacific Lutheran University

Patty Lee
University of Northern Colorado

OVERVIEW

In today's schools and businesses the focus is on improving communication through improved collaboration and teamwork. There are many definitions for teams in education and business. Collectively, these definitions stress that a team is two or more people who work together toward a common goal. The common goal and coordinated efforts to achieve the goal make them a team. To be successful, the teacher and the paraeducator must view themselves as a team. They need to form a "relationship" that is built on good communication, trust, respect, and recognition. In the school professional and paraeducator team, the team leader is always the certified supervisor.

Webster's Tenth Collegiate Dictionary defines *collaboration* as "to labor together; to work jointly with others, especially in an intellectual endeavor, to cooperate." Collaboration for the purpose of this text is defined as the act of the school professional and the paraeducator joining together to work on tasks in a cooperative and purposeful manner.

A common thread across definitions of collaboration includes the notion that collaboration is both interactive and dynamic. It is a process among partners who share mutual goals and who work together to make decisions and solve problems. Teamwork and collaboration are the main ingredients for facilitating change and solving problems because they allow people to discuss their work together and, as a result, to grow professionally.

To be successful, it is important that the school professional and paraeducator view themselves as partners in the educational process. Input from one another needs to be solicited. Questions need to be asked. Ideas need to be shared and appreciated.

One of the best examples of team building exists in athletics. Individual team members may have different backgrounds and attitudes. They develop into "teams" when their common purpose is understood by all of the members. For the most part, the purpose is to "win" the game or event. Within effective teams each member plays an important role using his or her talents to best advantage. When the members integrate their skills to accentuate strengths and minimize weaknesses, team objectives are achieved much easier.

In sports, feedback is immediate; when the players are individually focused, success as a team is impossible to achieve. Like their athletic counterparts, school professionals and paraeducators can accomplish far more when they work well together. Unfortunately, many school professionals fail to recognize and apply the same principles used in athletics. Some leaders do not always know how to transform a group into an effective team. A former coach of the University of Alabama, Paul Bear Bryant, said it best when he stated that there are five things a winning team member needs to know:

1. Tell me what you expect from me.

2. Give me the opportunity to perform.

3. Let me know how I am getting along.

4. Give me guidance when I need it.

5. Reward me according to my contribution.

Instructional Objectives

After studying this chapter and participating in discussions and case studies, the reader will be able to:

1. Define collaboration and teamwork and describe their characteristics.

2. Identify skills of effective communication critical for collaborating with paraeducators and other colleagues.

3. Define listening as a skill and name the factors that can interfere with listening skills.

4. Identify ways to improve listening skills.

5. Define attending and responding skills and give an example of each.

6. Understand the importance of collaborative problem solving as it applies to school professionals and paraeducators.

7. Be able to identify and apply the seven-step collaborative problem-solving process to situations that arise when school professionals and paraeducators work together.

8. Be able to discuss the nature and sources of conflict in a team.

9. Be able to identify and apply the six-step conflict resolution strategy to a variety of situations that might occur between school professionals and paraeducators.

. . . .

CHARACTERISTICS CRITICAL TO SUCCESSFUL TEAMS

The characteristics critical to successful teams can be found throughout social science literature and business research. The most common characteristics are discussed in the following sections.

Members Must View Themselves As a Team

Individuals cannot be effective members of a team unless they perceive themselves to be important to the team effort (Friend & Cook, 1996). Extending that notion further, team members must also be perceived by others as valued team members (Feldman, 1985). And, finally, team members must be committed to making the team process work.

All members of the team must be willing to work together and recognize the benefits of teamwork. Figure 5.1 lists several advantages of teams and Figure 5.2 lists the characteristics of successful teams. When team members work well together, many individual and group benefits emerge as a result of the process.

Teams Are Goal Focused

All team members must be focused in the same direction, with their efforts supporting one another. Successful teams have a clear understanding of their goals. The elements of a goal include (a) an accomplishment to be achieved—*what do we expect the outcome of our actions to be?*; (b) a measure of accomplishment—*how will we know when the outcome has been reached?*; and (c) the time factor—*when precisely do we want to have the goal completed?*

- Teams develop unique, creative, and flexible solutions to problems.
- Teams foster professional and personal growth by sharing knowledge and skills.
- Teams reduce the feeling of isolation.
- Teams support each other.
- Teams maximize each member's potential, strengths, and contribution.
- Teams establish goals together. Members feel a sense of ownership toward goals.
- Members are encouraged to openly express ideas, opinions, disagreement, and feelings. Questions are welcomed.
- Team members practice open and honest communication. They make an effort to understand each other's points of view. They operate in a climate of trust.
- Members participate in discussions affecting the team but understand their supervisor or leader must make the final decision.
- Members enjoy working together. A team spirit develops.

Figure 5.1. **Advantages of "The Team" concept.**

Typical goal-directed questions might include "What is the goal of Title I?," "What is the goal of inclusion?," and "How can we work together to achieve the goal?" The school professional and paraeducator need to maintain their focus on the needs of children and youth being served when writing goals.

Most school districts and/or school buildings have clearly defined mission statements (see Table 5.1). A mission is a general statement through

- Teams use their time and talents effectively.
- Teams are committed to skill development.
- Members build morale by showing respect and recognition to one another.
- Members give one another feedback.
- Members cooperate rather than competing.
- Members maintain positive attitudes toward each other's ideas.
- Teams communicate openly.
- Members mentor and learn from one another.
- Teams resolve conflicts effectively.
- Teams accept challenges.

Figure 5.2. **Characteristics of a successful team.**

Table 5.1
Common Terms Used in Mission Statements

Term	Definition
Mission	A statement of what the school district or team is about and the unique contribution it can make.
Goal	A result to be achieved.
Objective	A specific point of measurement that the team intends to meet in pursuit of its goals.
Strategy	A set of rules and guidelines to assist orderly progression toward a team's goals and objectives.
Plan	A time-phased action sequence used to guide and coordinate strategies in pursuit of objectives.

which an organization specifies overall strategy or intent that governs the goals and objectives of the team. The mission statement serves as the foundation all school district employees build on to establish goals and related actions. By focusing on goals, priorities can be established much more easily. Together, the school professional and the paraeducator determine what needs to be done, by whom, and by what deadline.

Teams Clarify Roles

To create an effective team, role distinctions of all team members need to be discussed and clarified. As noted previously, both school professionals and paraeducators need to know their roles in getting tasks done and how to use the skills and expertise of each member most effectively. Several factors need to be considered in determining the roles and responsibilities of team members. They include experience, training, comfort level, time constraints, and knowledge levels of individual team members.

EFFECTIVE LEADERSHIP

Leadership is a critical factor for team success. As stated previously, the leader is always the school professional who has been designated as the paraeducator's supervisor. The supervisor's role is similar to that of a coach. It involves assessing the paraeducator's skills and helping the paraeducator use them to the fullest. Paraeducators contribute more effectively when they are "coached" and encouraged to make optimal use of their strengths and resources. A supervisor provides direction and ideas, helps to identify alternatives, raises questions, and supplies feedback.

Whenever possible, the supervisor seeks input from the paraeducator. Effective team leaders have a sense of mission and purpose and they lead by example. They are committed to the role of leader, supervisor, or manager; they have good communication skills; and they clarify roles and expectations of all team members. A team leader is expected to provide on-the-job training, to mentor, and to coach others. They show respect to team members, are enthusiastic, and demonstrate organizational skills. Team leadership skills are outlined in Figure 5.3.

Team Effectiveness Is Established Through Shared Norms and Support

A team is an organized system of individuals whose behavior is regulated by a common set of norms or values (Friend & Cook, 1996; Sherif & Sherif,

---

Teamwork skills: The ability to interface with the paraeducator in a manner that promotes teamwork and develops commitment.

Communication skills: The ability to provide and receive information in an effective manner.

Problem-solving skills: The ability to identify problems and propose, evaluate, and analyze alternative solutions in order to develop ways of implementing the plan.

Interpersonal skills: The ability to recognize and demonstrate appropriate social behaviors, work with different interpersonal styles, appreciate the uniqueness of others, and manage conflict.

Feedback skills: The ability to monitor performance of the paraeducator through appropriate observation and feedback to ensure team effectiveness.

Technical and management skills: The ability to understand the mission of the team and program. The supervising professional must schedule, plan, and manage time, and handle the unexpected.

Delegating skills: The ability to communicate responsibilities effectively to the paraeducator.

Coordinating and planning skills: The ability to see that roles and responsibilities are scheduled appropriately, resources are available when needed, and conferences and meetings are used to their fullest advantage.

Figure 5.3.   Team leadership skills.

1956). Conflict or differences of opinion are dealt with openly, and authority and decision-making lines are clearly understood. In addition, team meetings have clear agendas and are organized for productivity and efficiency.

Sample norms or team member expectations include such things as arriving on time, being prepared, asking questions, listening to one another, respecting one another, and maintaining a positive attitude. Other expectations for success include providing support for each other professionally and personally, dealing with each other honestly and truthfully, and stressing the importance of being a good role model for children and youth. More than ever before, children need to see two adults working well together. School professionals and paraeducators should always demonstrate the skills of effective communication, respect, and integrity.

Norms are the common belief of the team regarding appropriate behavior for members. In other words, they delineate the expectations of all team members. For a team norm to influence a person's behavior, team members must recognize that it exists, be aware that other members accept and follow the norm, and accept and follow it themselves. Members accept and internalize norms in which they have a sense of ownership. Generally, team members will support and accept norms that they have helped create or that they consider valid. Figure 5.4 lists sample norms from one team. These could be applied to a school professional and paraeducator team.

Team effectiveness can be achieved by sharing expectations with one another, by allowing the paraeducator to give input and support into the planning process, by appreciating each other's unique personality traits, by respecting diversity, and by demonstrating a positive attitude. Once a team

---

- Team members will be present and punctual at all meetings.
- Team members will come prepared to meetings.
- Team members will ask questions if issues are unclear.
- Team members will listen to one another's ideas.
- Team members will contribute to the development of trust and openness.
- Team members will assume the responsibility to address concerns or ask for clarification.
- Team members assume the responsibility that their verbal contributions will move the team forward and will be pertinent to the topic.

Figure 5.4.   **Expectations of team members.**

works well together, the job is less stressful, more enjoyable, and more rewarding for all team members. The steps for effective teamwork are summarized in Figure 5.5.

Summary

If a team is to be effective, the team must agree on why it exists. Members must see the benefits of teamwork and collaboration, and the mission of the team must be developed with input from all team members. Responsibilities of each member should be clearly defined and the supervisor's role must be made clear. The importance of listening to one another is stressed and clear expectations are given in order to get the job done. Information is shared in a timely manner, and the time the team meets together is effective and productive (see Figure 5.6).

INTERPERSONAL COMMUNICATION SKILLS

Teaming and collaboration depend on effective interaction and communication. The skills of effective communication are critical for collaborating with colleagues and paraeducators.

Communication skills are both verbal and nonverbal. Effective communication expresses a speaker's beliefs, ideas, needs, or feelings. The listener must assimilate this information in such a way that there is agreement between what the listener understands and what the speaker intended to communicate.

Step 1: Define the purpose and goals of the team.

Step 2: Establish team composition and roles.

Step 3: Clarify team rules (norms) and responsibilities.

Step 4: Integrate individual personalities.

Step 5: Manage team performance.

Step 6: Evaluate team effectiveness.

Figure 5.5. **Team development.**

1. Goals for the team are established.

2. The team shares a clear vision of what needs to be done to accomplish the goals.

3. Roles and responsibilities of each team member are clearly established. Leadership role is clear.

4. Team expectations are communicated in a climate of trust and openness.

5. Members keep one another informed of issues affecting the team.

6. Problems are solved together.

7. Team members listen to one another. Effective communication strategies are employed. Questions are asked and input is solicited.

8. The meeting time is effective and productive.

9. Team members are recognized and appreciated for the work they do.

Figure 5.6.   **An assessment of team effectiveness.**

Effective Listening

Good communication starts with the ability to listen effectively. In collaboration, listening is especially critical. Listening is a primary way of getting information, as well as a means of conveying interest in the messages of all involved. Listening establishes rapport. Attention, willingness to listen, and desire to understand are important elements in establishing rapport, but accurate understanding is required to build and maintain a relationship. When team members demonstrate precise knowledge of what a person has said, they are then perceived as being both competent and genuine collaborators (Friend & Cook, 1996). The paraeducator and the supervisor need to develop listening skills so that they can obtain sufficient and accurate information necessary for an effective working relationship. Because many paraeducators have received little or, in some cases, no training for their job, it is especially important that the supervisor accurately and clearly describe the goals, lesson, and needs of the child being served. Both parties must have effective listening techniques in order to promote the essential understanding required for successful intervention.

Factors That Can Interfere with Effective Listening

Several factors can interfere with effective listening. Examine the following situation:

> Marla, the supervising teacher, met with Alison, the paraeducator, at the end of a typical workweek. Marla had planned for the meeting. She gave what she thought was a clear and precise description of next week's activity. Alison, on the other hand, left the meeting not sure of what had been said. She was not sure what she was to do next and regretted that she did not ask questions.

What went wrong here? DeVito (1994) describes several obstacles for effective listening, as discussed in the following subsections.

Daydreaming

Daydreaming can happen to all of us when we are supposed to be listening and receiving information. In many cases, our minds wander and we begin to think about picking up the children, getting to a meeting on time, or something else that is bothering us. Perhaps this is what happened to Alison when Marla was speaking. She may have lost track of Marla's message because she was thinking about a problem at home that was concerning her. It is important to concentrate on what a speaker is telling us. Giving undivided attention is not always easy and takes practice.

Stumbling on Trigger Words

Effective listening can stop when you are cognitively "triggered" by a particular word and its implications. Alison may have reacted to a word that she did not know the meaning of, a descriptor that could influence a change in her role or duties, or a term that was used in such a way that it created a response that distorted other things Marla was telling her.

Being Distracted

Any distractions may interfere with effective listening. Alison could have been distracted by a child in the room or a noise outside on the playground.

Distractions can be physical, verbal, mental, or environmental, such as an uncomfortable chair or temperature.

Filtering Messages

Friend and Cook (1996) point out that a frame of reference may cause a person to selectively attend to specific parts of a message and ignore others, thereby causing the listener to inaccurately perceive the message. In other words, your frame of reference may cause you to filter out the message.

Some people may simply not want to listen to a particular message and they "tune out." People tune out for various reasons. Alison may have found part of the message not relevant because she felt she already had knowledge of it, or part of the message had little relevance to what she perceived she needed to do. She might have felt the message contained too many details or too much information at once. Whatever the reason, when we filter the message we will perceive the message differently and mistakes could result.

Thinking About a Response or Questions

When Marla was speaking, Alison may have been thinking about what she would say when she had the opportunity to speak. Alison may have thought about some questions she wanted to ask Marla. Prior to the meeting she wrote these questions down and was reviewing her notes as Marla spoke. This caused her to miss some of the things Marla was saying.

Tips for Improving Listening Skills

To improve listening skills, you need to think about how you comprehend the verbal message. Comprehension involves patience, openness (being nonjudgmental, unbiased), and an intense desire to understand information from another point of view. Friend and Cook (1996) list several ways to improve listening:

1. *Mentally rehearse the information:* This can be done by identifying the main themes or keywords. The listener could practice repeating these themes as the speaker shares information. Sometimes people associate something with what the speaker is saying. Sometimes saying a keyword over and over to yourself will help you to remember it.

2. *Categorize the information:* This can be achieved by developing a scheme that helps to "map" the ideas (e.g., classifying case information according to behavior or instructional needs).

3. *Make notes of important details:* Both the supervisor and the paraeducator should use notes when information is shared. An outline, a plan of action, a list of questions, or an agenda will prove to be helpful. It is important to think about the issues and problems ahead of time. When notes are taken, jot down the most important concepts and details. The paraeducator should be reminded that asking for assistance is a strength, not a weakness.

4. *Use the listening process:* When we say there is a process to listening we are saying there are both *attending* and *responding* skills. This process will save time in the long run, even though it may seem time-consuming at first. By developing the process of listening you may save yourself from going back and redoing things or correcting the misunderstandings that can occur when one or both parties exhibit poor listening skills.

The Process of Listening: Attending Skills

Attending skills or active listening can be defined as the nonverbal things you do or the behaviors you exhibit to show you are listening. Your behavior can communicate to colleagues a clear message that shows you are interested in what they have to say. The opposite message can be sent when you show by your behavior that you do not care and are not interested. Note the following example, which demonstrates effective listening:

> Connie, the paraeducator, asked the supervising teacher about a student who has become withdrawn, unresponsive, and appeared to be depressed. The supervising teacher, Robert, without pause said, "Let's sit down and talk about this." Robert, who was correcting papers at the time, put the papers aside and focused on what Connie was telling him about the student.

What does this example communicate to you about this team and their ability to communicate? Let's change the story a bit with a focus on non-verbal cues:

> Ann, the paraeducator, asked the supervising teacher about a student she was working with who is having difficulty with his math. Although Sharon, the teacher, said she had several ideas, at the same moment she looked at her watch. Then she pointed to the math material cabinet and said as she

stepped out the door, "Help yourself to any of the materials. They should help. Let me know at our next meeting if he shows any improvement."

What does this example communicate to you about this team and their ability to communicate? What did the teacher's body language and nonverbal cues communicate to you?

In the first example, the teacher indicated through his actions that he was interested in what the paraeducator was saying. In the second example, the teacher's nonverbal message contradicted the verbal message. The following attending skills can be powerful tools for influencing and communicating with others:

- Eye contact
- Facial expressions
- Body language
- Gesturing
- Waiting to respond
- Leaning forward
- Resisting distractions and interruptions
- Nodding your head

The Process of Listening: Responding Skills

The act of responding also includes both verbal and nonverbal skills. Responding skills can encourage people to check the accuracy of the message being communicated. DeBoer (1995) defines responding skills as behaviors that you use when you are listening well. These responding skills include paraphrasing, clarifying, reflecting, summarizing, and perception checking. Occasionally, they can be used to seek more information. To use these skills effectively, the listener should avoid editorializing or adding any additional comments or information.

Paraphrasing

Paraphrasing can best be defined as restating in your own words what you think the other person just communicated. The main purpose of paraphrasing is to check the accuracy of the information, thoughts, and stated feelings of the speaker. After the listener states the person's ideas, the speaker approves and clarifies the paraphrase. Note the following example:

> *Speaker (teacher):* This was a great day today. We got everything done that was on my list. Thanks for your help.
>
> *Listener (paraeducator):* We got a lot accomplished today. I'm really glad you feel I contributed to the success of the day.

People are able to listen to themselves through paraphrasing by providing a restatement of their thoughts and ideas. Paraphrasing starts with phrases such as: "You are . . . ," "You believe . . . ," "It seems like you . . . ," "What you are saying is. . . ."

By restating the main points, the listener shows attendance to and accurate understanding of what the speaker was relating and thus conveys interest in the issue and in the speaker.

Reflecting

Reflecting involves careful listening, understanding, and concentration. The listener describes what the other person has said then tries to state (reflect) the meaning of the message. Note the following example:

> *Speaker (teacher):* How can I possibly get all this paperwork done? I don't have time to teach anymore.
>
> *Listener (paraeducator):* You are really frustrated with the paperwork, aren't you?
>
> *Speaker (teacher):* Yes, I really am.
>
> *Listener (paraeducator):* What can we do together to reduce the paperwork load? How can I help?

Keep in mind that a reflection focuses on the emotional side of communicating. Sometimes this can be an important tool for the person speaking because it captures a message that the listener can note through voice tone, quality, pitch, volume, speech rhythm, and pacing or tempo. Sometimes people are not aware of their feelings or how they are coming across without your help as a listener. Both the supervisor and the paraeducator become mutually supportive by demonstrating careful listening, which leads to shared understanding.

Clarifying

Clarifying is the skill of requesting more information. We can show interest in the speaker, as well as ensure that we understand accurately what is said, by seeking clarification through questioning. For example, if the speaker says, "This was a great day today. I completed many of the items on my list," the listener's response could be "What did you get done today that you are so happy about?" The question is not a judgment of the statement but rather a search for clarity.

Summarizing

Summarizing pulls together the key points in a discussion. Frequently we fail to see the whole picture, so summarizing allows us to refocus and clarify decisions. It also acts as a point for further discussion. An example of this is

> *Teacher (leader)*: "The key ideas we have covered so far are . . ." or "Let me review what we have discussed so far."

Summarizing consists of one or more statements or comments that restate in a concise way several preceding statements made by the individuals or team members involved in the discussion. It is a means to ensure that all individuals understand what is being said, and it functions in much the same way as a chapter summary section in a book or an abstract of a journal article.

Friend and Cook (1996) state that summarizing differs from paraphrasing in at least two significant ways. When you paraphrase, you are simply restating what another person has just said. Paraphrasing is usually immediate, and it is a response to a discreet self-contained piece of information. On the other hand, summarizing is a response to several pieces of information. Summarizing generally occurs at the end of a meeting or conversation. An example might be "Let's summarize what we covered today. . . ." A summary would then follow that includes the main points covered.

Perception Checking

Perception checking is checking for the accuracy of the information. It is very similar to reflecting. However, instead of making a statement that reflects what you sense a person is feeling, you check your perceptions by asking questions. If the speaker says "This was a great day today. I accomplished everything on my list," your response could be "Are you feeling really proud of your work today?" Or if the speaker says "I get so upset when parents don't show up for a conference," your response could be "You sound really frustrated with the parents. Are you frustrated with them?"

PROBLEM SOLVING WITH PARAEDUCATORS

As school professionals and paraeducators work together, problems will arise. Some of these problems are related to meeting the needs of individual children and youth, some are related to building issues and policies, others are related to parental concerns, and still others are connected to interpersonal relationships. When these problems are approached in a systematic manner, everyone benefits.

When school professionals and paraeducators work together as a team to solve problems, they build a respectful way of settling their differences. School professionals often use a step-by-step problem-solving process with students more frequently than with adult colleagues. In classrooms and educational settings, professionals take time to help students analyze problems, identify and weigh possible solutions for potential success, and then choose one to implement. The same problem-solving steps can be used effectively as professionals and paraeducators face the challenges of their work.

Collaborative Problem Solving

Most problem-solving processes consist of a series of steps. Many problem-solving strategies have been developed that can be adapted to meet the needs of school professionals and paraeducators who are working together (Dewey; 1993; Gordon, 1977; Elgin, 1989; Margolis & Brannigan, 1978; Senge, 1990; Schrage, 1990). This section examines a seven-step problem-solving process that applies the strategies from various sources:

1. Define the problem.

2. Determine the needs/desired outcomes.

3. Brainstorm possible solutions.

4. Select the solution that will best meet the needs.

5. Develop a plan of action.

6. Implement the plan.

7. Evaluate the solution and the problem-solving process.

By following each of the steps, identifying the importance of each, and developing ideas for accomplishing each step, participants will learn how the work of the team can be strengthened.

Define the Problem

It is important for the team members who are solving the problem to take time to define the problem at hand rather than just react hastily. Each person sees the problem from a unique perspective and each perspective contributes to developing team understanding. Answering questions such as the following promotes development of a common understanding of the problem:

1. What is not working in this situation?

2. What factors are contributing to this problem?

3. Who is involved (students, staff, parents)?

4. Who is affected and how are they affected?

Team members should individually consider these questions and list their own answers to be used in a discussion. When each member participates in defining the problem, it promotes respect for all contributions. Because the problem needs to be thoroughly described before a solution is implemented, it is important that no one feels they are suggesting the ultimate solution.

Once all members of the team have had a chance to contribute to defining the problem, a problem statement can be drafted. This brings the team to a consensus on just what it is they are attempting to solve.

Determining the Needs/Desired Outcome

Determining the needs of a situation means that you examine and clarify what the overall desired outcomes might be. This is not the same as developing a solution; rather it is a chance to talk about what should happen in the situation and what is the desired outcome. In doing this, it is helpful to address questions such as these:

1. What do we want to happen?

2. What do students need that they are not currently getting?

3. What is needed to improve our communication with each other?

4. What is needed in our communication with colleagues, parents, and students?

5. What is the overall desired outcome in this situation?

By answering these or similar questions, a team can focus on what they want to achieve. This helps bring team members to a positive and future-oriented approach. Now that the problem has been identified, the needs of the situation considered, and desired outcomes generated, it is time to begin the important step of brainstorming ideas.

Brainstorming

Brainstorming is a method for generating as many solutions as possible that might help to solve the problem. One way this can be accomplished is to have team members think of possible solutions for the problem at hand. Then the supervisor and paraeducator share their solutions to the problem. A list of the brainstormed solutions is written so that all participants can see the various ideas. To conduct a good brainstorming session, the following suggestions should be followed:

- Establish a time frame.
- Assign a note taker.
- Generate and accept all ideas—do not evaluate.
- Make sure everyone participates.
- Take more time if creativity is high or more ideas are needed.

Select the Solution That Will Best Meet the Identified Needs

Now the team selects a solution that will have the greatest chance for achieving the desired outcomes. The questions that can help team members arrive at mutually agreed-on solutions are as follows:

1. Which solution will meet the needs and achieve the desired outcomes?

2. Which solution is the easiest to implement?

3. Which solution is within the team's control?

4. Which solution would be least disruptive?

Discussion of these or similar questions will help to identify a solution that will be acceptable to all team members. Sometimes it is possible to combine two or more solutions to find a workable answer.

Action Plan: Who, What, Where, and When

After the solution has been agreed on by all team members, an action plan should be developed so that everyone knows what is to be done and by whom. It is best if the action plan is written out and copies made for everyone involved. This increases the likelihood that members will understand the solution and be accountable for clarifying their role in achieving the goals of the plan.

A sample form that may be used for the action plan is shown in Figure 5.7. The action plan provides a record of the decision, is a communication tool among team members, and serves as a reference for follow-up activities.

Action Plan		
for		
_____		
Staff Responsible: _____		
Supervising Teacher: _____		
Paraeducator: _____	Date of Meeting: _____	
Other: _____		
Action	**Person Responsible**	**Deadline**
_____		
_____		
_____		
_____		
_____		

Figure 5.7.   Sample action plan form.

Implement the Plan

By now each team member should know who is responsible for what actions or tasks and what the time frame is for carrying out the activity. Next team members discuss what support or resources are needed to achieve the goals of the plan. Questions to guide this discussion follow:

1. What resources are needed to implement the plan?

2. Are there any materials required that we do not currently have?

3. Who should know about this plan (students, parents, teachers, staff)?

4. Does the daily schedule need to change?

5. Do the daily schedules of the team members need to change?

6. When will the team meet to review the plan?

As the action plan is being implemented, each team member who participates in testing the solution should be keeping a record of how it is working. Observations about what is working well and not working well will help the team determine whether or not the goals of the plan are being achieved. These observations can be analyzed at the next meeting to determine what is more or less effective.

Evaluate How Well the Solution Worked and Satisfaction with the Problem-Solving Process

It is very important to complete the problem-solving process in two ways. The first is to determine whether the plan effectively achieved the desired outcome. This evaluation process should be carried out periodically and part of the results should be used to develop new strategies or alternative solutions. Questions that can guide this discussion follow:

1. What has been accomplished by the action plan?

2. Have there been any unexpected outcomes?

3. Does the plan need to be revised to address these outcomes?

4. Is there any sign that our actions are resolving the original problem?

5. Have any new problems arisen that we need to know about?

6. When will this action plan need to be reviewed again?

The second step is a review of the problem-solving process itself. This means that all team members who participated in steps 1 through 6 should now assess how well the process worked. The point of this evaluation is to determine if the problem-solving steps were helpful to the team and if there are any suggestions for improving them. The following questions can be used to guide this discussion:

1. How well did this problem-solving process work?

2. What should be changed next time, if anything?

3. What were the benefits to the team and students of a process for problem solving?

4. What have we learned from solving the problems this way?

The answers and discussion around these questions will provide direction for the next time professionals and paraeducators have problems to solve.

Summary

When school professionals and paraeducators work as a team, problems are a natural part of the job. It is helpful for teams to use a problem-solving process to address various issues that may include communication breakdown, parental concerns, student behaviors, scheduling conflicts, interpersonal relationships, and building or district practices and policies. Such a problem-solving approach respects the individual differences and the collective wisdom that exists on any educational team. The use of this mutual problem-solving process fosters cooperative working partnerships between school professionals and paraeducators and results in better services for students.

CONFLICT RESOLUTION

Conflict is a natural, though sometimes unwelcome, occurrence in any working relationship. In educational settings, conflicts may arise at any point. Potential areas of conflict are identifying the needs of students, integrating parental desires, scheduling, using different teaching methods, working with other staff, and measuring student success. When school professionals and paraeducators understand the nature of conflict and use a conflict resolution strategy, much of the confusion and personal misunderstanding can be avoided.

People who work together will often experience conflict as a result of opposing ideas or interests. For example, the paraeducator and the school professional might have different beliefs about the level of support a student needs to be successful. The professional might believe that a student needs less attention from adults and the paraeducator might believe the student needs more attention. When such a disagreement occurs, it is imperative that a conflict resolution strategy be implemented so that the student receives consistent support. Nearly all conflicts have an emotional component especially when any of the parties involved feels strongly that they are right and knows what is best. Using conflict resolution strategy lessens the emotional response and proves a more objective approach, which is respectful of everyone.

As in problem solving, conflict resolution strategies have a series of steps that assist in bringing the situation into focus, implementing each of the steps, and finally reaching a mutually satisfying outcome. The strategy outlined in Figure 5.8 can be used by all who are involved in the conflict or just one of the people.

Conflict Resolution Strategy

Step 1: Pause and Take a Breath

Stepping back helps to put the conflict into perspective and is the first step to resolving it. This step will help focus the energy in a productive manner rather than just getting caught up in the emotions of the issue at hand. The conflict may not have to be resolved at that very moment, and some time away gives people a chance to reorganize their thoughts.

This step is very important for diffusing the emotions of a conflict. In the fast pace of the school day, a disagreement can become exaggerated as

---

Step 1: Pause and take a breath.

Step 2: Name the conflict or source of the conflict.

Step 3: What part did I play in the conflict?

Step 4: What are our options?

Step 5: Choose the best one.

Step 6: Develop an action plan together.

Figure 5.8.   Conflict resolution strategy.

people feel pressed to get their work done and to get along well with their coworkers. Stepping back from the situation will offer each person the chance of a new perspective and prevent the conflict from escalating.

Step 2: Name the Conflict or Source of Conflict

Conflict can result from many sources as team members work together for the best interest of their students and clients. It is important at this step to recognize just what the source of the conflict is. The questions that follow will assist school professionals and paraeducators in assessing the sources of conflicts:

1. Do members of the team all have the same information?

2. Is the information we have complete?

3. Are the goals that we have compatible?

4. Are the methods we are using effective?

5. Is it comfortable for us to disagree openly with one another?

If the answer to any of the above questions is no, it indicates where the source of the conflict may be. In addition, the team members would consider who is involved in the disagreement, how it is affecting the people in their work, and what effect it is having on the students.

Naming the conflict or source of conflict can be done by all parties involved or just one individual who believes that there is a conflict and wants to think it through on his or her own. When this step is done in a thoughtful manner, there is more chance that the resolution will be effective and that the real conflict will be addressed. If this step is not carried out, the result can be a reactive, narrow-sighted response, which serves to confuse the issue and create further conflict.

Step 3: What Part Do I Play in the Conflict?

The third step is a time for individuals involved in the conflict to analyze what part they have in it. We all have varying responses to conflict and different approaches to dealing with it. Thomas and Kilmann (1974) identified five typical responses to conflict: avoidance, accommodation, compromise, competition, and collaboration. Each of the five responses is useful in its own right and can contribute to productive conflict resolution. By addressing the questions, each individual can determine which response is being used and whether there is a need for change.

Using avoidance. People avoid conflict for various reasons. It may be emotionally upsetting to some; it may be a matter of not taking the time or energy that is needed to resolve issues. It may be to provide a cooling off period so that the issue can be approached in a more rational manner. It is important to recognize when avoidance is being used as the response to conflict and for what reason.

Using accommodation. When people accommodate during a conflict, they tend to go along with the desire of another and give up their own. This is done to preserve harmony in the relationship or may be used when the issue is not of great importance to an individual. At other times accommodation is used because the individual is hesitant to assert a view that will be in disagreement with another. Although accommodation on the surface may appear to resolve a conflict, it may not be the best method for team effectiveness.

Using compromise. Compromise is characterized by individuals giving up some of their own demands and making concessions for the common goal. When using compromise, individual team members are willing to put aside some of their own outcomes and incorporate some of the other team members' ideas or suggestions into a mutually acceptable solution. The benefits of a compromise are many because each team member contributes to a resolution that is agreeable to all.

Using competition. When competition is used in conflict resolution, individuals are certain that they are right and rarely incorporate the thinking of others into their own. Sometimes this comes about as a matter of perceived authority (i.e., "I'm responsible for this program, therefore I need to be the primary decision maker"). At other times competition is used so that a quick solution can be reached. If competition is being used, it is helpful to recognize this and determine its effectiveness.

Using collaboration. Collaboration is the most cooperative and creative form of conflict resolution. Teams using collaboration contribute their individual ideas and are open to the ideas of others. A solution reached through collaboration is one that none of the individual team members could have developed without the others. Thus the outcome is mutually satisfying and all members feel involved in the resolution.

After the questions are addressed, it is time to move to the next step.

Step 4: What Are Our Options?

During this step of conflict resolution, it is important to determine what alternatives are available and to thoughtfully consider and evaluate the potential of each. Typically, team members can do one of three things:

1. Let things continue as they currently exist.

2. Address the issue with key people involved in the situation/conflict.

3. Develop a new way of thinking about the conflict.

We discuss each option next.

Let things continue as they currently exist. When teams choose to let things continue as they currently exist, there may be potential for the conflict to increase, or perhaps it will disappear after a certain amount of time. What are the benefits and liabilities of letting the current situation remain the same?

Address the issue with the key people involved in the situation/conflict. Teams may choose to address the issue with the key people involved so that the conflict is out in the open and discussion can be held to ascertain each person's experience and point of view. Not every conflict needs to be addressed in this manner. What are the benefits and liabilities of addressing the issue with key people involved?

Develop a new way of thinking about the conflict. Sometimes all that is needed is a shift in attitude about the conflict. Perhaps the conflict is not as intense or as important as we have made it. Rethinking or reframing a situation can result in a new approach that allows the individuals to proceed with other daily responsibilities. What are the benefits and liabilities of developing a new way of thinking about conflicts?

Step 5: Choose the Best Option

After evaluating the potential benefits and liabilities of the alternative choices, the team should deliberately and specifically choose the one that is most likely to resolve the conflict effectively. Which choice is best suited to this situation? If we choose to address this with other people, who are the key players? Have we exaggerated this conflict? If so, how can we think about it differently? Make a plan to take whatever steps are necessary to implement your choice.

Step 6: Develop an Action Plan Together

Whether a choice has been made to let things continue as they are, to address the conflict with others involved, or to develop a new way of thinking about it, putting the plan into action is the final and most important step. After the first five steps have been accomplished, the conflict is usually acted on in a more neutral and less emotional fashion. Such an approach shows respect for all team members.

Summary

Conflict is a natural occurrence when people work together. Having a conflict resolution strategy will assist team members in working through the problem in a way that is beneficial. It is important to discover the sources of conflicts, to identify one's own part in the conflict, and to think through possible ways of resolution. As school professionals and paraeducators learn to work through their conflicts, they grow in their strength as a team and the students are the benefactors.

Discussion Questions

1. List any team of which you have been a member. This could be an athletic team, a committee, and so on. Consider the ones that were most effective and list why. Consider the ones that were least effective and list why.

2. Think about any situation that you have been involved in where collaboration and teamwork were valued, encouraged, and demonstrated. Use this as a basis for a discussion with others to generate specific examples of the characteristics of collaboration.

3. Define leadership. What are the characteristics of an effective leader?

4. List the factors that could interfere with listening and give examples.

(Continues)

Discussion Questions (*Continued*)

5. Review the tips for improving listening skills and give examples. 6. Give examples of attending skills and responding skills that you have observed people using.

7. List the stages in the problem-solving process. Set up a role-playing situation where a problem has been identified. Role-play the problem-solving process.

8. Think about conflicts you have experienced in a work situation. How were these conflicts resolved? Now that you know about the problem-solving and conflict resolution strategy, explain how you would handle things the same or differently.

9. Identify two issues that school personnel might encounter where the problem-solving or conflict resolution strategy could be used.

10. Think about a small group meeting in which you participated that did not go as well as it might have. List the various blocks or hindrances that kept the meeting from being more successful.

Case Studies

Review the following case studies and answer the questions that follow.

Case Study 1: A Problem-Solving Exercise

Paraeducator Julie Brown

I am Julie Brown and I have been working as a paraeducator in special education for the past 3 months. I completed high school and was married soon after I graduated. My two children are now in high school and I decided to accept this job to supplement our income so that they can go to college. I really like working with children and have been active in elementary school PTA, was a Girl Scout leader, and taught in our local Sunday school. In fact, there was a boy in my class who had a developmental disability and I liked the challenge of finding ways to make him feel as though he was part of the group.

When I took this job, I was briefed on district policy with regard to salary, fringe benefits, working hours, vacation, and so on. In addition, I was

(*Continues*)

Case Studies (Continued)

told about the chain of command in the schools and the supervisor very briefly described my role and responsibilities as a paraeducator. I was told that Mr. White would be the classroom teacher I would be working with and that I would meet him when I reported to work. The supervisor said Mr. White would give me information about the specific tasks I would be expected to perform and the methods and strategies he would expect me to use to carry out the activities.

From the day I walked into the classroom, we have never had a formal discussion about what he expects me to do; there is always some reason why we can't sit down and talk. We can never meet during his prep periods because he is always too busy doing lesson plans to talk to me. When I suggested we meet after school, he told me that would be impossible because he either has graduate classes or meetings to attend. Then on one of the days when he was "free," I really had to get home to take one of my kids to the doctor.

I never know in advance what he wants me to do or how he wants it to be done. Just before he does something in the class, he will say, "Julie, take this group and follow my plans." I have no real idea about what to do, except to try to do what I see him doing while I sit in the back of the room watching him teach the lessons as he has asked me to do. When I am teaching, he frequently breaks into what I am doing and corrects me right in front of the students. I don't have the guts to tell him how this makes me feel—so I save it up until I get home, and my family bears the brunt of all my frustrations.

But what really has me worried is what his correcting me in front of the students might be doing to my ability to work with them. Today it came to a head when he had to leave the room and I was left alone with the group. I asked one of the students who is rather difficult to work with to join us for an activity. He responded by looking straight at me and saying, "No, I don't want to, and I don't have to because you're just the 'para,' and you can't tell me what to do." I wanted to cry and quit right then—but I didn't. Where do I go from here?

Teacher Ken White:

I am Ken White, a high school teacher who has been assigned my first paraeducator after teaching for 12 years. This was done because several special education students were assigned to my class as part of the dis-

(Continues)

Case Studies (Continued)

trict's efforts to place them in what the district calls the "least restrictive" environment. I wish they had asked me whether I wanted someone or not because I am really a loner and have very strict rules about how things are to be done in my classroom. I've never worked with anyone before in my classroom and I'm not really sure that I think it is worth the time to plan for another adult, especially someone who is not trained to be a teacher much less to work with students with special needs.

At any rate, Julie walked into my room 3 months ago, just before school began, and said she was the paraeducator assigned to me. I asked her if she had been told what her duties were and she informed me that they had been explained to her at a meeting at the district office. I wish they had told me what I could expect her to do because I have no idea what goes on in those "briefing" sessions nor have I seen a copy of a job description for paraeducator. I asked her to sit in the back of the room and watch for a while so she could get the hang of how I work. I told her that we'd get together later when I had some free time to talk to her.

During the first few days, I never had time to talk to her. I had lesson plans to develop. I have four different preparations which really take a lot of time. I'm also taking a second master's and I have to leave 3 days a week almost immediately after school, so for me, just sitting down to talk is a problem. I wish there was time during the day to do this, but I'm just too busy with the kids and the planning to talk to her.

I finally decided that I'd let her review some of the skills I had already taught the students. So I gave her my plans and told her to follow them religiously. But she never did it exactly the way I wanted it to be done—she apparently thought it didn't make much difference how she did it as long as she felt comfortable. So what was I to do? I told her to do it the way I had written it and not to use her own methods.

Three months have gone by and I'm still as harried as I was before if not more so. And to make matters worse, she seems to be having problems controlling the kids in the classroom. It started when I had to leave for an emergency meeting and Julie was left in charge. I'm not sure what she did wrong but she is having real trouble dealing with one of the kids and it seems to have an impact on the way some of the other students are responding to her. Maybe I should find the time to talk to her about how she deals with the problems of integrating the paraeducator into the program.

(Continues)

Case Studies *(Continued)*

Case Study Discussion Questions

1. Describe the problem from the paraeducator's point of view. (This may include attitudes, actions, and other factors described in the case study.)
2. Describe the problem from the teacher's point of view.
3. What behavior(s) does the teacher need to change?
4. What behavior(s) does the paraeducator need to change?
5. Discuss and list desired goal(s) for the team.
6. How can they work together to achieve the goal and to be a better instructional team? What additional information, skills, or other resources will they need to achieve the goal?

Case Study 2: Conflict Resolution Strategy

The following case study applies the six-step conflict resolution strategy to a situation that might be encountered by school professionals and paraeducators.

The Situation

Dan is a speech–language pathologist who works with Madeline, a speech–language assistant. Madeline works with students in small groups to reinforce their practice of articulation skills. Dan has become increasingly frustrated because Madeline has been arriving late to work with the students. The regular classroom teachers have told Dan that Madeline often comes to their classrooms 10 to 15 minutes late then only works with students for 10 minutes instead of the scheduled 20-minute session. Dan wishes that Madeline would recognize the importance of being punctual and giving students their full time, but he realizes that she may not change if he continues to avoid the situation. Knowing that he needs to intervene, Dan believes that it will probably be more positive if he thinks though the conflict resolution steps he has leaned.

Case Study Discussion Questions

1. How does the conflict resolution strategy help Dan in this situation?
2. How does the strategy support Madeline in this situation?
3. What would you do if this does not resolve the situation?

(Continues)

Case Studies *(Continued)*

Case Study 3: Collaborative Problem Solving

The Situation

Jeff, a student who has a learning disability, is in fourth grade. The special education teacher has worked closely with the fourth-grade teacher so that Jeff does most of his school work in the fourth-grade classroom. Recently Jeff has had difficulty staying on task for more than a couple of minutes. He can be a behavior problem. The fourth-grade teacher is at a loss as to what to do and asks the special education teacher and the paraeducator who support Jeff in the regular classroom to help solve this problem. The special education teacher tells the paraeducator about the fourth-grade teacher's concern and sets a time for a meeting that is convenient for all three of them. At this meeting, the special education teacher asks the fourth-grade teacher to share details of her concern.

Role-play this case study using the collaborative problem-solving process.

Case Study Discussion Questions

1. How well did this problem-solving process work for the team?

2. What would we change next time, if anything?

3. What were the benefits to our team and to Jeff?

4. Do we think all seven steps are necessary all of the time?

Case Study 4: Developing Expectations

To develop expectations for communications is to think ahead about the desired outcomes of an interaction, to anticipate behaviors that might interfere with or enhance mutual understanding, and to predict possible needs that will arise.

Sue, a speech–language professional is going to meet with Monica, a paraeducator, for their first planning meeting. She wants them to "get off on the right foot" and wants Monica to feel free to ask questions as they come up. She knows that Monica is a bit shy and may be hesitant to speak up.

Case Study Discussion Questions

1. What can Sue do so that Monica will feel comfortable?

(Continues)

Case Studies (*Continued*)

2. How can Sue approach the meeting so that they begin as partners, not as boss and employee?

3. What behaviors might intimidate Monica?

4. What are the issues they need to discuss at this first meeting?

5. How many issues should Sue try to cover at this meeting?

Thinking ahead about this meeting and answering the questions given here will increase the likelihood that Sue and Monica will get off to a good start in their communication.

Case Study 5: Understanding Perspectives

To understand perspectives during communication is to recognize that people see issues, situations, and ideas through their own points of view and that knowing and respecting these diverse views can serve the discussion in positive and productive ways.

Beth, a resource teacher, works with Joseph, a paraeducator, who assists her with students when they are in the regular classroom. She believes that Joseph is becoming frustrated in trying to adapt to so many different classroom teachers' expectations of him. She wants to have a discussion with Joseph and two of the classroom teachers so that a common understanding can be reached.

Case Study Discussion Questions

1. What should Beth tell the teachers when she invites them to the meeting?

2. How should Beth approach Joseph so that he knows the purpose of the discussion?

3. What can Beth do at the meeting to get everyone's perspective of the current situation?

4. How can Beth make sure that each person is heard and understood?

5. How can Beth facilitate the development of a mutually accepted plan?

As individual perspectives are taken into account by professionals and paraeducators, communication is enhanced and the capacity for part-

(*Continues*)

Case Studies *(Continued)*

nership increases significantly. Answering the questions given here will promote the possibility of including everyone in decision making and will decrease misunderstanding.

Case Study 6: Asking Questions

Asking questions during interpersonal conversations is to inquire further and demonstrate a sincere interest in learning from another.

Sabrina, a vision specialist who is only in the elementary school once a week, relies on Ryan, a paraeducator, to provide three students practice sessions in Braille. As part of her weekly visits, Sabrina meets with Ryan for a half-hour. Lately she has felt that she has done too much of the talking and that Ryan is not contributing as much as he used to. She hopes that the next meeting will be more balanced in participation.

Case Study Discussion Questions

1. What can Sabrina do at the next meeting to solicit Ryan's participation?

2. What questions would encourage Ryan without putting him on the spot?

3. How can Sabrina make sure that she doesn't end up doing all of the talking?

4. If Ryan gives a brief response, what can Sabrina ask to get him to say more?

5. How can Sabrina find out about the students' progress from Ryan?

When professionals learn to ask questions of paraeducators, the communication is two way and the needs of students are better served.

Case Study 7: Listening

Listening actively is making a conscious effort to hear the words and understand the meaning of a spoken message. It is one of the most empowering communication skills a person can learn.

Ralph has become aware that whenever Yuko, the paraeducator, is explaining something to him, he is distracted by trying to get several other things done in his classroom. Consequently, he doesn't remember what she

(Continues)

Case Studies (*Continued*)

*says and has to ask her to repeat herself. He wants to give her his full atten-
tion next time.*

Case Study Discussion Questions

1. What could Ralph do to make sure that he is paying attention to Yuko?

2. What should Ralph *stop* doing to improve his listening?

3. How will better listening skills improve his relationship with Yuko?

4. How can Ralph make sure that he doesn't lapse back into his old non-
   listening habits?

5. How will Ralph know if he has become a better listener?

   When professionals practice good listening skills during interpersonal
communication with paraeducators, a climate of trust is established and
the partnership is greatly enhanced.

Case Study 8: Speaking Clearly

Speaking clearly in conversation is to express oneself in such a manner that
the receiver's understanding closely matches what the speaker meant to
convey.

   *Jamica, an occupational therapist, is to meet with the paraeducator
Connie, who works with her. They have been discussing an inservice they
will present on serving students with special needs in the regular classroom.
Jamica wants to be sure that they are coordinated in an efficient and
effective manner. She has been leading most of the conversation and
Connie has been appearing to agree. Now she wants to be sure that she's
made herself clear and that Connie has understood what Jamica meant.*

Case Study Discussion Questions

1. How can Jamica check to see if Connie is understanding what has
   been said?

2. What questions can Jamica ask that will elicit Connie's perspective?

3. How will Jamica know if she got her points across?

(*Continues*)

Case Studies (*Continued*)

4. What should Jamica do if Connie has misunderstood some of the discussion?

5. How frequently should Jamica check for Connie's understanding?

REFERENCES

DeBoer, A. (1995). *Working together: The art of consulting and communicating.* Longmont, CO: Sopris West.

DeVito, J. A. (1994). *The interpersonal communication book* (7th ed.). New York: Harper Collins.

Dewey, J. (1993). *How we think.* Boston: Heath.

Elgin, S. (1989). *Success with the gentle art of verbal self-defense.* Englewood Cliffs, NJ: Prentice Hall.

Feldman, R. S. (1985). *Social psychology: Theories, research, and applications.* New York: McGraw-Hill.

Friend, M., & Cook, L. (1996). *Interactions. Collaboration skills for school professionals* (2nd ed.). White Plains, NY: Longman.

Gerlach, K., Pickett, A. L., & Vasa, S. F. (1992). *Strengthening the partnership: Paraeducators and teachers working together. Issues, roles, and responsibility.* A guide for the teacher and the paraeducator. Bremerton, WA: Olympic Educational Service District No. 114.

Gordon, T. (1977). *Leader effectiveness training.* New York: Wyden Books.

Margolis, H., & Brannigan, G. (1978). Problem solving with parents. *Academy Therapy, 22,* 423–425.

Reisberg, L., & Gerlach, K. (1992). *Strengthening the partnership: Collaboration and teaming.* A guide for paraeducators and the teacher (rev. manual). Bremerton, WA: Olympic Educational Service District No. 114.

Schrage, M. (1990). *Shared minds.* New York: Random House.

Senge, P. (1990). *The fifth discipline.* New York: St. Martin's Press.

Sherif, M., & Sherif, C. (1956). *An outline of social psychology.* New York: Harper & Row.

Thomas, K., & Kilmann, R. (1974). *Thomas–Kilmann conflict mode instrument.* Tuxedo, NY: Xicom.

CHAPTER 6

• •

Professional and Ethical Responsibilities of Team Members

• •

William Heller
University of South Florida, St. Petersburg

OVERVIEW

The role of paraeducators and their relationship to the professional in the same setting has been described and analyzed in great detail in this text. No attempt is made in this chapter to further delineate the roles of these two critical adults in education or other settings. The purpose of this chapter is an attempt to consider roles and their professional and ethical implications. This is important because each individual brings into a setting his or her own values, personalities, strengths, weaknesses, and ideas. What role does one's personal values play in interactions as a paraeducator with children and youth, with professionals, with parents, and with other school personnel? What ethical responsibilities and rights do children and youth, parents, teachers, and paraeducators have? What unique ethical dilemmas present themselves in a paraeducator role? Are there ethical issues to be addressed in settings where paraeducators and professionals work together? These and many other similar questions are legitimate ones to pose for the professional and paraeducator because they have largely been previously ignored.

Instructional Objectives

After studying this chapter and participating in discussions and case studies, the reader will be able to:

1. Describe how organizations are dependent on effective relationships among and between those who work within them.

2. Explain the criteria for determining whether or not an occupation warrants recognition as a profession.

3. Recognize that educators are considered professionals as a consequence of the public's perception of their role, not as members of an occupation meeting the criteria for status as a profession.

4. Know that the most distinguishing characteristic of a profession is a code of ethics.

5. Describe the code of ethics for educators adopted by the National Education Association in 1975.

6. Describe the paraeducator code of ethics.

7. Recognize the major sources of ethical dilemmas for school professionals and paraeducators.

8. Discuss the seven steps for making decisions when ethical dilemmas are confronted.

9. Recognize that ethical dilemmas are situational and therefore variable to a given or a group of common situations.

10. Recognize that there are not always right or wrong answers to ethical dilemmas.

AN ORGANIZATIONAL PERSPECTIVE

Organizations, including educational systems, are affected by complex internal and external forces. These forces include, but are not limited to, laws, litigation, and social concerns. The development of such forces is founded, in part, on the ethical beliefs of our diverse society.

Relationships exist between the individual and the organization in which the individual affiliates. The importance of these relationships lies within the organization and has an impact on the individual in proportion to the strength of his or her identification with the organization. Marlowe (1971) summarized this phenomenon as it relates to the individual in the following ways: "The organization generally tries to get the individual to absorb certain beliefs as well as do certain things. These beliefs facilitate his performance in the organization and, hence, the performance of the organization as a whole" (p. 477). Marlowe (1971) indicated that a reciprocal relationship needs to exist if the organization and the individual are going to fulfill their respective needs. It is through individuals that an organization achieves its goals and objectives; and it is through the organization that the individual works to improve and advance. Within this relationship the organization, through key members, enacts policies, procedures, and standards to govern the members at large. As noted by Albanese (1975), it is not the organizations that behave, it is the individuals within that do. Because individuals have differing degrees of identification with an organization, they will also have differing relationships with each other even in similar roles. That is why some individuals within an organization may complain openly about their organization's leadership, its direction, and other factors while their colleagues do not. The person whose own values and goals are matched most closely with those of the organization will be the most comfortable and supportive of the organization's policies and procedures.

It is important for the organization to expect behaviors from its members that are considered to be appropriate within the context of the organization. It is just as important for the individual to be informed of these desired behaviors in order to act accordingly (Robbins, 1976). In addition to the relationship between the organization and the individual, relationships also exist among the organization, the individual, and the public. This is especially true of education, which is an enterprise operated by educators for students and supported by public funds. As a consequence of this triadic relationship, the public has required educators to conduct more research, train more personnel, and provide more service than at any other time in the history of education. The public is demanding accountability matching the public's expectations for the schools with the behavior (outcomes) of the school as an organization.

The moral principles on which our country was founded are delineated in the U.S. Constitution. Specifically, the 14th Amendment to the Constitution guarantees all citizens of the United States due process and equal protection under the law (Weintraub & Abeson, 1974). According to P.L. 94-142, the Education for All Handicapped Children Act of 1975, as amended in 1990 by P.L. 101-476, the Individuals with Disabilities Education Act, educational services must be provided to all children and youth with disabilities in the United States, without regard to the nature and severity of their disability. The implementation necessary to comply with this goal becomes the responsibility of the educator. Prior to implementation, the educator must establish objectives. Once completed, if educators fail to implement objectives, then they violate the moral principle of providing education to all children and are, as a consequence, unethical. If education services provided are inappropriate then, by definition, they, too, are unethical.

Konnert and Graff (1976) related the establishment of goals and objectives to the individual when they stated, "With the increasing interdependence of all activities throughout the world, worthy organizational goals cannot be set in isolation, if man is to survive. The value one puts on these interdependent variables directly reflects the feelings and beliefs one has relative to the nature and welfare of man, the nature and uses of knowledge, and other fundamental questions. In short, one cannot establish worthy goals without revealing individual philosophical beliefs and values" (p. 2). Konnert and Graff (1976) further stated that their use of the term *philosophy* and its derivations is interchangeable with such terms as *morality* or *ethics*. If Konnert and Graff's premise is accepted, then it is impossible for personnel in education and related services to establish goals and objectives without revealing their personal ethics.

It is through the implementation of these goals and objectives that services are provided. Horn (1976), in differentiating between enactment and implementation, stated that enactment is an administrative process, whereas implementation is an instructional process. The instructional process is where the service is provided. If an individual enacts service goals and objectives without the subsequent implementation of the services, then the individual is merely engaging in the administrative process. If the goals and objectives are based on the ethical beliefs of the profession and/or society, then failure to implement the goals and objectives is unethical.

EDUCATION AS A PROFESSION

Most educators consider themselves professionals by virtue of their degree and certification or licensure to practice as a teacher, administrator, counselor, or other key educational role. However, the field of education does not meet the criteria necessary for earning the distinction of being a profession. If education is not a profession, how can its members be professionals? The answer to this question is one that has concerned the discipline of education for years and continues to do so.

In other professions, differentiated roles and responsibilities have gradually emerged as a means of balancing the requirements of supply and qualifications. Those not fully certified or less extensively trained are limited to performing tasks for which they have been prepared, and they practice under supervision. Complex decisions are reserved to those certified to make such judgments. A suggestion made by the Holmes Groups in 1986 that untrained college graduates be hired only as instructors who practice under the supervision of certified teachers is a step toward protecting the public interest. (Darling-Hammond, 1990, p. 269)

It is important that educators and paraeducators understand the characteristics of a profession and the extent to which the discipline of education embodies them.

A review of the literature regarding the characteristics of a profession reveals four that are often cited among authors (American Association of School Administrators, 1960; Leiberman, 1956; Moore, 1970; Myers, 1973). First, the profession must possess a specific body of knowledge. Second, the profession must have an organization that represents the profession. Third, the profession must have a formal code of ethics developed by the members and enforced in cases in which the code is violated. Finally, the profession, through its members, should be dedicated to providing quality service to its clients.

The characteristics used to define a profession vary from author to author. Heller (1983), in an effort to provide an argument for having professional standards for special educators, used the following characteristics by Reynolds and Birch (1982) to define a profession:

1. The activity is identified by a distinctive and commonly recognized name, the improper use of which is illegal.

2. The work done is acknowledged to be a vital public service.

3. Learning to do the work calls for extended and specialized education based, in part, on undergirding disciplines.

4. Performance of the activities requires major public trust and accountability.

5. The application of the thinking process to the solution of problems (intellectuality) is a predominant ingredient.

6. Decisions and procedures are based on reliable knowledge that is constantly refreshed by new facts and ideas (learnedness) from the arts and sciences and from other professions.

7. The activity has a practical object, a definite and useful purpose in the eyes of both the practitioner and of society.

8. Communicability is represented by an agreed upon corpus of knowledge and skills essential for carrying out the object of the profession, and organized in such a way that it is passed on to new entrants as an orderly discipline.

9. Procedures exist to ensure that all members are qualified to perform a basic and common body of practice at a safe level.

10. The already qualified members prescribe and apply standards governing admission (organization) to their group.

11. A licensing body or similar, recognized authority exists to perform certain functions and is governed largely by the members themselves.

12. There is a code of ethics adopted and enforced by the profession itself.

13. Members are motivated primarily by concern about other individuals' and society's objectives rather than their own rights and interests.

14. Recognized and accredited higher education institutions exist to prepare members for the profession.

15. Members are eligible to conduct private practice and consultation with other professionals and the public.

16. There are associations made up exclusively of members of the profession that are aimed at maintaining and elevating its standards and its public accountability.

Whether or not education is considered a profession, the educator is viewed by those he or she serves as a professional. Consequently, the expectations by a parent for an educator are no different than those that parent has for a physician or attorney. Those expectations are that educators know their subject matter, can effectively teach children this subject matter in an educational setting, and are accountable for their performance and achievement of those taught. Education is at best a semiprofession in terms of the critical criteria used to judge a profession, but to the public, to the student, and to the parent, education is a profession and they expect its teachers, administrators, and others to be professionals. Educators may well feel that what the public perceives and expects them to be is discrepant with what they accord other professions and this feeling on the part of educators may well be right. However, as long as education remains the domain of the public, the discrepancies between it and nonpublic-controlled professions will continue but the fact remains that in the eyes of the public, education is a profession. This perception is really all that matters. The educator must meet all the expectations that are inherent in the title "professional." It is within this expectation and context that professionalism is defined.

ETHICS DEFINED

The preceding discussion has tried to answer the question of whether or not education is a profession. While it is at best a semiprofession from a criterion-based analysis, it is a profession in terms of the public's expectations. Basic to these expectations, and an element required of all professionals, is a code of ethics. All professions are based on an accepted set of ethical standards or principles set by their members.

Ethics and its associated terms, morals, values, and religion deal with the conduct of humans. Understanding the differences between various terms associated with ethics requires the examination of definitions.

Ethics may be viewed from three perspectives (Edwards, 1967). First, ethics is viewed from a philosophical perspective called *mataethics*. This perspective focuses on the inquiry *about* ways of life and rules of conduct. Second, ethics may be viewed as a way of life or the manner in which people live. This view is commonly associated with religious beliefs. A third viewpoint is more professional in nature and emphasizes the pursuit of a set of rules, conduct, or moral code. Common examples are found in the various professions, such as law or medicine.

Some philosophers have simply defined ethics as the body of knowledge concerned with the conduct of humankind (Copeland, 1928; Everett, 1918; MacKenzie, 1925; Symonds, 1928). Dewey (1962) viewed ethics as "the principles that will tell us what is the *right* thing to do, or what things are *worth* doing, no matter what people in fact approve or disapprove and no matter who will be damaged by the decision. It is not concerned with what public opinion on moral matters actually happens to be, just as the scientist is not concerned with what people believe about the shape of the earth but with its actual shape" (pp. 6–7).

The concept of ethics is viewed differently based on the terms associated with it. The purpose of this chapter is to discuss the ethical and professional responsibilities of school professionals and paraeducators. Ethics is best viewed from the professional perspective because the teacher and paraeducator are a team. Together, they are the ones responsible for what occurs in the classroom or related environment. The definition for this purpose was developed by Hartoonian (1976): "Ethics . . . have to do with the relationships that exist between and among people, with the modes of conduct that exist within a profession, and with the moral principles of the cultural heritage to which a society or civilization makes reference" (p. 2).

One characteristic of a profession is the development and governance of a code of ethics. According to Leiberman (1956), a code of ethics provides several advantages. First, it provides a mechanism to separate the competent professional from the incompetent. Second, it provides the newly trained professional with information regarding rights, privileges, and obligations. Third, it establishes a foundation for the interaction between the professional and the client. Finally, it provides the public with a guide to understand the conduct of the professional. Moore (1970) not only supported Leiberman but added that a professional code of ethics is equivalent to a private system of law.

The National Education Association (NEA) adopted, in 1975, a Code of Ethics for the Education Profession, which serves as a guide for the individual educator as well as a basis for enforcement by NEA of any violations of professional conduct. The NEA code is presented in Figures 6.1, 6.2, and 6.3. It is the author's view that ethics is basic to professionalism and any judgments made of professional practice must be considered against an established code of ethics approved by educators. The reader should pay particular attention to the preamble of the NEA code (Figure 6.1), which asks all educators to accept responsibility for adhering to the highest ethical standards.

Education, like many other professions, has numerous specialties. Those in education include elementary education, special education, counseling, school administration, and related services, to name only a few. Each of these

---

The educator, believing in the worth and dignity of each human being, recognizes the supreme importance of the pursuit of truth, devotion to excellence, and the nurture of democratic principles. Essential to these goals is the protection of freedom to learn and to teach and the guarantee of equal educational opportunity for all. The educator accepts the responsibility to adhere to the highest ethical standards.

The educator recognizes the magnitude of the responsibility inherent in the teaching process. The desire for the respect and confidence of one's colleagues, of students, of parents, and of the members of the community provides the incentive to attain and maintain the highest possible degree of ethical conduct. The Code of Ethics of the Education Profession indicates the aspiration of all educators and provides standards by which to judge conduct.

The remedies specified by the NEA and/or its affiliates for the violation of any provision of the Code shall be exclusive and no such provision shall be enforceable in any form other than one specifically designated by the NEA or its affiliates.

Figure 6.1. **Code of Ethics of the Education Profession—preamble.** From *Code of Ethics of the Education Profession*, by National Education Association, 1975, Reston, VA: Author. Reprinted with permission.

PRINCIPLE I
Commitment to the Student

The educator strives to help each student realize his or her potential as a worthy and effective member of society. The educator therefore works to stimulate the spirit of inquiry, the acquisition of knowledge and understanding, and the thoughtful formulation of worthy goals.

In fulfillment of the obligation to the student, the educator

1. Shall not unreasonably restrain the student from independent action in the pursuit of learning.

2. Shall not unreasonably deny the student access to varying points of view.

3. Shall not deliberately suppress or distort subject matter relevant to the student's progress.

4. Shall make reasonable effort to protect the student from conditions harmful to learning or to health and safety.

5. Shall not intentionally expose the student to embarrassment or disparagement.

6. Shall not on the basis of race, color, creed, sex, national origin, marital status, political or religious beliefs, family, social or cultural background or sexual orientation, unfairly

   a. Exclude any student from participation in any program.

   b. Deny benefits to any student.

   c. Grant any advantage to any student.

7. Shall not use professional relationships with students for private advantage.

8. Shall not disclose information about students obtained in the course of professional service unless disclosure serves a compelling professional purpose or is required by law.

Figure 6.2. **Code of Ethics.** From *Code of Ethics of the Education Profession*, by National Education Association, 1975, Reston, VA: Author. Reprinted with permission.

specializations has its own respective code of ethics. Each will also address a commitment to students, commitment to quality practice and performance, and commitment to the profession. Thus, they conform to the NEA code in content and differ only in terms of their specificity to a group of professionals serving a particular population of children or school system role.

The NEA code of ethics emphasizes two major areas of responsibility for the professional school person: the student and the profession. The responsibilities related to students include the broad areas of respect, health (mental and physical), safety, confidentiality, discrimination, exclusion and inclusion, and assessment. The individual school professional responsibilities to

---

PRINCIPLE II
Commitment to the Profession

The education profession is vested by the public with a trust and responsibility requiring the highest ideals of professional service.

In the belief that the quality of the services of the education profession directly influences the nation and its citizens, the educator shall exert every effort to raise professional standards, to promote a climate that encourages the exercise of professional judgment, to achieve conditions that attract persons worthy of the trust to careers in education, and to assist in preventing the practice of the profession by unqualified persons.

In fulfillment of the obligation to the student, the educator

1. Shall not in an application for a professional position deliberately make a false statement or fail to disclose a material fact related to competency and qualifications.

2. Shall not misrepresent his/her professional qualifications.

3. Shall not assist any entry into the profession of a person known to be unqualified in respect to character, education, or other relevant attribute.

4. Shall not knowingly make a false statement concerning the qualifications of a candidate for a professional position.

5. Shall not assist a noneducator in the unauthorized practice of teaching.

6. Shall not disclose information about colleagues obtained in the course of professional service unless disclosure serves a compelling professional purpose or is required by law.

7. Shall not knowingly make false or malicious statements about a colleague.

8. Shall not accept a gratuity, gift, or favor that might impair or appear to influence professional decisions or action.

—Adopted by the 1975 Representative Assembly

Figure 6.3. **Code of Ethics.** From *Code of Ethics of the Education Profession,* by National Education Association, 1975, Reston, VA: Author. Reprinted with permission.

the profession address the broad areas of qualifications, honesty, competence, standards of practice, confidentiality, collaboration, and cooperation.

The paraeducator's role is impacted by the NEA code of ethics in a number of significant ways. The obligations of school professionals relative to their students really do not differ from the obligations that a supervised paraeducator has to students. A delineation of these obligations by the paraeducator is presented in Figure 6.4, a suggested code of ethics for paraeducators developed by Vasa and Steckelberg (1991).

A code of ethics defines and describes acceptable practices. A code for paraeducators would examine specific responsibilities of the paraeducator, as well as the relationships that must be maintained with students, parents, teachers, school and community.

Accepting Responsibilities:

Recognize that the supervisor has the ultimate responsibility for the instruction and management and follow the directions prescribed by him/her.

Engage only in activities for which you are qualified or trained.

Do not communicate progress or concerns about students to parents unless directed to do so by the supervising teacher.

Refer concerns expressed by parents, students, or others to the supervising teacher.

Relationships with Students and Parents:

Discuss a child's progress, limitations, and/or educational program only with the supervising teacher in the appropriate setting.

Discuss school problems and confidential matters only with appropriate personnel.

Refrain from engaging in discriminatory practices based on a student's disability, race, sex, cultural background or religion.

Respect the dignity, privacy, and individuality of all students, parents, and staff members.

Present yourself as a positive adult role model.

Relationship with the Teacher:

Recognize the teacher as a supervisor and team leader.

Establish communication and a positive relationship with the teacher.

When problems cannot be resolved, utilize the school district's grievance procedures.

Discuss concerns about the teacher or teaching methods directly with the teacher.

Relationship with the School:

Accept responsibility for improving skills.

Know school policies and procedures.

Represent the school district in a positive manner.

Figure 6.4. **Suggested code of ethics for paraeducators.** Adapted from *Issues and Responsibilities in Utilizing, Training, and Managing Paraprofessionals*, by S. F. Vasa and A. L. Steckelberg, 1991, Lincoln: Department of Special Education and Communication Disorders, University of Nebraska.

As the reader will note, much of the language used in the code of ethics for paraeducators is analogous to that used in the NEA code of ethics for professional school personnel. The one notable distinction is the section labeled "paraeducator relationships with teacher." Interestingly, the code of ethics for paraeducators addresses the supervising relationship directly, whereas the code of ethics for professional school personnel does not at this time. There is reason to believe that this will change. It is already beginning to change in the legal profession as paralegals become more widely utilized and valued, and has for years been recognized in allied health areas. The next revision of the NEA code of ethics will likely address the supervision of paraeducators and, thereby, expand on statement number 5 in the NEA code relating to assisting a noneducator. Are paraeducators noneducators? No, they are members of the educational team, and like paralegals, who work under the supervision of licensed attorneys, paraeducators work under the supervision of certified/licensed professionals.

The problem facing educators regarding the role and utilization of paraeducators is one of definition and delegation. The lines of demarcation between the work of school professionals and paraeducators are somewhat blurred and difficult to judge on a continuum, whether the latter addresses authority or instruction. Some school professionals will delegate more authority and autonomy to a paraeducator than another. Just as important, that is why the understanding of ethics is so critical. The individual (educator and paraeducator) must, in many cases, determine whether or not what has been delegated is within the role of the professional to delegate or the role of the paraeducator to accept. The degree and amount of delegation not only determines roles but, without equivocation, precipitates the formulation of ethical dilemmas.

PREPARATION OF EDUCATION PERSONNEL TO DEAL WITH ETHICAL DILEMMAS

A variety of instructional materials exists for preparing teachers for the everyday aspects of service delivery to children and youth. However, at every level there is an absence of comparable materials available for preparing teacher educators, school administrators, supervisors, and teachers to deal with everyday ethical issues in the classroom (Bateman, 1982; Heller, 1982, 1983; Howe & Miramontes, 1992; Kauffman, 1992; Maple, 1983; Stephens, 1985; Turnbull & Barber, 1984). This lack of information probably has contributed to the current limited focus on ethical issues in preservice and graduate teacher education curricula in special education. "The ethics of special education has so far received scant attention, either as a field of ethical inquiry or as a topic in teacher education" (Howe & Miramontes, 1992, p. 1). Special education professionals are not the only professional educators voicing concern regarding the lack of ethics in education. In *The Moral Dimensions of Teaching*, Goodlad, Soder, and Sirotnik (1990) address professionalization issues from ethical perspectives and they advocate reorienting teaching and teacher education around ethical relationships. Goodlad et al. (1990) believe that teachers need to prepare all children to live in a democratic society that embraces dialogue and debate about those things that make lives and living worthwhile. Although many leaders in education have voiced concern over the lack of attention to ethics in general and special education, only a few empirical studies have been undertaken and the results of those studies are less than encouraging.

The results of several studies as well as the issues involved in "educational reform," "restructuring," and "excellence in education" have caused many educational professionals to note that "education, and especially special education, is rife with ethical problems—problems concerning how to treat individual students, how to ensure equal educational opportunity for all, how to respect the views of parents, how to effectively work with colleagues, how to supervise and manage paraeducators, how to train paraeducators and how to do all these things while maintaining one's personal integrity and allegiance to the practices of education" (Howe & Miramontes, 1992, p. 1). Kauffman (1993), in discussing how radical reform might be achieved in special education, agrees with Sarason (1990): "Attempts to reform education will make little difference until reformers understand that schools must exist as much for teachers as for students. Put another way, schools will be successful in nurturing the intellectual, social, and moral development of children only to the extent that they also nurture such development of teachers. The notion that what is good for students is also good for teachers applies not only to the conditions under which they work but also to the way they approach problems" (p. 7). Kauffman's and Sarason's basic premise is that lasting reform in special education can only be achieved if special education leaders/professionals use the same problem-solving strategies they recommend for special education teachers. Among others, these strategies include "devotion to ethical decision making" (Kauffman, 1993).

NEEDED: MORE ETHICS EDUCATION

"Presently, most personnel preparation programs provide little if any preparation and information about professional expectations. Evidently, reliance is upon whatever standards students happen to have acquired on their own" (Stephens, 1985, p. 191). Even if it could be assumed that most teacher education preparation programs introduce students to either the NEA code of ethics or the codes of various specialty groups within education, knowing a code of ethics and knowing how to respond to situations containing ethical dilemmas are not necessarily correlated. Usually, the principles articulated in ethical codes are very general. The resulting problem is that "they provide little by way of guidance regarding what to do in specific cases of ethical controversy" (Howe & Miramontes, 1992, p. 121). The lack of ethics preparation typically has been justified on the basis that the existing curricula are demanding enough given the wide range of education needs of children. Handelsman (1986) has questioned the ethical soundness of this rationale by asking: "Is it ethical to train people to do a variety of skills without training them to perform these skills in an ethical manner?" (p. 371).

The basic premise underlying this chapter is that a knowledge of professional ethics is especially essential to school professionals with responsibilities for the supervision and management of paraeducators in education and related services, and the fact that both professionals and paraeducators may receive little or no preparation in ethics. Teachers and paraeducators must follow professional and ethical guidelines in their relationships with students, students' families, colleagues, policymakers and administrators, the public, and each other. Such a diversity of relationships creates an area for competing interests among all concerned that can result in major ethical dilemmas. When dilemmas involve decisions that impact the lives of children, including their safety, well-being, and quality of education, we cannot afford to resolve them without serious ethical deliberation.

All educators, including related services professionals, paraeducators, and paratherapists, knowingly or not, have responsibility for safeguarding the human and legal rights of children and youth and their families, as well as providing quality services. A code of ethics by itself cannot provide sufficient guidance for educators who are confronted with ethical dilemmas. It is open to serious question whether administrators and supervisors are sufficiently knowledgeable concerning ethics to adequately assist teachers, paraeducators, and related support personnel in dealing with ethical dilemmas.

SOURCES OF POTENTIAL PROBLEMS FOR TEAMS OF SCHOOL PROFESSIONALS AND PARAEDUCATORS

The school professional–paraeducator relationship provides numerous opportunities for ethical dilemmas. The following are some potential sources of these dilemmas. The issue of classroom authority and who is the one, to put it in terms of the vernacular, "in charge" remains a major source of professional and ethical problems. Although the teacher is held responsible and accountable by the school system for what occurs in a classroom, the teacher may in reality not be in charge. For example, a teacher may be more passive and nondirective and the paraeducator may be more structured and assertive. A potential result is blurred or unclear lines of authority in the classroom. Chances are that anyone observing such a classroom would notice this and perhaps feel the paraeducator is the authority figure.

The nature of preparation for school professionals and paraeducators may create dilemmas. Few teacher education programs prepare those seeking to become teachers to work effectively with paraeducators. Many find themselves working with a paraeducator before they have ever had a serious thought about what role such an individual might perform in a classroom and other settings. Paraeducators usually receive limited preparation also in terms of learning about the role of the school professional. The paraeducator may well be versed in the "process of instruction" but not in determining educational needs of students, deciding which instructional strategies to implement, or evaluating the effectiveness of these strategies— the things teachers must do many times in a given day. These decisions are based on years of formal preparation by the school professional with a focus on decisions being made unilaterally in a classroom managed by a single individual, the teacher. What a teacher knows and understands about the role of a paraeducator is extremely important and should not have to depend solely on inference or on-the-job experience. Unfortunately, the latter is currently more the rule than the exception.

The concept of "team" is important to an effective professional and paraprofessional relationship; yet, this is a difficult concept to achieve. The team concept requires sharing, cooperation, collaboration, mutual understanding, shared goals, and a respect for the role(s) of everyone on the team. It is easy to talk about teaming and teamwork, but achieving a true team practice in reality is seldom so easily accomplished.

A variable, especially in classroom settings that constitute a source for possible dilemmas, is the human element. Not only are there professional–

paraeducator relationships, but equally as significant, there are relationships with children and parents, who may choose to align their affections and judgments with either the teacher or the paraeducator, or possibly both. Children and parents may actually vie for the affection or attention of the teacher or paraeducator. Unfortunately, this competition for favor more often than not divides rather than unifies,which could lead to the destruction of a quality professional–paraeducator relationship.

Inclusive settings also frequently require the use of teacher consultants or resource teachers to assist in the accommodation of children with disabilities. Introduction of additional adults, including paraeducators and related services personnel, into a classroom changes the concept of classroom autonomy for the teacher and introduces the need to team or collaborate. The majority of teachers have not been prepared to cope with such situations.

Another issue that could cause some professional and ethical concerns is when paraeducators are not assigned to a team of professionals as a program but rather to a specific student or students. Frequently the paraeducator has full responsibility for modifying the plans and works with the student exclusively. Could we actually be segregating both the paraeducator and student when assignments such as these are made? If a regular teacher feels that the paraeducator has the responsibility for this student, planning and supervision by the teacher may be nonexistent.

Two other related sources of ethical dilemmas pertain to substitute teachers. Substitutes, like other teachers, have received little preparation to work with paraeducators. Whereas some substitute teachers are skilled in the subjects they are assigned to teach, others are not. Even when substitutes are skilled in the subject matter, they typically enter the classroom with little knowledge of the routines, procedures, and learning needs of students in the class. When a substitute teacher works in a classroom served by a paraeducator, many potential ethical dilemmas may arise. In this situation, it is clear that the paraeducator is more familiar with the routines, procedures, and learning needs than the substitute teacher. The paraeducator may be inclined to assume the lead role, or the substitute may tacitly initiate such an arrangement. Either way, the outcome is that the substitute teacher passes the day without assuming the principal responsibility for the class.

In contrast, the paraeducator may fail to provide essential information to the substitute teacher about routines, procedures, and learning needs of students, expecting that a substitute teacher should know what to do. Or, the substitute teacher may fail to request such information from the paraeducator. In either case, the substitute is working at a distinct disadvantage, deprived of information that is readily available.

Of even greater ethical concern is the situation wherein no substitute teacher is employed and the paraeducator is placed in the position of substitute teacher. There are various reasons for this circumstance. For example, in some localities, few substitutes are available. In others, the cost of hiring substitute teachers strains the budget of the school or district. Whatever the reason, the paraeducator is placed in a role that may violate the codes of ethics for professionals and paraeducators.

Finally, volunteers provide valuable contributions to schools throughout the country. Volunteers may be parents, community leaders, business personnel, or other individuals who want to help in schools. Some volunteers are very well prepared, some may even be former school professionals, and others are not well prepared and bring only a sincere desire to help to the educational setting. When volunteers and paraeducators are in the same classroom, it is often difficult for a casual observer to differentiate one from the other. This apparent lack of differentiation gives rise to ethical dilemmas. There are, however, three clear distinctions that may be made between paraeducators and volunteers. First, volunteers are not employed by the district. Paraeducators, in contrast, are school employees who are paid to perform specific duties at specific times. Second, school districts and school professionals have less control over the attendance, actions, and ethical behavior of volunteers than they do over the attendance, actions, and ethical behavior of paraeducators. Thus, some tasks that must be performed in specified ways, that require specific behaviors, or that must be performed at specific times are better performed by paraeducators than volunteers. Finally, volunteers have no right to access certain confidential information about students. Thus, some tasks that require knowledge of confidential information may not be safely assigned to volunteers and should be assigned instead to paraeducators. Teachers need to be aware of the distinctions in roles of volunteers and paraeducators in order to delegate appropriately and create appropriate plans for the duties of each. Without question, all school professionals should be prepared to recognize and understand the value and roles of paraeducators. School professionals also need to know how the employment of paraeducators and use of volunteers may give rise to certain ethical dilemmas in their practice.

PARAEDUCATOR ETHICAL AND PROFESSIONAL DILEMMAS

Tymchuk (1982, p. 170) listed seven steps for making ethical decisions:

1. Describe the parameters of the situation.

2. Describe the potential issues involved.

3. Describe the guidelines already available that might affect each issue (e.g., values, laws, codes, practice, research).

4. Enumerate the alternative decisions for each issue.

5. Enumerate the short-term, ongoing, and long-term consequences, as well as the probability of their occurrence.

6. Present evidence (or lack thereof) for those consequences, as well as the probability of their occurrence.

7. Rank order and vote on the decision.

Using these steps, the reader is asked to analyze five ethical and professional dilemmas and answer a number of discussion questions related to each dilemma. Critical to the analysis is accurately assessing all elements of the situation evoking the dilemma. Please remember that situations are seldom simple and the more complex, the greater the need for accuracy in analyzing the situation.

Situations

Situation 1

Mary is a teacher of a primary classroom that includes two students who have learning and sensory disabilities. Mary grades the latter students on effort and they always receive A's based on their hard work. All the other children are graded on what they learn and while they may work hard, most do not receive A's. The paraeducator feels Mary's grading procedure is unfair. She speaks to Mary and discovers they have a very different philosophy. The paraeducator shares her concerns with one of her friends, who happens to be a parent of one of the students in that class.

(Continues)

Situations (Continued)

Situation Discussion Questions

1. Has Mary violated any of the NEA code of ethics statements? If so, which one(s)?

2. What should the paraeducator do if she believes a breach of ethics has occurred? What should the teacher do?

3. Are some things right for students with disabilities that may not be right for others?

4. Whose responsibility is it to assign grades to students in a classroom? Who is ultimately accountable and can accountability be shared from the viewpoint of the employer and the school system?

5. Do you feel inclusion requires a different procedure for evaluating the performance of students with disabilities?

6. What are the major professional and ethical issues in this case?

Situation 2

The school professional, Rodger, has planned a field trip for his class to a local restaurant's main offices to learn about business and management techniques. This chain has recently been criticized for sexual harassment of its employees and the paraeducator (Sharon) refuses to go. Rodger notes that the criticism has never been validated and that the paraeducator's values have an impact on his ability to expand learning experiences for the students. The plans for the field trip continue on schedule. This is not the first time Rodger and Sharon have had a discussion on values and differences of opinion.

Situation Discussion Questions

1. Are any of the NEA or paraeducator code of ethics statements violated? If so, which one(s)?

2. As an employee, what might the consequences of a refusal be? Do you feel a dismissal would be warranted if you were the principal of the school?

3. If ultimately ordered to go, does the order constitute sexual harassment?

(*Continues*)

Situations (*Continued*)

4. Is the question of values relevant here and, if so, how does one deal with it professionally and ethically?

5. The paraeducator code of ethics indicates that the supervisor has ultimate responsibility for instruction. Is this an instructional issue or a relationship issue?

6. Should the paraeducator go? If yes, why? If no, why not?

Situation 3

John, a school professional, and Janet, the paraeducator with whom he has worked for years, have had a major disagreement. John has taken a few days off as sick leave when he actually went to baseball games. Janet knows what he did and has informed John that she'll not cover for him anymore. This has happened several times before. Frequently he leaves class and allows her to take over. John tells Janet that she is being disloyal and that others do it regularly. Janet feels it is bad for the classroom because the substitute teachers are barely satisfactory and she feels uncomfortable when John is not there.

Situation Discussion Questions

1. Does either Janet or John violate any ethical principle advocated by the NEA or the paraeducator code of ethics? If so, which one(s)?

2. If Janet has known about the reasons for John's absences before and not reported them, what are the ethical implications?

3. Where does loyalty fit into a relationship and what really constitutes loyalty?

4. Have you ever known of someone who called in sick but wasn't? What were your feelings?

5. Since John has Janet as a paraeducator, do his absences have less of an impact than his absence might if he had no paraeducator? Should this be given consideration in determining the ethical implications?

6. What if Janet was the one who was absent and John found out she was not sick? Is it as serious?

(*Continues*)

Situations (*Continued*)

7. What will happen to this instructional team if Janet follows through on her decision to report John's sick leave deception and her concerns about him leaving her with the class?

8. Can and should it be settled between John and Janet and never reported to administration?

Situation 4

Juan Ortiz, a teacher of a very diverse class of children with learning disabilities, had been ill for 2 days recently and Marci, the paraeducator, worked with a substitute teacher who delegated almost everything for the 2 days to her. In addition, the substitute teacher seemed to avoid the Hispanic children in the classroom and when he did interact with them, he was very rude and condescending. Juan has called in sick again and although the paraeducator asked for a different substitute, she was informed that teacher selection was not within her purview. The substitute she previously had concerns about was the one selected to substitute again.

Situation Discussion Questions

1. Are there any ethical violations of either the NEA or paraeducator code of ethics in this situation? If so, which one(s)?

2. If a substitute teacher is not a very confident teacher, would it not be better to let the paraeducator do the teaching?

3. Should paraeducators have a role to play in selecting and evaluating substitutes? If so, how should this role be fulfilled in terms of ensuring that personal differences are not conflicting with professional competence concerns?

4. If the substitute teacher feels uncomfortable teaching Hispanic children, would it not be acceptable for Marci to teach them?

5. Would it be justifiable for Marci to take personal leave and let another paraeducator work with the substitute?

6. Is there a point where commitment to children becomes secondary to one's personal integrity and survival? If so, how does one justify this

(*Continues*)

Situations (*Continued*)

within the stated parameters of either the NEA code of ethics or the paraeducator code of ethics?

Situation 5

Josephine is a first-year teacher and has never worked with a paraeducator. Marie, the paraeducator assigned to her classroom, has 15 years of experience and is only a few hours from having earned her own BA via a career ladder program. Josephine is somewhat in awe of Marie and has essentially taken a back seat to her. Marie is a dominant personality, she knows the children, knows the school system, and does not hesitate to assume any responsibilities Josephine might relinquish. The question to others, and especially to Josephine's induction year mentor, is who is really teaching the class?

Situation Discussion Questions

1. Are any of the NEA or paraeducator code of ethics principles being violated? If so, which one(s)?

2. If you were Josephine's mentor, what would you advise or how would you help Josephine?

3. What could Marie do to help Josephine without making it appear she is taking over or being too directive?

4. Does the fact that Marie almost has her BA degree make a difference in this situation? After all, they are almost identical in terms of preparation.

SUMMARY

The purpose of this chapter has been to provide professionals an understanding of ethics and professionalism as these relate to their work with paraeducators. More and more professional educators and others in related disciplines are emphasizing the study of ethics as a means of coping with serious dilemmas occurring in educational settings among and between professionals. Because education is a people-oriented activity, the need to establish and maintain effective ethical relationships and practice is critical. These relationships motivate not only professionals and support personnel but also children, parents, and a variety of others. The concept of a team is predicated on relationships; eliminating ethical dilemmas which impair the purity of these relationships is crucial. The professional without a knowledge of ethics is a professional in trouble. The professional who knows ethics and practices in an ethical manner is a professional who will always be in demand and command of those relationships and experiences that foster success.

Discussion Questions

1. From an ethical perspective discuss why teacher supervision is essential for working with paraeducators.

2. What do the school professional and paraeducator need to know about professionalism and ethics?

3. What are some important ethical considerations when planning to integrate a paraeducator into a team where she will be supervised by a number of teachers?

4. Review the NEA code of ethics. How does this code of ethics impact the school professional–paraeducator team?

5. If the job of a paraeducator is to be considered a new career choice, how do you feel about a nationally accepted code of ethics for paraeducators?

6. What are the ethical issues involved in scheduling, conferencing, delegation, lesson planning, large group instruction, and training of the paraeducators?

7. What are some of the professional and ethical considerations that should be discussed with paraeducators when they are employed?

8. What are some possible issues connected with the supervision of paraeducators that have professional and ethical implications? Present any you know about and discuss how they might have been resolved or prevented.

Exercises

1. The importance of confidentiality is paramount. If you were to develop a 1-hour inservice program for paraeducators on this topic, what would you include? Develop an inservice outline containing the content you think is important.

2. Ask your local school district for guidelines and standards (code of conduct) for school professionals and other employees. How does the code relate to paraeducators?

3. Review the following six case studies and discuss, in a group, the professional and ethical implications of each situation.

Case Studies

Case Study 1

It is one o'clock in the afternoon and the teacher became ill. The principal sends the teacher home and asks the paraeducator to be in charge of the class for the rest of the afternoon. The paraeducator was told to teach the lessons to the entire class as scheduled in the lesson plan book.

a. How do you feel about this situation?

b. Discuss this case from the perspective of the administrator, teacher, and paraeducator.

c. What are the professional and ethical implications of this case?

Case Study 2

John, a student with special needs, has disrupted the classroom several times this semester. The teacher has just about given up on him. Today, the teacher said to Jane, the paraeducator, "Take him, keep him busy. I want to work with students who really want to learn. I'm assigning you to work just with him."

a. How do you feel about paraeducators working with the most challenging students?

b. What should have been done differently?

c. What are the professional and ethical implications of this case?

(Continues)

Case Studies (Continued)

Case Study 3

Karen Adams has been assigned to David Bowen's classroom. On the first day of school, Mr. Bowen introduces himself and the paraeducator by saying "I am Mr. Bowen, your teacher, and this is Karen. Karen is a helping teacher for Tommy, Susan, and Mark."

a. *How do you feel about Mr. Bowen introducing Karen by her first name?*

b. *Discuss the potential problems that could result by assigning the paraeducator to work with a child rather than a class or program.*

c. *How could this be handled differently?*

d. *What are the professional and ethical implications of this case?*

Case Study 4

Fred, a second-grade teacher, works with two paraeducators in his classroom, Jesse and Joann. Fred has decided he needs to talk with both of them about a problem that is developing. He has heard Jesse and Joann discussing students outside the classroom and believes that they are violating confidentiality. He wants to be clear in stating the guidelines about confidentiality without being punitive with the paraeducators.

a. *What should Fred bring to the meeting that outlines confidentiality?*

b. *How should he begin the meeting so that Jesse and Joann feel that the meeting is friendly and yet professional?*

c. *What material should he give to Jesse and Joann for future reference?*

d. *What can Fred do to make sure that Jesse and Joann understand the issues of confidentiality?*

e. *What are the professional and ethical implications of this case?*

Case Study 5

There are several students in a class who have very limited English. The paraeducator is fluent in their native language. Because the paraeducator is so competent and understands the needs of the children so well, the teacher asks the paraeducator to tutor these children. The paraeducator plans the lessons, translates classroom material, and adapts the curriculum when appropriate. The teacher and the paraeducator meet

(Continues)

Case Studies (Continued)

weekly to discuss how things are going. In addition to the instructional duties, the teacher asks the paraeducator to visit the parents of these children at the home in order to strengthen the school–home relationship. The paraeducator feels comfortable with her job and enjoys the interaction with the students and families.

a. How do you feel about this situation?

b. Do you feel the assigned role is appropriate for this paraeducator since she understands the needs of the children and families?

c. What could be done differently?

d. What are the professional and ethical implications of this case?

Case Study 6

The teacher and the paraeducator have worked together for several years. The teacher knows that the paraeducator has exceptional music talents. She asks the paraeducator to decide what the class should do for the Spring Music Festival and to plan and rehearse the program.

a. How do you feel about the situation?

b. How do you feel about paraeducators teaching an entire class?

c. What are the professional and ethical implications of this case?

REFERENCES

Albanese, R. (1975). *Management: Toward accountability for performance.* Homewood, IL: Richard D. Irwin.

American Association of School Administrators. (1960). *Professional Administrators for American Schools* (38th Yearbook). Washington, DC: Author.

Bateman, B. (1982). The special educator as a professional person. *Exceptional Education Quarterly, 2*(4), 57–69.

Copeland, J. R. (1928). *Natural conduct: Principles of practica; ethics.* Stanford, CA: Stanford University Press.

Darling-Hammond, L. (1990). Teachers and teaching: Signs of a changing profession. In W. R. Houston, M. Haberman, & J. Sikula (Eds.), *Handbook of research on teacher education.* New York: Macmillian.

Dewey, J. (1962). Reconstruction in philosophy: Reconstruction in moral conceptions. In W. T. Jones, F. Sontag, M. O. Beckner, & R. J. Fogelin (Eds.), *Approaches to ethics: Representative selections from classical times to the present*. New York: McGraw-Hill.

Education for All Handicapped Children Act of 1975, 20 U.S.C. § 1400 *et seq.*

Edwards, P. (1967). *The encyclopedia of philosophy* (Vol. 3). New York: Macmillan & Free Press.

Everett, W. G. (1918). *Moral values: A study of the principles of conduct*. New York: Henry Holt and Company.

Goodlad, J. I., Soder, R., & Sirotnik, K. A. (1990). *The moral dimension of teaching*. San Francisco: Jossey-Bass.

Handelsman, M. M. (1986). Problems with ethics training by "osmosis." *Professional Psychology, 17*, 371–372.

Hartoonian, H. M. (1976). *The ethics of our profession: The student and schooling*. Washington, DC: National Council for the Social Studies Annual Convention. (ERIC Document Reproduction Service No. ED 132 083)

Heller, H. W. (1982). Professional standards for preparing special educators: Status prospects. *Exceptional Education Quarterly, 2*(4), 77–87.

Heller, H. W. (1983). Special education professional standards: Need, value, and use. *Exceptional Children, 50*(3), 199–204.

Horn, C. J. (1976). Differentiation in special education. *Education and Training of the Mentally Retarded, 11*, 335–336.

Howe, K. R., & Miramontes, O. B. (1992). *The ethics of special education: Professional ethics in education series*. New York: Teachers College Press.

Individuals with Disabilities Education Act of 1990, 20 U.S.C. § 1400 *et seq.*

Kaufmann, J. M. (1992). Foreword. In K. R. Howe & O. B. Miramontes (Eds.), *The ethics of special education* (pp. xi–xvii). New York: Teachers College Press.

Kaufmann, J. M. (1993). How we might achieve the radical reform of special education. *Exceptional Children, 60*(1), 6–16.

Konnert, W., & Graff, O. B. (1976). The sine qua non of organizational effectiveness. *Educational Administration Quarterly, 12*(3), 1–8.

Leiberman, M. (1956). *Education as a profession*. Englewood Cliffs, NJ: Prentice-Hall.

MacKenzie, J. S. (1925). *Manual of ethics* (4th ed.). New York: Noble and Noble.

Maple, C. C. (1983). Is special education certification a guarantee of teaching excellence? *Exceptional Children, 49*, 308–313.

Marlowe, L. (1971). *Social psychology: An interdisciplinary approach to human behavior*. Boston: Holbrook Press.

Moore, W. E. (1970). *The profession: Roles and rules*. New York: Russel Sage Foundation.

Myers, D. A. (1973). *Teacher power—Professionalization and collective bargaining*. Lexington, MA: D. C. Heath.

National Education Association. (1975). *Code of ethics of the education profession*. Reston, VA: Author.

Reynolds, M. C., & Birch, J. W. (1982). Special education as a profession. *Exceptional Education Quarterly, 2*(4), 1–13.

Robbins, S. P. (1976). *The administrative process: Integrating theory and practice*. Englewood Cliffs, NJ: Prentice-Hall.

Sarason, S. B. (1990). *The predicted future of educational reform. Can we change before it's too late?* San Francisco: Jossey-Bass.

Stephens, T. M. (1985). Personal behavior and professional ethics: Implications for special educators. *Journal of Medical Ethics, 11*, 47–53.

Symonds, P. M. (1928). *The nature of conduct*. New York: Macmillan.

Turnbull, R. H., & Barber, P. (1984). Perspectives on public policy. In E. L. Meyen (Ed.), *Mental retardation: Topics of today—Issues of tomorrow* (Vol. 1, pp. 5–14, Serial No. 1). Reston, VA: Division on Mental Retardation of the Council for Exceptional Children.

Tymchuk, A. J. (1982). Strategies for resolving value dilemmas. *American Behavior Scientist, 26*, 159–175.

Vasa, S. F., & Steckelberg, A. L. (1991). *Issues and responsibilities in utilizing, training, and managing paraprofessionals*. Lincoln, NE: Department of Special Education and Communication Disorders, University of Nebraska.

Vasa, S. F., Steckelberg, A. L., & Sundermeier, C. (1990). Supervising paraprofessionals in special education programs: The teacher's role. Lincoln, NE: Department of Special Education and Communication Disorders, University of Nebraska.

Weintraub, F. J., & Abeson, A. (1974). New education policies for the handicapped: The quiet revolution. *Phi Delta Kappan, 55*, 526–529, 569.

CHAPTER 7

• •

Paraeducators in School Settings: Administrative Issues

• •

Stan Vasa and Allen Steckelberg
University of Nebraska–Lincoln

OVERVIEW

While local educational agencies have considerable latitude in the development and administration of paraeducator programs, common concerns and tasks must be addressed. Securing funding, allocating a budget, determining wages and fringe benefits, conducting needs assessments, and developing procedural and policy handbooks are important initial tasks.

Administrators play a critical role in establishing effective education and related services programs. This is especially true for programs in which paraeducators are employed. Policies and procedures are established by district and building administrators and are important in creating a climate that promotes the value of the services provided by paraeducators. Administrative leadership is necessary to clearly establish roles for paraeducators and to provide the support necessary to ensure that they are prepared to work with children and youth. Administrators must also support professionals so that they can be effective classroom and instructional managers. This chapter addresses policies and administrative issues in establishing and maintaining quality school programs that include paraeducators. Topics discussed are establishing district policies and practices; conducting needs assessments; developing job descriptions; recruiting, interviewing, selecting, and assigning paraeducators; identifying ethical and legal responsibilities for paraeducators; developing training policies and programs; developing supervisory policies; and evaluating the impact of paraeducators on school programs.

Instructional Objectives

After studying this chapter and participating in discussions and exercises, the reader will be able to:

1. Describe why district policies and standards for paraeducator employment, supervision, and training need to be established.

2. Describe why needs assessments are important tools for determining policies and standards and facilitating administrative decision making.

3. Describe the need for and components of three levels of job descriptions: (a) district wide, (b) program, and (c) personalized job descriptions for individual paraeducators.

4. Describe effective procedures for paraeducator recruitment, selection, and placement.

5. Describe district and building administrator's responsibilities for developing supervisory procedures and evaluation criteria for paraeducator performance.

6. Describe district and building administrator's responsibilities for developing and implementing staff development opportunities for paraeducators and school professionals.

7. Describe the value of a district-wide handbook to share information about policies and procedures connected with paraeducator employment.

. . . .

ESTABLISHING POLICIES AND STANDARDS

Administrators should establish policies and procedures that recognize paraeducators/paratherapists as vital members of the school's educational team. Reasons for employing and the expected impact of paraeducators/paratherapists should be an element of the district's strategic planning process. District and school staff should begin by working together to identify expected outcomes that will result from the assignment of paraeducators to a program and use this information to guide the development of policies and the allocation of resources.

Establishing District Policy

The first step in establishing guidelines for paraeducator employment is to identify the need and expected benefits. These guidelines establish a common vision for all school personnel and provide direction in allocating resources, setting standards for employment, training, supervision, and evaluation of the contributions paraeducators make to programs. Typically, outcomes target decreasing costs of education and more efficient use of educational resources. Yet, the aim of paraeducator employment must be more than just reducing costs. Indeed, the primary and perhaps the only reason must be to improve the quality of education for students. The many benefits of employing paraeducators include but are not limited to

- increased availability of positive adult role models for students,
- expanded student learning opportunities,
- increased availability of individual and small group instruction,
- additional time for professionals to plan, provide instruction and related services, and evaluate program outcomes,
- increased on-task student behaviors in the classroom,
- improved teacher morale, and
- better monitoring and evaluation of the educational process.

Needs Assessment

Conducting a systematic needs assessment is a valuable tool for administrative decision making regarding the employment, placement, training, and supervision of paraeducators. Issues commonly addressed include (a) needs of students for individualized attention; (b) extent of professional/supervisory staff needs for paraeducator support; (c) training required by teachers to supervise paraeducators; and (d) paraeducator training needs.

Establishing the education needs of students and the support required by school professionals to meet these needs is critical. In tandem, they provide the basis for determining whether paraeducator employment should be initiated, expanded, or reduced. Determining where and how paraeducators should be assigned is affected by many factors including the number of students in the district who (a) have learning, physical, and sensory disabilities,

(b) have limited English proficiency, or (c) come from economically disadvantaged families or other backgrounds that place them at risk. Changes in school programs related to inclusion of children and youth with special needs in general education place increased program and curriculum management responsibilities on school professionals that warrant additional support from paraeducators. Training needs of paraeducators and professionals and the resources available to support a paraeducator training program can also be identified through a needs assessment. Figure 7.1 provides an example of school district paraeducator policy statements.

Paraeducator Job Descriptions

A natural outgrowth of a needs assessment is the development or amendment of job descriptions for paraeducators. Job descriptions validate the importance of paraeducators, clarify teacher–paraeducator role distinctions, serve as a reference point for evaluating paraeducator performance, and identify skills and training needs for paraeducators. Written job descriptions at both the district

---

Teacher Responsibilities

Teachers are trained and certified to perform certain functions in the education of children and youth. Responsibilities that are reserved for teachers involve (1) analyzing the instructional needs of students, (2) prescribing educational activities to meet student needs, and (3) supervisory responsibilities consistent with established school policy.

Teachers working with paraeducators in either classrooms or community-based settings must rely on their professional judgment when assigning duties to paraeducators. These duties should not infringe on the responsibilities reserved for teachers, however, paraeducators may assist teachers in meeting their responsibilities.

The building principal retains the responsibility for supervision of the school and the entire staff.

Paraeducator Duties

Paraeducator roles are to assist teachers or other school professionals to carry out their instructional, administrative, and other program responsibilities. Paraeducators who do not have teaching certification may not replace classroom teachers. Paraeducators may not be assigned to perform and may not assume teachers' professional duties (e.g., assessing student performance, establishing program and student goals and objectives, and developing lesson plans).

Figure 7.1.   District policy statement on paraeducators.

level and at the program level promote job satisfaction by eliminating paraeducator and teacher apprehensions about what is expected of team members.

Job descriptions are often constructed at three levels to provide guidance to staff and paraeducators (see Figure 7.2). District-wide job descriptions provide guidelines for duties, supervision of paraeducators, and minimum requirements for employment. Program-level job descriptions are used to delineate paraeducator roles in unique settings and programs that may include general, bilingual, and special education; early childhood programs; community-based training; and related services (i.e., occupational and physical therapy, speech–language pathology). The third level occurs at the team level where the school professional develops a personalized job description for a paraeducator/paratherapist.

District job descriptions specifically delineate paraeducator duties. Included are the duties that paraeducators are to perform as dictated by school district policy and ethical and legal considerations. Administrative concerns such as working conditions, training requirements, supervision procedures, and evaluation should appear in a written job description.

District-Wide Job Descriptions for Paraeducators

District-level job descriptions should provide the foundation for program and school professional-generated job descriptions. They contain instructional paraeducator roles and responsibilities, define supervisory responsibilities, and experiential/education requirements for different paraeducator positions.

Program Job Descriptions

Job descriptions for specific program areas identify tasks unique to the setting and student needs. Program-specific job descriptions should also address supervisory responsibility, roles, duties, and criteria for formal evaluations.

School Professional-Developed Personalized Job Descriptions

School professionals who supervise paraeducators are responsible for establishing a personalized job description that includes tasks the paraeducator will perform, where they will occur, individual student needs, materials required, and instructional strategies to be used. These job descriptions should be modified as changes occur in student goals and objectives.

Figure 7.2.   Levels of job descriptions.

Program job descriptions serve as both communication instruments and organizational tools. These job descriptions include information relevant to the specific program where the paraeducator is placed. Roles can be delineated more specifically and expectations for on-the-job training and evaluation criteria can be more directly related to the duties performed by individual paraeducators than in district-level statements.

Personalized job descriptions (PJDs) for paraeducators developed by school professionals allow them to communicate information about their personal philosophies for teaching and management style. Paraeducators themselves may often take an active role with the professional in the development of PJDs. This collaboration provides an opportunity for discussion and the development of understanding, and ownership of the roles and responsibilities for the team. (Development of program and team job descriptions were discussed more fully in Chapter 4.) Figure 7.3 provides an example of district-wide job descriptions.

RECRUITMENT AND SELECTION
OF PARAEDUCATORS

Services provided by schools are directly affected by the quality of all personnel including paraeducators. Procedures for recruitment, selection, and placement of paraeducators require attention from policymakers and district and building administrators.

Recruitment

One effective recruitment practice is to establish the positive aspects of being a paraeducator. Positive aspects include assignments that encompass a variety of interesting duties, opportunities for personal growth and career advancement, various benefits offered by many districts, high levels of responsibility given to many paraeducators, and the personal satisfaction provided by working with children and youth. Sources for recruitment of paraeducators include parent–teacher associations, senior citizen centers, civic and community organizations, school volunteer programs, community colleges, high school occupational/vocational training programs, and retired military personnel.

Position Title: General Education Paraeducator

Position Setting: Elementary/Secondary Classroom

Qualifications for the Position:

1. Must be 18 years of age or older.

2. Meet experiential/education criteria established by district.

Purpose: Assist the teacher in providing learning experiences for students.

Duties and Responsibilities:

1. Carry out instructional activities with students as planned and directed by the teacher.

2. Assist teacher in implementing the classroom behavior management program.

3. Provide objective feedback to teacher on student progress and behavior.

4. Assist in the preparation and care of instructional materials and equipment.

5. Perform clerical duties assigned by the teacher.

6. Follow district procedures for maintaining healthy and safe environments for students.

7. Practice legal and ethical standards of conduct established by the district.

Training Requirements:

Attend 20 hours of inservice training during the school year including a 3-day orientation session at the beginning of the school year. Work with the teacher for on-the-job training.

Supervision Guidelines:

The teacher will supervise the daily work of the paraeducator, provide a schedule and daily plans, and conduct regularly scheduled planning conferences. The paraeducator will be responsible to the teacher in instructional support role matters. The paraeducator will be responsible to the building principal in district policy matters.

Evaluation Guidelines:

Paraeducators are responsible for all assignments given to them and for carrying out the instructions of the supervising school professional or administrator. All paraeducators will be continuously evaluated with a written evaluation by the supervising teacher and/or administrator. Each paraeducator will develop an individualized training plan for the year in conjunction with his or her supervisor.

Figure 7.3.   Sample district paraeducator job description.

Qualifications

An important component of school policies regarding paraeducator utilization is establishment of qualifications for employment. Qualifications should be established to ensure that candidates have education and/or life or work experience that will enable them to perform assigned duties and protect student and parent rights. Commonly used entry-level employment criteria for paraeducators include a high school diploma or GED. In some locales a community college AA degree in a specific discipline may be required (i.e., physical or occupational therapy). Increasingly, states and local districts are requiring fingerprinting and background checks for all staff.

Selection and Hiring

Previous job experience, references, educational level, literacy, language skills, and skills applicable to the specific position (e.g., word processing, computer knowledge, understanding of students' cultural and ethnic heritages) are important in selecting the best qualified candidate. Research shows, however, that interpersonal skills and attitudes of applicants and an interest in self-improvement may be even better indicators of how well a candidate will fit into the team (Kansas State Department of Education, 1983; Vasa, Steckelberg, & Ulrich-Ronning, 1982).

Although it is difficult to assess objectively a potential employee's attitudes, values, and interpersonal skills, they are, nonetheless, important to the paraeducator's ability to work effectively in the classroom. The importance of conducting a systematic interview cannot be overstated as a tool for assessing self-confidence, patience, empathy, concern for children, and other personal qualities that indicate that a candidate will be an effective team member. A good practice is to include the potential supervisor in the pre-employment interview with prospective paraeducators. Including the supervising professional in the interview can help to minimize possible conflicts between team members and ensure that the applicants clearly understand the duties they will be expected to perform. As part of the interview process, the candidate should be given the job description, information about the school's organization, and information about the students to be served. A written set of performance competencies and ethical responsibilities and duties expected of the prospective employee should also be available.

PARAEDUCATOR SUPERVISION POLICIES

Both district and building policies and administrative practices need to acknowledge and support the supervising roles of school professionals. Developing standards and guidelines for paraeducator supervision involves determining the roles and duties of school professionals in (a) selecting paraeducators; (b) planning, assigning, and delegating tasks to individual paraeducators; (c) identifying a paraeducator's skills and training needs; (d) planning and providing paraeducator on-the-job training; and (e) participating in formal (annual) paraeducator performance evaluations. Figure 7.4 provides an example of a district-level policy statement that addresses these issues. It is divided into two parts. Part I describes the supervisory roles of classroom teachers. Part II describes the supervisory roles of school professionals who direct paraeducators assigned to vocational or other community-based programs.

Principals and/or program administrators, in particular, play important roles in enabling teachers, occupational and physical therapists, and speech–language pathologists to supervise and integrate effectively paraeducators/paratherapists into education and related services teams. It is the responsibility of building principals to

- ensure that school professionals and paraeducators understand the distinctions in their roles and are aware of district policies;

- involve school professionals in the selection of paraeducators;

- schedule opportunities for school professionals and paraeducators to meet regularly for on-the-job coaching and planning;

- develop, in collaboration with school professionals, criteria and instruments for assessing the performance of paraeducators and guidelines for involving teachers in annual performance reviews of paraeducators;

- provide support that will assist team members to resolve interpersonal or other problems that may occur in classrooms or programs; and

- provide teachers and paraeducators with information about career development opportunities and support services available through the district or institutions of higher education. (Pickett, Vasa, & Steckelberg, 1993)

I. Supervision of Paraeducators in Building-Based Programs

1. The supervising professional shall be responsible for planning and assessing all aspects of instructional programs.

2. When supervising paraeducators, school professionals shall:

   a. plan and assign paraeducator duties;

   b. direct and delegate paraeducator responsibilities;

   c. establish methods for evaluating and communicating student progress;

   d. provide systematic on-the-job training, related to the particular services provided by the paraeducator; and

   e. evaluate the impact of activities on performance carried out by the paraeducator.

3. The supervising professional shall keep written records of paraeducator evaluation and training and provide copies to the paraeducator and building administrator.

II. Supervision of Paraeducators in Nonschool Sites

The utilization of paraeducators in vocational, transitional, and other community-based programs is critical to the successful implementation of these programs. To ensure that paraeducators are appropriately supervised:

1. The supervising school professional is responsible for providing on-the-job training before the paraeducator accompanies a student to any site. Training should focus on detailed instructional plans, prepared or approved by the supervising teacher, and data-collection methods documenting student performance.

2. Regular on-site visits to community placements will be made by the designated supervising teacher. This time will be spent observing, evaluating, planning, and/or training with the paraeducator and on-the-job training.

3. Student progress will be monitored by the supervising teacher. Supervisors will review data and make changes in instructional plans as required. All changes in the student programs will be discussed with paraeducators.

4. A clear line of communication shall be established between paraeducators and supervising teachers. Emergency communication procedures should be developed, implemented, and monitored by building principals.

Figure 7.4.   **District-level supervision policy statements.** Adapted from job descriptions developed by the Lincoln, Nebraska, public schools, 1993.

Evaluating Paraeducator Performance

Evaluation of paraeducator performance is twofold: (a) informal evaluation of paraeducator performance by the supervising professional, which occurs throughout the school year, and (b) formal (annual) evaluation that involves the observations and ratings of administrators or other designated personnel in addition to those of supervising professionals.

When effective supervision is provided, informal (functional) evaluation combined with feedback takes place almost daily. In fact, in such situations the supervision and evaluation processes are almost inseparable and provide a basis for on-the-job training. Regularly scheduled conferences are important components of the functional assessment process because they provide opportunities for the supervising professional to discuss how well the paraeducator implements program strategies and objectives, follows instructions, and establishes rapport with students. Conferences also provide an opportunity to talk about the teacher's observations regarding strengths and readiness of the paraeducator to take on new tasks. The monitoring checklist shown in Figure 7.5 is an example of a format for recording the results of observations.

In contrast to these functional assessment activities, formal evaluations are usually more standardized and take place either annually or semiannually. The formal evaluation process is frequently shared by teachers and administrators (Vasa et al., 1982). Components of a formal evaluation process incorporate (a) preobservation activities, including defining concerns, establishing criteria for acceptable performance, and developing evaluative instruments; (b) data gathering through formal observations, using rating scales, questionnaires, or other instruments; (c) analysis of results and identification of behaviors to maintain or change; and (d) conferencing with the paraeducator being evaluated to provide positive feedback about performance and outline plans or strategies to improve the performance of the paraeducator when it is required.

Items appearing on observation forms and rating scales should match duties and responsibilities outlined in the job description. Local needs and expectations determine the specific content of evaluation instruments.

Figure 7.6 is a sample paraprofessional evaluation form/rating scale to be completed by an administrator, teacher, or other supervising personnel.

Evaluating the Quality of Supervision of Paraeducators

In addition to rating the performance of an individual paraeducator, an important outcome of the evaluation process is the determination of how

Instructions: This form is completed by the supervisor in order to provide feedback after observing the paraeducator conducting an instructional activity.

Date _____   Activity _____

Skills	Well Developed	Needs Improvement	Comment
1. Prepares for the session			
2. Establishes rapport with student			
3. Gives clear instructions			
4. Uses appropriate questions and cues			
5. Uses materials effectively			
6. Keeps lesson focused on objective			
7. Keeps student on task			
8. Gives appropriate feedback to student			
9. Uses reinforcement effectively			
10. Records student responses			
11. Follows lesson as planned			
12. Stays on task and uses allotted time effectively			

Figure 7.5.   **Monitoring checklist.**

well the paraeducator is being integrated into the instructional team. Questions and issues that require the attention of a principal or program administrator to determine the effectiveness of supervision include the following:

1. Are there district and building structures and guidelines for supervision?

2. Does the school professional provide appropriate direction and support for the paraeducator?

3. How does the presence of the paraeducator impact the productivity of the professional?

4. How does the presence of the paraeducator impact the students?

Name _____   Placement _____

Evaluator _____   Date ____/____/____

Instructions: Complete the following form for each paraeducator employed in the district. The rating scale of 1 to 5 is employed with 1 being low and 5 being high. Make narrative comments where they would be appropriate in evaluating the paraeducator. (NA refers to not applicable.)

I. **Interpersonal Skills**	**High**				**Low**	
1. Rapport with children/youth	5	4	3	2	1	NA
2. Communication with supervising teacher	5	4	3	2	1	NA
3. Communication with other staff members	5	4	3	2	1	NA
4. Communication with parents of children	5	4	3	2	1	NA

II. **Personal Characteristics**						
1. Interest and enthusiasm for the job	5	4	3	2	1	NA
2. Self-control in stress situations	5	4	3	2	1	NA
3. Initiative and work habits	5	4	3	2	1	NA
4. Friendliness and cooperativeness	5	4	3	2	1	NA

III. **Performance**						
1. General assistance to the teacher	5	4	3	2	1	NA
a. Student supervision and monitoring	5	4	3	2	1	NA
b. Attendance taking, etc.	5	4	3	2	1	NA
c. Recordkeeping of student progress	5	4	3	2	1	NA
d. Operation of multimedia equipment	5	4	3	2	1	NA
e. Operation of word processing equipment	5	4	3	2	1	NA
f. Bulletin board assistance	5	4	3	2	1	NA
2. Instructional assistance	5	4	3	2	1	NA
a. Instructional skills	5	4	3	2	1	NA
b. Group supervision and instruction	5	4	3	2	1	NA
i. small group (1–5)	5	4	3	2	1	NA
ii. large group (5 or more)	5	4	3	2	1	NA
c. Behavior management	5	4	3	2	1	NA
d. Observation of student performance	5	4	3	2	1	NA
e. Reporting information to teacher	5	4	3	2	1	NA

(*Continues*)

Figure 7.6.   **Paraeducator evaluation form.** Adapted from *Guide for the Effective Utilization of Paraprofessionals in Special Education*, by S. F. Vasa, A. L. Steckelberg, & L. Ulrich-Ronning, 1983, Lincoln: Department of Special Education, University of Nebraska–Lincoln.

IV. General Observations	High				Low	
1. Carries out assigned responsibilities	5	4	3	2	1	NA
2. Follows ethical guidelines	5	4	3	2	1	NA
3. Takes part in inservice opportunities	5	4	3	2	1	NA
4. Is punctual	5	4	3	2	1	NA
5. Carries out student learning contracts	5	4	3	2	1	NA
6. _____						

Comments:

Figure 7.6.   Continued.

The checklist in Figure 7.7 provides a guide for administrators in planning and evaluating the supervision and integration of paraeducators into education and related services teams.

Sharing Information About District Policies and Practices

Districts employing paraeducators have the responsibility for developing and implementing policies and procedures that maximize the benefits of paraeducator employment to ensure that student needs are met and their rights are protected. Carefully written policies contribute to an environment that recognizes the contributions and value of all staff, provide a common vision for all school personnel, establish the basis for allocating resources, and serve as

The following checklist is designed to evaluate the quality of supervisory policies and practices for paraeducators.

I. Are there district and/or building policies and procedures present?

_____ Policies on supervisory procedures and responsibilities?

_____ Time in daily/weekly schedules for team meetings?

_____ Guidelines for functional (informal) assessment?

_____ Criteria for formal (annual) performance evaluations?

_____ Procedures for conducting paraeducator evaluations?

_____ Plans for structured inservice linked to on-the-job training?

II. Does the supervising professional do the following?

_____ Prepare classroom and lesson plans that designate teacher and paraeducator tasks?

_____ Clarify expectations for paraeducators?

_____ Observe paraeducator performance?

_____ Provide ongoing on-the-job training?

_____ Document meetings and topics discussed?

_____ Provide flexibility and variety in assignments?

_____ Provide adequate information about student needs and program goals?

_____ Show respect for the paraeducator?

_____ Serve as a mentor for paraeducators?

III. How does the presence of a paraeducator affect school professionals and students? Is there more time for the following tasks?

_____ Consulting with other education and related services personnel?

_____ Assessing/diagnosing student needs?

_____ Curriculum development?

_____ Lesson and program planning?

_____ Achieving student goals and objectives?

_____ Providing individualized attention?

Figure 7.7.   **Evaluation checklist for supervision of paraeducators.** Adapted from *Using Paraeducators Effectively in the Classroom* (Fastback 358), by A. L. Pickett, S. F. Vasa, and A. L. Steckelberg, 1993, Bloomington, IN: Phi Delta Kappa Educational Foundation.

a foundation for evaluating education quality and student progress at both the district and building levels.

One of the most effective means of communicating policies and practices is a handbook. Policy handbooks include information about paraeducator duties, ethical and legal responsibilities of paraeducators, supervisory responsibility, personnel practices, and other district policies that are important to staff employed in the district. Figure 7.8 outlines the content for a paraeducator handbook. The components of a school policy handbook frequently contain definitions, rationale, job requirements, role descriptions, training provisions, benefits/working conditions, supervision policy, evaluation procedures, emergency procedures, and confidentiality/ethics matters.

TRAINING POLICIES

Administrators at the district and building levels have responsibility for ensuring that both school professionals and paraeducators/paratherapists have the skills and knowledge base they need to work as members of education and related services teams. This section discusses (a) the components of a comprehensive training system for paraeducators; (b) the roles of district and building administrators and school professionals in implementing the training plan; and (c) the training needs of school professionals to enable them to supervise and work effectively with paraeducators.

Components of a Comprehensive System of Professional Development for Paraeducators

Effective training for paraeducators should be based on professional development opportunities that provide a continuum of experiences including (a) initial orientation for paraeducators; (b) structured on-the-job coaching in classrooms or other learning environments; (c) formal inservice sessions to supplement the workplace training; and (d) opportunities for paraeducators to earn academic credit or enter professional preparation programs based on career preferences (French & Pickett, in press; Pickett et al., 1993).

Ideally, training should be provided at the district, building, and classroom levels. In addition to more traditional approaches to training, opportunities for professional development for paraeducator staff could include conference attendance for paraeducators, self-instruction using resource

A. **Definitions**
Statutory provisions
State and district policies

B. **Rationale/need for paraeducators**
Purpose of position
Benefits for students
Benefits to school
Benefits for school professionals

C. **Requirements for employment**
Education (minimum level)
Age (minimum)
Interest in working with students who have different ability levels

D. **Job description**
Position title(s) and setting(s)
Duties and responsibilities
Supervision guidelines
Evaluation procedures and criteria

E. **Staff development**
State and district training policies and standards
Rationale for training
Training goals/competencies
List of training resources (building, district, community colleges)
Types of training: orientation, on-the-job, inservice

F. **Benefits/working conditions**
Salary
Hours
Absence procedures
Benefits (i.e., sick leave, insurance, personal leave, vacations)

G. **Supervision policy**
Definition of supervision
Supervision responsibilities (role and responsibilities of school professionals and
administrators)

H. **Evaluation procedures**
School district policy
Person(s) responsible
Frequency of evaluation
Criteria for evaluation
Feedback/reporting guidelines
Appeal/grievance provisions
Dismissal procedures

I. **School and emergency procedures**

J. **Paraeducator professional/ethical responsibilities**
Maintaining confidentiality
Relationship to students
Relationship to supervisors, colleagues, and parents

Figure 7.8.   Paraeducator policy handbook outline.

materials provided by the district, and distance learning. In addition, by developing collaborative efforts with 2-year and 4-year colleges, professional organizations, and education service/resource centers, school districts will find it easier and cost effective to expand the availability of opportunities for career development and professional growth for paraeducators.

Initial orientation for paraeducators must provide them with an overview of district and building policies (e.g., who is to be called if a paraeducator will be absent or late; what is the role of the supervising professional; what are the professional and ethical responsibilities of paraeducators; what are the district's emergency procedures; whether the students they will work with have special needs, and if they do, what are they?). Many of the skills paraeducators need to learn are appropriately taught in an on-the-job setting by the supervising educator. On-the-job training may be particularly effective in enhancing behavior management and instructional and other skills related to the program/classroom where the paraeducator is assigned. A training/planning guide developed by the supervising professional helps organize and document the training activities. Planning and documenting on-the-job training efforts formalizes the training, helps ensure continuity, and provides a way to monitor progress.

Establishing a Training Plan

Paraeducator training programs should be long range, comprehensive, and systematic. Often the impact of training is lessened because it is based on available speakers or the current "hot topic" rather than on progressive development of an identified set of knowledge and skills. Paraeducators deserve a well-defined set of training competencies and incentives for achieving them. To develop opportunities for structured approaches to on-the-job training and ongoing inservice training programs, school districts should consider establishing a committee of administrators, teachers, and paraeducators to identify competencies and instructional needs for paraeducators. Involving teachers and paraeducators in designing and providing training often results in more relevant training. Their participation also contributes to improved job satisfaction and better staff morale and provides added incentives to improve skills.

Training competencies should be based on skills paraeducators require to carry out instruction and other program duties in different curriculum areas and levels of paraeducator positions. Training should also prepare paraeducators to maintain confidentiality; respect the human and legal rights of children, youth, and their families; and provide safe and secure learning environments. (Typical training competencies for paraeducators and para-therapists working in different programs are described in Chapters 2 and 3.)

In addition to establishing competencies, the district must develop a plan for achieving the identified skills. An annual training plan provides a systematic way of focusing on the skill development of paraeducators. The training plan should include the competencies, the method for demonstrating mastery, and a time frame for completing the program. Flexibility to allow alternative methods for learning and demonstrating competence and developing skills should be incorporated into the plan.

The annual training plan should also provide for accountability and management of the training program. A training plan such as the example in Figure 7.9 can be included in paraeducator personnel records for charting their progress. Completion of all or portions of the planned activities often serves as the basis for advancement to a higher level and receipt of additional benefits.

Training for Supervising Professionals

In addition to developing paraeducator training opportunities, districts must also support the supervisory roles of school professionals by preparing them to assume these responsibilities. To fully tap the benefits provided by paraeducators, teachers, and other licensed practitioners, they require training that enables them to

- describe reasons for the employment of paraeducators;
- identify key distinctions in the roles of paraeducators and supervisory professionals;
- describe professional, ethical, and legal factors that impact paraeducator employment;
- participate in interviewing applicants for paraeducator positions;
- communicate effectively with paraeducators;
- develop and implement on-the-job training activities for paraeducators;
- plan, assign, and delegate paraeducator tasks;
- provide feedback about paraeducator performance; and
- use effective problem-solving techniques.

	Target Date	Date Completed	Evaluation
Name _____		Date _____	
Orientation			
Orientation to the building and introduction to other staff members	_____	_____	_____
Goals of the school program	_____	_____	_____
State rules and regulations and local education agency policies regarding paraeducators	_____	_____	_____
Ethical considerations in work with students	_____	_____	_____
First aid and emergency procedures	_____	_____	_____
Inservice			
Instructional strategies	_____	_____	_____
Legal, ethical, and confidentiality standards	_____	_____	_____
Behavior management	_____	_____	_____
Communication and problem-solving skills	_____	_____	_____
Human growth and development	_____	_____	_____
Technology and computer skills	_____	_____	_____
Appreciating diversity	_____	_____	_____
On-the-Job Training			
General content of instructional materials	_____	_____	_____
Daily routines and schedules			
Systems of reporting student progress and other recordkeeping and clerical duties	_____	_____	_____
Instructional strategies	_____	_____	_____
Behavior management	_____	_____	_____
Classroom management	_____	_____	_____
Observation and recording strategies	_____	_____	_____
Other:	_____	_____	_____

Figure 7.9. **Annual training plan.**

Effective supervisors of paraeducators should have an understanding of management and supervisory procedures which includes (a) planning and evaluating instructional activities, (b) establishing priorities and scheduling resources, (c) clarifying expectations and establishing performance standards, (d) delegating paraeducator assignments, (e) providing training and support for paraeducators, (f) evaluating paraeducator performance, and (g) providing a supportive work environment.

It is important for school administrators along with school professionals to join forces with graduate and undergraduate professional development programs, state departments of education, and other agencies with jurisdiction over credentialing to develop standards that will ensure that school professionals are prepared to perform these tasks.

SUMMARY

Administrators provide a climate of high expectations for performance and leadership in promoting quality educational programs. Paraeducators can play important roles in education if they are supported by professionals and administrators.

Paraeducator contributions are directly related to well-planned programs that recognize student needs and provide appropriate guidelines for their performance and the necessary training and supervision. It is disheartening to see educational resources squandered when paraeducators are hired and placed in classrooms with little or no orientation, given schedules that do not include time for planning with the teacher, are not compensated for time spent developing job-related skills, and are assigned to supervising teachers who have little training or support as managers. In the final analysis, effective paraeducator programs rely on direction provided by school administrators.

Paraeducators should be recognized in district policies as important members of the team who increase the quality of education and related services. District polices should delineate the roles of paraeducators, identify training requirements, and clarify supervision policies.

Job descriptions serve a number of administrative functions. The job description is used to communicate expectations to the paraeducator, to develop formal inservice and on-the-job training goals for paraeducators, to form the basis for evaluating paraeducator performance, and to set standards for supervision.

Administrators have the responsibility for the recruitment, selection, hiring, and assignment of paraeducators. School professionals make positive contributions to the selection process and should be included in paraeducator interviews.

Regular evaluation of paraeducator contributions is an important element in determining how to fine tune the program. Administrators need to establish criteria for evaluation and involve both the professionals and the paraeducators in the process.

Administrators have a leadership role in establishing training policies and working with school staff to develop a plan for a long-range training program. Systematic training programs include a defined set of competencies and a plan for achieving the competencies, and provide accountability for both paraeducators and administrators .

Paraeducators cannot be ethically employed in classroom settings without appropriate supervision by school professionals. Clear guidelines for supervision are important to both paraeducators and teachers. Administrators must support supervision by making sure that teacher and paraeducator schedules allow time for planning, on-the-job training, and activities that evaluate classroom duties. Providing professionals with strategies for planning and documenting conferences with paraeducators also supports effective supervision. Recognizing the training needs of professionals to be supervisors and providing them with opportunities to learn skills that will enable them to work with paraeducators impacts both the educational achievement of students and the effectiveness of the teams.

Discussion Questions

1. What are the primary responsibilities of district and building administrators for developing strategies and mechanisms for supporting school professionals and paraeducator/paratherapist teams?

2. Does your district have job descriptions for paraeducators and paratherapists? When were they developed? Are they similar to the roles and responsibilities described in this text? If not, what are the differences?

3. Who provides the staff development for paraeducators in your district? Is it the district, the supervising school professional, a community college, or another agency?

Exercises

1. Divide into groups of four or five participants. Assume that you are members of a committee that has been asked to plan a 2-day orientation session for both new and experienced paraeducators. The goal of the workshop is to prepare paraeducators for assignments in inclusive classrooms and community-based learning settings. What topics and issues should be on the agenda? What kind of follow-up training will the paraeducators need during the year? Who should provide the training?

2. Interview a new and an experienced paraeducator to identify paraeducator training priorities. You may want to ask the following questions (however, do not limit yourself to these): What would you have liked to have been told prior to starting your job? What topics would you like to learn more about (instructional strategies, legal issues, career development, curriculum content, working with students with special needs)?

3. Assume you have been asked to interview several candidates for the paraeducator position in your classroom. Develop a list of questions that will help you elicit information in order to choose the person with whom you would prefer to work.

4. Working with your group, use the Job Description Analysis (Worksheet 1) that follows the case study to develop a model district-wide job description for paraeducators.

5. Continue to work as a group. Assume that you are members of a committee appointed by the district superintendent to design a policy handbook for paraeducators. Use the questions in Worksheet 2 (which follows the case study) and the outline in Figure 7.8 in this chapter as a discussion guide to identify the information that all staff need to know about paraeducator employment, supervision, and training. Then work as a team to develop the contents of a paraeducator handbook.

Case Study

Assume your group makes up the shared decision-making council in your school. After you read the case study, work as a team to develop a list of suggestions the principal could implement to provide regular opportunities for the team to meet.

Ms. Pressler is the principal of a middle school that serves a student body with diverse education and related service needs. Students with learning, physical, and sensory disabilities are assigned to inclusive class-rooms. During the last 3 years the demographics of the neighborhood where the school is located have changed and now Vietnamese and Korean are the primary languages spoken in many students' homes. Still other students come from family backgrounds that place them at risk and will benefit from personalized attention that helps them master new academic skills. As a result, the instructional team in most classrooms includes one or more paraeducators.

Recently, several teachers and paraeducators spoke to Ms. Pressler and shared a concern that affects their ability to work together effectively. It is a lack of time for team members to meet to share information, plan activities, and discuss student needs and progress.

Shared decision making has proven to be an effective way for school staff and parents to address mutual concerns. Therefore, Ms. Pressler decided to ask the school-based council to discuss ways to schedule opportunities for instructional teams to meet regularly. As the council began to study the situation, they quickly discovered that this problem could not be solved easily or in a vacuum. As they began to study the issues the council discovered the following information: (a) Paraeducators are paid on an hourly basis, they arrive when the students arrive and they leave when the students are dismissed; (b) budgetary cutbacks district wide make it difficult to extend the number of hours paraeducators work; and (c) during teacher's planning periods, paraeducators are assigned other duties (e.g., monitoring the playground or lunchroom, escorting students with special needs to music, gym, math, assisting the librarian).

The council (your group) is holding their second meeting. Brainstorm a list of ideas and strategies that you could suggest to Ms. Pressler that might help her find the time for the instructional teams to meet regularly.

Worksheet 1
Job Description Analysis

Instructions: Analyze job descriptions from different districts and programs to determine if they contain the components listed below. Check those items which are included in the job description.

_____ 1. Are the following subtitles included within the job description?

_____ Position title

_____ Position setting

_____ Qualifications

_____ Rationale/purpose for the position

_____ Orientation/training requirements

_____ Duties and responsibilities

_____ Hours of employment

_____ Evaluation and supervision methods

_____ 2. Is the title appropriate and reflective of current trends in paraeducator employment?

_____ 3. Does the job description include enough detail about expectations for the position (e.g., what the paraeducator will be doing)?

_____ 4. Does the job description show a true relationship to what paraeducators are currently doing?

_____ 5. Does the description prevent the paraeducator from performing certain educational tasks? Does it demand too much?

_____ 6. Is the description of the teacher–paraeducator relationship sufficiently detailed? Are line-staff relations with other personnel described?

_____ 7. Are the paraeducator's responsibilities to students detailed? Are limits to authority identified?

_____ 8. Does the supervision section adequately inform paraeducators about how they will be supervised?

_____ 9. Does the job description provide direction for the development of paraeducator training programs? Are on-the-job training goals identified?

_____ 10. Does the description allow for the paraeducator to plan for and participate in the evaluation process? Is information included on the methods of evaluation of the paraeducator?

Page 1   (*Continues*)

Worksheet 1 (*Continued*)

In the space provided below, write suggestions for improving the job descriptions.

Worksheet 2
Paraeducator Policy Handbook Issues

Activity

1. Why is a district policy handbook for paraeducators important?

2. Should there be a building program handbook for paraeducators?

3. How will a handbook benefit all team members?

4. What information should be in the different handbooks?

5. Which handbook do you feel would be most beneficial to team members?

REFERENCES

French, N. K., & Pickett, A. L. (in press). *Paraeducators in special education: Issues for teacher education*. Reston, VA: Teacher Education Division, Council for Exceptional Children.

Hale, J. M. (1972). *Administrators guide to training paraprofessionals*. Englewood Cliffs, NJ: Prentice Hall.

Hilbrunner, C. L. (1976). *Using instructional paraprofessionals with exceptional children*. Slow Learner Workshop.

Kansas State Department of Education. (1983). *A manual for the implementation of the facilitator's model*. Topeka, KS: Author.

Lincoln Public Schools. (1993). *Policy and regulation manual*. Lincoln, NE: Author.

Pickett, A. L., Faison, K., & Formanek, J. (1993). *A core curriculum and training program for paraeducators working in inclusive classrooms for school age students*. New York: National Resource Center for Paraprofessionals in Education and Related Services, Center for Advanced Study in Education, The Graduate School and University Center, City University of New York.

Pickett, A. L., Vasa, S. F., & Steckelberg, A. L. (1993). *Using paraeducators effectively in the classroom*. Fastback 358. Bloomington, IN: Phi Delta Kappa Educational Foundation.

Vasa, S. F., & Steckelberg, A. L. (1987, November). *What teachers need to know about utilizing paraprofessionals: Higher education's role*. Paper presented at the annual conference of National Council of States Inservice Education, San Diego, CA. (ERIC Document Reproduction Service No. ED 293 230)

Vasa, S. F., Steckelberg, A. L., & Hoffman, P. (1986). *Resource guide for the development of policies and practices in the use of paraprofessionals in special education*. Lincoln, NE: Department of Education and Communication Disorders, University of Nebraska–Lincoln.

Vasa, S. F., Steckelberg, A. L., & Ulrich-Ronning, L. (1982). *A state of the art assessment of paraprofessional use in special education in the State of Nebraska*. Lincoln, NE: Department of Education, University of Nebraska–Lincoln.

Vasa, S. F., Steckelberg, A. L., & Ulrich-Ronning, L. (1983). *Guide for the effective utilization of paraprofessionals in special education*. Lincoln, NE: Department of Special Education, University of Nebraska–Lincoln.

CHAPTER 8

. . . .

Paraeducators in School Settings: The Future

. . . .

Anna Lou Pickett
National Resource Center for Paraprofessionals
in Education and Related Services,
City University of New York

Kent Gerlach
Pacific Lutheran University

OVERVIEW

A more accurate title for this chapter is probably "The Future Is Now." This text has provided an in-depth look at the policy questions, systemic issues, and personnel practices that influence the roles, supervision, performance, and preparation of paraeducators and paratherapists. In today's schools and other education provider agencies, paraprofessionals are key members of education and related services teams. For this and other reasons described in the different chapters, policymakers and implementers in SDEs, LEAs, and IHEs do not have the luxury of waiting until some distant time in the future to establish standards and infrastructures that will effectively address these issues.

The purpose of this chapter is to provide learners with information they can build on to develop proactive collaborative efforts to investigate state and local needs and to implement policies and systems to meet these needs.

Instructional Objectives

After studying this chapter and responding to the discussion questions, readers will be able to:

1. Describe policy questions and systemic issues that need to be investigated cooperatively by SDEs, LEAs, IHEs, and other stakeholders to provide direction for developing and implementing standards and infrastructures to improve paraprofessional performance, supervision, and preparation.

2. Describe support systems that exist in their state for the development of policies, standards, and mechanisms to improve paraprofessional performance, supervision, and preparation.

3. Discuss barriers that exist in their state to the development of policies, standards, and infrastructures to improve paraprofessional performance, supervision, and preparation.

4. Explain roles for different stakeholders in these development activities.

. . . .

ISSUES

The efforts of several researchers indicate that the employment of paraeducators and paratherapists will probably continue unabated into the foreseeable future (Council for Exceptional Children, 1996; Ebenstein & Gooler, 1993; Genzuk, Lavadenz, & Krashen, 1994; Hales & Carlson, 1993; Haselkorn & Fideler, 1996; Innocenti, 1993). The results of these and other investigations reveal that the areas of greatest need for paraprofessional staff will continue to be inclusive general and special education programs, compensatory and remedial education, linguistic-minority education and support services, and early intervention and preschool programs. This continuing reliance on paraprofessionals in programs serving children and youth who can benefit from individualized education programs, related services, and student support systems is supported by several demographic databases (*Education Daily*, 1994; National Center for Education Statistics [NCES], 1995, 1993; Office of Special Education Programs and Rehabilitation Services, 1993).

Policymakers and implementers in state departments of education are confronted with a multitude of issues as they grapple with finding effective methods for improving the quality of education practices and systems. One of the most critical areas of need is preparing school professionals and paraprofessionals to work together as effective instructional and related services teams.

Nationwide, SDEs, LEAs, IHEs, and other stakeholders have worked cooperatively to forge systems that empower teachers, by involving them more directly in determining education priorities and developing curriculum content to prepare students for the rigors of today's world. These same partners have also worked together to set new standards for teacher education that recognize the redefined and restructured roles of teachers.

These efforts have, for the most part, ignored the need to prepare teachers and other school professionals to supervise and work effectively with paraeducators/paratherapists.

The resurgence of interest in policy questions surrounding the paraprofessional workforce is fairly limited and these issues remain "afterthoughts" in the public policy arena. To ensure that school professionals and paraprofessionals are prepared for their new, more demanding roles, it is important for these issues to be more closely tied to major education reform initiatives that currently are being tested and assessed.

The various agencies and organizations with responsibility for and interest in improving the quality of education systems must work in concert to develop relevant policies, standards, and permanent infrastructures for the employment, supervision, and preparation of paraprofessionals. This includes gathering and assessing information they can use to

1. clearly delineate teacher and paraeducator roles;

2. determine distinctions and similarities in skills required by paraeducators to work in different programs;

3 identify the core skills required by all paraprofessionals and the hierarchy of skills required by paraeducators employed in different position levels;

4. identify curriculum content standards for comprehensive systems of paraeducator preparation that include structured on-the-job training, ongoing staff development opportunities, and access to articulated undergraduate and graduate programs that will facilitate career advancement;

5. develop credentialing systems or other mechanisms that will ensure paraeducators have mastered the required skills;

6. set standards for the supervision and evaluation of paraeducator performance; and

7. develop curriculum content and activities to prepare school professionals to supervise and work effectively with paraeducators.

These issues cannot be addressed in a vacuum. Several factors must be taken into account by the stakeholders. They include the following:

- federal legislative mandates and availability of categorical funding for different programs,

- state policies for reimbursing local school districts (How are funds allocated? Are they linked to specific programs? Can they be used to supplement salaries? Do they support staff development?), and

- the impact of collective bargaining issues on individual district policies and practices with regard to paraprofessional preparation, career development, and professional growth.

SUMMARY

Policymakers and implementers are confronted with myriad challenges as they prepare for the 21st century. As always, our nation's schools are respondents to and initiators of change. It is important that the contributions paraeducators and paratherapists make to improving the quality and productivity of education and related services not be overlooked; and that standards for their employment, roles, supervision, and preparation be established and opportunities for staff development and professional growth be institutionalized.

Discussion Questions

1. What barriers to or support for the development of standards and mechanisms to improve the performance, supervision, and preparation of paraprofessionals exist in your state?

2. How do federal mandates and funding, state reimbursement, or collective bargaining influence paraprofessional employment, roles, supervision, and preparation in your state?

3. What are the roles of your state department of education and other state agencies, local school districts, 2- and 4-year colleges and universities, professional organizations, and unions in developing and implementing standards and infrastructures?

4. How can links among the various partners mentioned in question 3 be strengthened?

REFERENCES

Council for Exceptional Children. (1996). *Report of the consortium of organizations on the preparation and use of speech–language paraprofessionals in early intervention and education settings.* Reston, VA: Author.

Ebenstein, W., & Gooler, L. (1993). *Cultural diversity and developmental disabilities workforce issues.* New York: Consortium for the Study of Disabilities, City University of New York.

Education Daily (1994, October 12). *Special education personnel shortages to worsen, researchers predict, 27*(196), 1, 3.

Genzuk, M., Lavadenz, M., & Krashen, S. (1994). Paraeducators: A source for remedying the shortage of teachers for limited-English-proficient students. *The Journal of Education Issues of Language Minority Students, 14.*

Hales, R. M., & Carlson, L. B. (1993). *Issues and trends in special education.* Stillwater, OK: National Clearinghouse of Rehabilitation Materials.

Haselkorn, D., & Fideler, L. (1996). *Breaking the class ceiling: Paraeducator pathways to teaching.* Belmont, MA: Recruiting New Teachers.

Innocenti, M. (1993). Paraprofessionals in early intervention: Some information and some ideas. *Utah State Educator, 13*(3).

McDonnell, L., & Hill, P. (1993). *Newcomers in American schools.* Santa Monica, CA: RAND.

National Center for Education Statistics (1993). *Language characteristics and schooling in the United States: A changing picture.* Washington, DC: Office of Educational Research and Improvement, U.S. Department of Education.

National Center for Education Statistics (1995). *Projection of education statistics to 2005.* Washington, DC: Office of Educational Research and Improvement, U.S. Department of Education.

Office of Special Education Programs and Rehabilitation Services. (1993). *Fifteenth annual report to Congress on the implementation of the Individuals with Disabilities Act.* Washington, DC: U.S. Department of Education.

Index

About the Editors

Anna Lou Pickett is the director of the National Resource Center for Paraprofessionals in Education and Related Services (NRCP). She has held this position since the NRCP was established almost 20 years ago as an operating unit of the Center for Advanced Study in Education located at the Graduate School and University Center of the City University of New York. She provides technical assistance to state and local education agencies and to professional organizations to help them build systems and practices to improve the employment, supervision, and preparation of paraeducators. She is also the author of journal articles, instructional programs, and resource materials concerned with enchancing the status, professional development, and performance of the paraprofessional workforce.

Kent Gerlach is a professor of special education at Pacific Lutheran University in Tacoma, Washington. His research interests include collaboration and teaming and paraeducator issues. He has conducted numerous seminars and staff development workshops throughout the United States and Canada. He has taught a course on supervising paraeducators for 12 years at Pacific Lutheran University. In 1996, he received the Faculty Achievement award for his work with the Washington State Legislature and the Washington Education Association for his efforts in the preparation of legislation affecting the welfare of exceptional students and those who educate them.